the boy

on the back

of the turtle

Wherein our Narrator sees Things both Astounding and Wondrous, and in doing so
draws near the Heart of a Great Mystery; and also hears many
Questions on the subject of Dogs, addressed to him by his beloved Daughter; and also
looks at the beginning of Time in the company of his own Father;
and also drinks Ale that is exceeding Warm.

the boy
on the back
of the turtle

Seeking God, Quince Marmalade and the
Fabled Albatross on Darwin's Islands

PAUL QUARRINGTON

GREYSTONE BOOKS
DOUGLAS & McINTYRE

03 04 05 06 07   5 4 3

Greystone Books
A division of Douglas & McIntyre Ltd.
2323 Quebec Street, Suite 201
Vancouver, British Columbia
Canada V5T 4S7
www.greystonebooks.com

National Library of Canada Cataloguing in Publication Data
Quarrington, Paul.
    The boy on the back of the turtle

    ISBN 1-55054-584-1 (cloth) 1-55054-701-1 (pbk.)

    1. Quarrington, Paul—Journeys—Galápagos Islands. 2. Galápagos Islands—
Description and travel. I. Title.

Library of Congress Cataloging-in-Publication data is available.

Editing by Barbara Pulling
Cover design by Tom Brown
Text design by Val Speidel
Typesetting by Brenda and Neil West, BN Typographics West, and Val Speidel
Printed and bound in Canada by Friesens
Printed on acid-free paper
Distributed in the U.S. by Publishers Group West

We gratefully acknowledge the financial support of the Canada Council for the Arts,
the British Columbia Arts Council, and the Government of Canada through the Book
Publishing Industry Development Program (BPIDP) for our publishing activities.

To Dorothy, for making Carson, and Mary, for making me

One day a ship's captain spied a sea turtle swimming in the seas that surround the Galapagos Islands. Or the Encantadas, as the sailors called the archipelago, bothered as they were by the inexplicable calmnesses. So this captain—his own ship stonestill and stayed—tied a rope to his boy and sent him overboard to get the animal for the crew's table. As soon as the lad climbed onto the barnacled back, the wind picked up and the ship was pulled away. The last the captain saw, the boy was still clinging to the sea turtle and waving, not frantically, but farewell.

—A TALE TOLD BY THE MERRY BOYS

One

On March twenty-fifth of the year nineteen hundred and ninety-six, with my spirit made dull and muzzy by so long spent ashore, I embarked upon a voyage of the Encantadas, the storied, shrouded archipelago that lies some six hundred miles to the west of the southern Americas. For companionship upon my travels I had with me my daughter Carson, aged seven years, and my father Bruce, ten times that. The sun, punctual and prompt upon the equatorial line, was withdrawing behind the globe as we first stepped onto our vessel, the mighty *Corinthian*, not five years out of the wrightyard but no less worthy for that. It had been our design to set to sea by midday, but we had been made behind time by some hopeless dickwads—oops. Well, I would never have lasted the whole book anyway. I had hoped to break a paragraph before descending into the vulgate, but there you go.

Delayed we had been, unaccountably, forced to sit in a departure lounge in the Quito airport for some five hours, staring at the craft from SAN airline that sat idly on the tarmac. Rumour had it that the machine needed mechanical attention, but we saw no grease-covered fly-boys ministering to it. My father sat with his large fingers curled around his armrests, nodding in and out of sleep. My daughter worked on her journal, inscribing the single word "bored" over and over again. I read from the small library of books I was carting with me: *A Traveller's Guide to the Galápagos Islands*, *Field Guide to Birds of the Galápagos*, *Darwin's Islands: A Natural History of the Galápagos* and a small dog-chewed paperback edition of *The Origin of Species*. That last book assumes some importance in these pages, so allow me to remind you: it was written by Charles Darwin (1809–1892), who, sailing aboard a "coffin-brig" named the H.M.S. *Beagle*, visited the Galápagos Islands in 1835. He saw something there that caused him to give voice to the Theory of Evolution by Means of Natural Selection. This in turn caused people to squabble savagely. That squabbling has bothered me throughout my life; I heard it even as a small child, angry adult voices muted behind closed doors and thick walls.

So when, many months ago, the Publisher asked what I had in mind to follow a very modest success (significantly, a book about a fishing trip where no fish were caught), my answer was quick. "The Galápagos."

The Publisher is a man of boyish enthusiasms. Almost any place name would have elicited some reaction, but this one caused his head to snap upwards, his eyes to widen with wonder. Mind you, we were both holding wine glasses at the time. "Yes," he enthused. "Why?"

"Well ..." I couldn't tell him the truth, which involved Dr. Moody and a makeshift movie theatre. I couldn't tell the Publisher that visiting the Galápagos Islands was, in effect, the Prime Directive. It wouldn't have been at all professional, for one thing, to claim that I had been somehow "programmed" to visit the archipelago. I am by nature a private man, even with more wine inside than is absolutely necessary, so I sighed and started upon the road to something not quite as near the truth. "My father is a psychologist, a professor," I told the Publisher. "He is an academic. And, for my whole life, he has told me about Charles Darwin. He is a huge Charles Darwin fan."

"Yes!" the Publisher enthused. "Why?"

Good question. It was not always easy to read a moral or a lesson in some of the stories my father told me. Like this one: Darwin was fascinated with worms. Of course, Darwin was fascinated with every living thing, but he had his favourites and passions, worms being one of them. And in his tiny poop cabin on the *Beagle*, he devised and built an earth-filled drawer beneath his berth. Charles would wake up in the middle of the night, lean over and pull out the drawer, so that he could watch the nocturnal activity of the worms. That is a story my father told me. I have reasons to doubt that the story is true—for example, there would be no light in the tiny poop cabin, and the story lacks a certain credibility when we picture Darwin fumbling with a lantern just to aid whimsical worm-inspection —but that is hardly the point. What did my father mean for me to learn from it? So I put to the Publisher that my aim was to answer just that sort of question. Darwin and the Galápagos had become connected with the issue of *fatherhood*. Therefore, I wanted to take with me my elder daughter (the other was then too wee), and I would use the experience as an opportunity to meditate on the joys and mysteries of paternity. Most publishers would bolt in terror, but not this one, who considers the subject of fatherhood underrepresented on the bookshelves. He sipped his wine and appeared thoughtful.

I didn't mention to the Publisher that I'd tried a few dry practice runs, meditation-wise, sitting up in my office with a furrowed brow, the fusty air filled with appropriately brooding music, Bruckner, Brahms and Mahler. I hadn't really been able to generate much. Still, I wasn't worried. All this would change in the Galápagos. Cruising about the Encantadas, I would be granted an Insight. After all, the one granted to Charles Darwin is one of the great Insights, perhaps the greatest ever. It was an Insight—as opposed to a discovery, or a creation—because the Theory of Evolution by Means of Natural Selection had always been lying in plain sight. As Darwin's great defender and advocate Thomas Huxley (1825–1895) remarked, very famously, "How extremely stupid not to have thought of that."

There's competition on the Insight front, no doubt. Archimedes shouting "Eureka!" for example, although I'm sure whoever was in charge of cleaning that particular bathroom floor wandered away muttering, "*Eureka*, your fat ass. It happens every time you take a bath." Or Einstein and his E=mc², although I don't think that was properly an "Insight," I think it was something Albert and his wife Mileva hashed out over breakfast.

No, the Great Insight was had by Charles Darwin—admittedly some years after he had visited the Galápagos—and set down in *The Origin of Species*.[1]

So, I elaborated to the Publisher—wine lapping over the top of the stemware—if Charles Darwin could be smacked about the head by the Great Insight, then surely I, while not a particularly observant or intelligent fellow, well—you know. Fish have been caught on empty hooks before.

This is what I told the Publisher. He seemed convinced.

It was late in the afternoon when my father, my daughter and I finally boarded the plane that would take us to the Galápagos Islands.

---

1 "I think I have found out (here's presumption!) the simple way by which species become exquisitely adapted to various ends."

We had flown to Quito on SAETA airlines, an experience that was delightful in every way. The plane was big and roomy, the attendants fervently attentive. This shorter domestic flight, from Quito to Puerto Baquerizo Moreno on San Christóbal Island, was on SAN, and the craft was too small and nearing retirement, the attendants disinterested in anything involving aviation. For instance, at the Quito airport I had been given boarding passes, with seat assignments written in the appropriate boxes, but aboard the plane these were more than meaningless. Frequent-flying Ecuadorians, knowing the scoop, were enthroned in the choice seats. The rest of us, clutching our boarding passes and waving them frantically, charged up and down the aisles like cake-crazed children at a birthday party. The attendants regarded all this activity with icy dispassion, shrugging whenever a complaint was registered, telling people to deal themselves with the pituitary giant sitting in 6-B, who was returning from a butcher's convention in Guayaquil to his home in Puerto Baquerizo Moreno. (I mean no disrespect to butchers, but I don't think this man was one, at least not professionally.) And all this mayhem unfolded five full hours behind schedule.

The plane landed on San Christóbal Island and the Ecuadorians disappeared into the hills, leaving behind a mob of disoriented tourists. The airport was an unusual outdoorsy affair, an overgrown gazebo with little wooden huts in the centre where uniformed men checked your passport and made sure that you had paid the park entrance fee back at the Quito airport and charged you some other fee just for fun.

A cruise through the Galápagos Islands is more affordable than you might think, although once there the tourist is subjected to a series of somewhat indiscriminate levies and taxes. The big one is the eighty-dollar entrance fee, which goes to the

Galápagos National Park Service. The park service operates in tandem with the Charles Darwin Research Station (which we were scheduled to visit on the last day of the week-long cruise), where scientists labour hard trying to save endangered species, most visibly the vanishing trademark tortoises.

So I don't begrudge them the money one little bit, and didn't at the time. Mind you, at the time I was feeling pretty punchy; I would have thrown any amount of money at the uniformed men in the little huts if they would only let me go somewhere and lie down. We'd gotten up at dawn—which always comes at 6:00 A.M. in Quito—and gone to the airport for our 11:00 flight, because that's how things are done in Ecuador, and that flight was, as I believe I've mentioned, five hours late, and then we were an hour and a half in the bumpy air, so eighty dollars (forty for the kid) seemed a small price to pay if it meant we were finally drawing near our destination.

I wanted to be well rested throughout the voyage, not simply so as to be as receptive as possible to Insight but because of a little piece of legend or lore that I'd picked up during my pre-trip reading, especially from Herman Melville's *The Encantadas, or Enchanted Isles*, with its tales of the hermit Oberlus and the murderous Dog-King. The notion was this: a visit to the Encantadas might drive one insane.

The archipelago was first called Las Encantadas—likely because of the way the winds will suddenly pick up and blow away a curtain of mist, making an isle seem to appear out of thin air—but people kept referring to "the Enchanted Isles" long after the place was officially designated the Galápagos. This might have to do with the proliferation of tortoises, because sailors believed that tortoises were their old shipmates, cursed and transformed. I've heard also that it was sort of a practical joke perpetrated by the Spanish: a buccaneer once asked directions to the "Galipoloes," and some Spanish seadogs laughed and replied that they were "Inchanted"—"shadows and noe reall Islands." But an explanation that seems to have a lot of evidence supporting it is that the islands are "enchanted" in that visitors come away spellbound and tranced.

Captain Robert FitzRoy, for example, all of twenty-three years old when he took command of the H.M.S. *Beagle*, ended his life poorly, delirious and babbling. Granted, he was always a little bit unstable, given to black moods and silences. Ironically, this propensity for depression gave us, indirectly, the Theory of Evolution by Means of Natural Selection, because Charles Darwin was originally retained not as the ship's official naturalist (a position held customarily by the surgeon) but as companion to Captain FitzRoy. There were some sixty-odd people sailing on the *Beagle*, but FitzRoy could not, because of his rank and station (his father had been prime minister, his uncle was the foreign secretary Lord Castlereagh), associate with any of them. So he would take meals in his quarters with young Darwin, a man close to his own tender age, whom FitzRoy identified fondly as "Philos," the ship's philosopher.

The *Beagle* put into the Galápagos, actually touching upon only four of the islands. Both men saw what they saw, and then sailed back to England in 1836.

Charles Darwin settled in London but found that he could not abide the bustle and clamour. So he took his wife Emma and the first few of his children and moved into Down House near the town of Farnborough. Here he wrote books on various subjects: the voyage of the *Beagle*, coral reefs, barnacles.

But all this time, it seems, his mind was working on another problem. Darwin had with him at Down House the remains of finches collected from the Encantadas, and he'd noticed that they were different one to another. Unfortunately, Darwin had not recorded which island any one individual was from, so he sat there and rubbed his chin and wondered what it all could mean.

Then Charles Darwin had the Great Insight, but was wary of setting it down (other than in a series of notebooks which he kept hidden away), perhaps fearing a challenge that he hadn't been able to predict, perhaps fearing the outrage that he knew would greet his Theory of Evolution. Or, perhaps, because he knew he now possessed a power never before granted a mortal man.

Darwin became reticent and withdrawn. He also became ill, quite severely and quite often, although the specific symptoms and ailments changed, afflictions leaping willy-nilly from one part of his body to another. His skin flaked and peeled like the hide of a marine iguana. Darwin's stomach knotted in pain; his head ached and throbbed so that it could hold no thought. Charles's heart pounded in panicked irregularities and his body swelled and distended. Some scholars think that he was suffering from the tropical disease Chagas, picked up during his voyages about the globe. Darwin himself thought that he was somehow flawed, profoundly, and worried that the condition might be inherited by his children. These days we would probably ascribe much of this to stress; after all, Charles was grappling all this time with the Great Insight. Or, I sometimes wonder, was his post-Galápagon madness manifesting itself physically? Charles Darwin was a kind man, people maintain, a devoted husband and doting father (especially to his eldest daughter Annie), but he didn't care to go out much—he was, in his own words, "a hermit"—preferring to spend time in his study, all alone with his books and his specimens, the remains of little birds.

As for Captain FitzRoy, he sailed away from the Encantadas convinced of the literal truth of the Great Flood. After all, he had seen the world floating about in the sea, down in the Encantadas, black spires sticking up through the surface, hideous lizards clinging desperately to the rocks.

Captain FitzRoy became obsessed with the weather and its predictability. He became the government's first official meteorologist, and I've heard the actual term "forecasting" attributed to him. Although not the creator of the barometer, FitzRoy was one of its earliest and most passionate advocates, relying on the instrument, sometimes even ignoring his own senses, putting out to sea during hellish storms because the needle of his mechanism trembled toward "FAIR SKIES."

In 1858, more than twenty years after the voyages of the *Beagle*, Charles Darwin, spurred by a letter from a young naturalist and collector named Alfred Russel Wallace (1823–1913), who had lived long in the Malay Archipelago and had arrived at essentially the same conclusion, finally published a paper, sharing credit with Mr. Wallace, entitled "On the Tendency of Species To Form Varieties; and on the Perpetuation of Varieties and Species by Natural Means of Selection." Darwin also wrote an abridged version of his proposed major work, which was published in the fall of 1859 and entitled *On the Origin of Species By Means of Natural Selection, or, The Preservation of Favoured Races in the Struggle for Life.*

The first Great Squabble took place on June 30, 1860. Seven hundred people crammed themselves into a hall in the Zoological Museum, Oxford, to hear a Dr. Draper speak on the "intellectual development of Europe considered with reference to the views of Charles Darwin." After the lecture, two opponents rose to debate the Theory of Evolution; it was defended by Thomas Henry Huxley and damned by the Bishop of Oxford, Samuel Wilberforce. Wilberforce got in first licks, snidely demanding to know if Huxley were descended from an ape on his grandfather's, or his grandmother's, side. Huxley, according to well-worn legend, clapped the knee of the man beside him and whispered excitedly, "The Lord hath delivered him into mine hands," whereupon he stood up and tore a strip off the bishop's butt, which culminated in his famous assertion that he'd rather be descended from an ape than from a brilliant man who got involved in scientific questions about which he knew nothing.

The Zoological Museum erupted into chaos, which might best be described by this sentence of Victorian gentility, borrowed from Ruth Moore's *Charles Darwin*: "Lady Brewster fainted."

At the end of that first debate in Oxford, a man rose from his seat, an aging, wasted man with the Bible clutched between bony fingers. "Here is the truth," he shouted at the assembled, "here in this Book, not in the mouth of that evil snake in the grass." This was Captain Robert FitzRoy. Five years later, he slit his own throat.

My father, my daughter and I were labelled, there at the San Christóbel airport, actually and physically labelled. We all wore little stickers that said *Corinthian*. There were others with *Corinthian* labels; a few middle-aged, well-heeled couples, two young women travelling together, a couple of singleton young males, and a trembling clutch of old people. No children as far as we could see, which was a little unfortunate, although I had stopped far short of promising Carson that there would be playmates aboard the ship. I had reason to suspect there wouldn't be. Ingrid the travel agent had placed a call, sitting behind her desk in downtown Toronto, securing her cigarette between her lips to free her hands, punching at her telephone with power and accuracy. "Hello, Julio," she said, the name coming from deep down in her throat, rolling across her tongue with authentic Spanish curves. "Could you do me a favour?" She bid Julio to check the guest register for the *Corinthian*, which he did only on the condition, I gather, that he report nothing other than passengers who had declared themselves to be children. There were none. Ingrid cradled the phone and resumed her cigarette smoking. "Mind you," she suggested, "there could still be children. They're just not recorded as children."

I nodded, but was rightfully unconvinced. So I made no promises to Carson that she would have friends and playmates. She is a social creature, my daughter is, ever eager to be in company. "Can I bring a friend?" is a constant refrain with her.

Indeed, that was one of the driving forces behind the trip, at least, one of the more practical purposes, to establish a friendship, a *chumminess*, with my daughter, because many times I've said, "Hey, Carson, let's you and I go out to a ballgame, a movie, the museum, whatever," only to have her demand, "Can I bring a friend?"

"Well, you know, I thought it would be fun, just the two of us."

Carson's constant response is to allow little creases to inform her features, just enough to warp her face with doubt and concern for my sanity. *Why would that be fun?*

So, as I say, I had guaranteed no other children, and was even relieved that there were none. Because this, by god, was going to be fun.

Meanwhile, a host of healthy young people, wearing tight blue shorts and white golf shirts that said *Corinthian*, corralled everyone with the proper label and pushed us over into one corner of the outdoor airport. More paperwork was done. We were then ushered onto a bus, an ancient white beast of a bus, and driven down to the sea.

The sun was sinking.

Two

Here's the story I didn't tell the Publisher:

When I was thirteen years of age, I received permission to go to the Ex by myself. The Ex being the Canadian National Exhibition, an annual phenomenon here in Toronto, an outsized version of Ontario agricultural fairs. It consists of many old buildings, long resident near the grey Lake, each dedicated to some sphere of human endeavour. There is the Agricultural Building, for example, which didn't (and doesn't today) smell at all nicely. There is a Better Living Building, where, for many decades now, they have predicted upcoming boons and benisons, few of which have materialized. The builders and stockers did accurately predict the advent of the vibrating chair thirty-odd years ago, several examples of which adorned the ground floor. This made the Better Living Building a mecca for the tired and weary. The Ex consists largely of the midway, a garish avenue of carnival amusements. There are whirligigs, humbugs and tawdry diversions. When I was a lad, there was even a Freak Show, where I saw a family with flippers instead of arms, a man with green and scaly skin, people variously tiny and huge, and a Rubber Man. (The first time I saw the Rubber Man, I was eight or nine years old and pressed up to the apron. The Rubber Man opened his act by grabbing his forefinger and bending it until it lay flat against the back of his hand. I took hold of my own finger and pushed, trying to gauge the pain involved. Surprisingly—to both me and the Rubber Man—my finger folded backwards obediently. I didn't pursue this career opportunity, which is just as well, because my finger stiffened in my twenties, and I would have been a washed-up carnival freak very early in life.)

The Better Living Building lay at the far end of the midway, and people who'd survived the traverse gathered there to settle into the vibrating chairs. On that day in late August, when I was thirteen years of age, I entered the Better Living Building only to find all of the vibrating chairs occupied. Children and old people languished in the Naugahyde comfort. None showed any inclination to move and many were fast asleep. This is what sent me outside again, through the nearest exit.

I was sweaty and exhausted. My journey through the midway had been long and arduous, consisting of a stop at the Freak Show, multiple turns on the Flyer and the Wild Mouse, several Belgian waffles with slabs of ice cream sandwiched between them. I had thrown and gambled away most of my money and had only managed to win a single minute plastic gewgaw. I won this by letting a thin man with the history of the world tattoo'd upon his face attempt to guess my weight. He was unsuccessful, lowballing by many pounds, but I suspect he was merely being kind, any more accurate assessment of my weight likely to wound and insult. For I was a pudge of a boy, bespectacled and pimply.

Attending the Ex alone was a badge of maturation and independence, even though our parents' reluctance to allow it was a little ill-thought. *No, don't go to that place by yourself, where you will be quieted by fear and cowed into obeisance of the public laws; go instead in packs and hordes, so that you may be the very instruments of violence and mayhem.* My friends often claimed that going alone increased their chances of picking up girls, but this was an audacious and preposterous statement for the coolest of them, so I never even attempted it. Mostly I wanted to go alone so that I could travel at my own pace (my friends didn't stop to eat as often as I did) and pursue my own interests (they didn't much like the Freak Show; I tended to make a beeline for it).

It was an extremely hot mid-afternoon and I was spent. I mostly wanted to go home, although this would have been a humiliating defeat, because it was customary to remain at the Ex until closing at 10:00 P.M.

Now, I knew my way around the Ex as well as any young man, keying not only on the common landmarks—the Shell Tower, for example—but several more idiosyncratic ones. (The Belgian waffle stand figured large.) But I'd left the Better Living Building through the handiest exit, impatient and frustrated, and I found myself somewhere foreign. There was a building immediately before me, one I'd never seen before, a strange edifice that seemed to have been transported from Victorian England. There was a cobblestone pathway surrounding it, bordered by gas lamps that burned even in the day. The building was corniced and friezed, much more complicated architecturally than the rest of the Ex, which was rendered in the no-nonsense Presbyterian style so admired in Ontario.

This was, if memory serves (and it doesn't, often, I just thought you should know), the Boosey & Hawkes Museum of

Brass and Woodwinds. Or something like that. I dutifully entered, being the first clarinetist for the school band, the Concertmaster, which brought me honour much like that accorded Torquemada, Chief Inquisitor. So I entered, made a quick revolution of the exhibits and found myself back outside.

Beside the main door, huge and wooden and thrown open invitingly, was a smaller one, painted a dull red. I noticed a sign suspended above it, swaying and creaking in the breeze. It announced, "The Moody Theatre of Nature." (I actually think it may have been "Moodie," but I have decided to go with the former spelling. This isn't to avoid possible legal entanglements, it just seems a much more apt rendering.) What actually caught my attention, I'll confess, was another sign creaking in tandem with this one. It read, "AIR CONDITIONED."

I pushed open the door and mounted a shadowed staircase. In years to come, I was to enter many squalid dens and squats; I won't go into the details, but my point is, for gloomy forbiddenness this staircase remains a clear winner. At the top were shadows of a deeper hue. I stepped gingerly, half-expecting the final riser to give way to nothingness. But then there was a sudden illumination and Dr. Moody was addressing me. "The world of nature," he announced, "is wondrous and astounding."

Dr. Moody's image was being projected onto a screen, or at least a plastic groundsheet or something that had been pressed into service as a screen. He was a fleshy man, possessed of an unnatural healthiness. Across a face that was tanned the colour of mahogany spread a dazzling smile. What dazzled about the smile was not so much the whiteness (although it was indeed angelic and incandescent) as the energy and earnestness with which the smile was fashioned. You and I would probably have a hard time coming up with such a smile, certainly on our own. We might manage with advanced intoxicants, or a group of our closest friends adhering to specific and complicated instructions, but we couldn't manage what Dr. Moody did, to flash this smile perpetually, for no apparent reason. Dr. Moody affected the dress of an insurance salesman: a sober suit, a white shirt, a tie knotted so tightly that it shot colour into his jowls. Despite the fact that he seemed to be situated in an office, Moody tramped and kicked about the place as though hiking through the Alps, although he'd periodically place a buttock gingerly on the edge of the desk, fold his hands, and bend over slightly to address the camera with especial import. This is what he did as I entered what I shall graciously call the theatre. Dr. Moody placed a ham on the edge of his desk, smiled at the camera lens (making the unseen operator pull back abruptly) and said, "Suppose I were to find a pocket watch on a deserted beach ..."

I took a seat in the back row. This is indicative of a congenital demureness, because the place was deserted. Dr. Moody continued talking about this watch he'd found, or supposed that he had, but I didn't really pay attention, basking blissfully in the shower of cold air leaking from the vent above. Then there was music, gushing with peppy grandeur, and the titles went and came. Because I'd walked in on the end of one film, you see, and now watched another from the beginning. "The world of nature is wondrous and astounding," Dr. Moody assured me.

But I didn't have to take his word for it. Dr. Moody had film footage, which he introduced (he'd changed clothes for this second film, altering the tone of his suit and tie, although his face was no less woody, his smile undiminished) and then seemed to watch for himself, turning his head to the right as though the world of nature existed just beyond the edge of the movie screen.

I certainly cannot remember all that I saw that day. I spent the rest of the afternoon and that evening there, until the Exhibition's closing. People entered the darkened room during this time, drawn, like me, by the siren call of air conditioning, but few stayed longer than ten minutes, twenty minutes tops. Twenty minutes was the approximate length of one of Dr. Moody's films, and no one other than myself stayed for a second.

The films had a sameness. After Dr. Moody's proclamation— the words would change, but the "wondrous and astounding" theme was restated again and again—there would be a short documentary. Dr. Moody had obviously gathered these up from disparate sources. Some were grainy, and the hands that held the camera trembled. In others the images were crystal clear, and obviously made with much more sophisticated equipment, lenses that roamed and zoomed everywhere. Many of the documentarians favoured time-lapse photography, and any number of wondrous and astounding flowers exploded out of the earth and struggled toward heaven. Then these films would end, abruptly. Dr. Moody would appear and turn toward the camera, away from all the wonder. "Suppose I were walking along a deserted beach," he'd say, hiking a cheek over the lip of his desk, folding large hands over his crotch, "and I found a pocket watch. Suppose I'd never seen a pocket watch before. Now, I might be able to convince myself that this watch was simply a happenstance amalgam of molecules, that they had aligned themselves this way by purest chance. But how then would I explain the beauty and functionality of the pocket watch? No, the simplest logic would tell me that someone had *made* it. So it is with the wonders of nature ..."

I'm sure you are beginning to see Dr. Moody's point. You are likewise beginning to understand why no one stayed for more than the one film, because Dr. Moody was the ordained representative of some Christian sect (I forget which, perhaps the Church of Jesus Christ, Naturalist) and his true desire was not to educate, rather to convert. His success rate must have been rather low, I think. Most evangelists have figured out that the easiest targets are the downtrodden and twisted, people with lives so unblest that organized religion becomes the last refuge and sanctuary. The evangelists are on television late at night only partly because the rates are low. Late at night is when the Truly Wretched are sitting there on their sofas, blue-eyed and unthinking, a bottle of their favourite poisonous beverage clutched in both hands. Dr. Moody was out to convert others of his ilk, the Perpetually Beaming, but others of his ilk were not in attendance at the Exhibition. So the closest he got to a spiritual transformation was the chubby little thirteen-year-old sitting in the back row.

In the pocket-watch speech, Dr. Moody was, in fact, paraphrasing William Paley and his seminal work *Natural Theology, or, Evidences of the Existence and Attributes of the Deity, Collected from the Appearances of Nature*, published in 1802, many years before anyone thought that books needed snappy titles. (I suppose Moody was not paraphrasing so much as stealing, but that's all right, as Paley had borrowed much of this watch business from a Dutch philosopher named Bernard Nieuwentyt.) William Paley is very elaborate in the analogy, much more so than Dr. Moody, making a leisurely appraisal of the timepiece. "We next observe a flexible chain," he writes, "artifically wrought for the sake of flexure, communicating the action of the spring from the box to the fusee." Paley then asks the reader to consider an eye; is it any less complicated, is there any less evidence of contrivance? He comes to the same place as Dr. Moody, that there is an obvious intelligence, "adequate," as Paley puts it, "to the appearances which we wish to account for." And both men, Moody and Paley, turn their eyes Heavenward. "Upon the whole," concludes *Natural Theology*, "after all the schemes and struggles of a reluctant philosophy, the necessary resort is to a Deity. The marks of *design* are too strong to be gotten over. Design must have had a designer. That designer must have been a person. That person is God."

I bought it.

I walked away from the Museum of Brass and Woodwinds with the argument folded neatly and tucked into my breast. I had been struggling with questions of *belief* since early childhood—not with the actual belief itself, because I'd long accepted God as my Father Who Art in Heaven—but with a justification for it. This (what I've since learned is referred to in theological circles as the "Argument from Design") was just what I needed. I became a whiz in high-school science classes, and when dissecting frogs would often step back and take a blissful look skyward. I didn't go so far as to study natural sciences in university, concentrating instead on Beer Consumption and the Intricacies of 9-5-2. But I read about nature, I was an inveterate visitor of zoos and museums, and certainly, most certainly, whilst powering through the television channels, I could be stopped in an instant by the image of a bird or insect. And thus I remained convinced of God's existence.

Shortly after the birth of our first daughter, my wife and I were lying in bed (the infant cradled at our feet) fretting anxiously and watching television. I had possession of the channel changer, which I rarely relinquish, and was traipsing through the frequencies when an image caused my hand to relax, my thumb to leave the button. A pile of black rubble rose out of the water. Huge turtles and lizards romped upon it. "The Galápagos," I said, with the authority of personal recognition. I somehow have always been able to recognize the Encantadas.

"You know," I said, "when Carson is seven years old, I think I'm going to take her there."

"Why?" yawned my wife.

I shrugged. "I don't know." And I didn't, at least, I wouldn't have been able to give it voice. But the answer has since made itself clear: *To introduce her to God.*

Three

We huddled in the Zodiac, shoulder to shoulder, twenty people, strangers to me, except of course for my father and my daughter. My father sat with one hand on his hat. He had a brand-new Panama, the largest he could find, although that was still a little small for his skull. My daughter likewise had a new Panama—they actually come from Ecuador, you see—although hers was oversized. She, too, was forced to raise an arm and paste the thing down, setting the brim a-flapping in the evening sea breeze.

Our little boat snaked through the bay, which was full of yachts and fishing vessels. Beyond all these other ships, silhouetted against the darkening sky, sat the *Corinthian*. It was easily the biggest craft in the harbour (it is actually the second largest ship cruising the archipelago) and seemed capable of riding the roughest waters. It looked to me like a warship, oversized and ironclad. The weathervane above the fo'c's'le spun around at quite a clip.[1] A pelican did its best to rest upon it,

---

1 It may not have actually been the fo'c's'le, but how often do you get a chance to use a word with three apostrophes in it?

a study in blissful self-denial, because every gust threatened to hurtle the bird from its perch.

The bird was reluctant to give up its roost, treacherous as it was, because competition for resting places was fierce. Flying creatures, black slashes against the departing sun, filled the welkin with fluid design. Creation was abundantly evident in this empyrean; I could almost sense His hand at work. I nudged my daughter in the side with my elbow.

She yawned.

Here's my thinking: If God's existence is proven by the presence of wondrous and astounding things, then, where things are most wondrous and astounding, He Himself must be manifest.

The Galápagos has always felt like that place. After all, Dr. Moody made large use of the archipelago in his little films. He would show us a close-up of the marine iguana, the beast with the peeling hide, so hideous as to seem accursed. The marine iguana is the only seagoing lizard in the world, Dr. Moody stated, and he demonstrated with underwater footage, the creatures undulating through the surf, grazing on large quantities of seaweed. Wondrous and astounding. Dr. Moody also featured the lummoxy tortoises, the lithe sea lions. "Here on these islands," Dr. Moody seemed to be saying, "you can really see God doing His stuff." Darwin himself seemed to sense something of this, writing, "Both in space and time, we seem to be brought somewhat near to that great fact—the mystery of mysteries—the first appearance of new beings on Earth."

It was not lost upon me, however, that Carson and I were journeying to the place where God suffered His greatest personal defeat. *God Is Not Dead, But He Is Not Feeling Well* reads a bumper sticker I once saw, and if that is the case, the Galápagos is where He took ill. Because Charles Darwin countered

Paley's watch argument—he'd read *Natural Theology* in his school days, and found that the logic gave him "as much delight as did Euclid"—with the assertion that wondrous and astounding things could be fashioned by means of Natural Selection. It was, Darwin conceded, absurd to imagine that something as wondrous as (to use Paley's own example) an eye had exploded into being via a chance meshing of the appropriate molecules. But over eons, starting with a tiny cluster of light-sensitive cells (something like the sensitized spot on the flagellum of the fresh-water plant Euglena), Natural Selection would eventually fashion an eye. Several types of eyes, indeed, for there are eyes in the astounding and wondrous animal kingdom that work on different principles than, say, our own.

The mechanics of the process are easily understood; that is, if you read a good writer on the subject (Richard Dawkins is very good, even if he makes the reader feel *just* a little bit thick[2]), you will come away with understanding. My own grasp is not so sure, and I probably wouldn't get into it at all, except that this stuff is important if we are to fathom all the squabbling. So here goes. I give fair warning, do not defend any scientific theory put forward in these pages, especially not late at night in barrooms. I may well be misrepresenting the theories of others, and any that are original to me should probably remain that way.

Humans have long bred animals for certain characteristics— an acute sense of smell in hounds, say, or stamina in homing pigeons[3]—so no one, two to three hundred years ago, had a

---

2   *The Selfish Gene* was Dawkins's first book; *The Blind Watchmaker* is perhaps his best.
3   Charles Darwin, entering his middle age, the adventures aboard the *Beagle* all behind him, spent a great deal of time talking to pigeon breeders. He asked them about the various types of birds; he took copious notes about the breeders' strategies and methods. He became a member of the Columbarian and Philoperistera Clubs, where

problem with the concept of specific mutability, change within a species. But they did not know the mechanism by which these changes occurred. Darwin's answer to the problem was at once simple ("How extremely stupid not to have thought of that!") and mind-boggling, because it solved a much greater riddle: how species themselves come into being.

One of the first people to unequivocally state a Theory of Evolution was, oddly enough, Charles's grandfather, Erasmus Darwin (1731–1802). In his masterwork *Zoonomia, or, The Laws of Organic Life* (1796),[4] Erasmus very sensibly argued that all life was descended from the same primitive organism, which he termed the "one living filament," and was altered by external influences, such as climate. Unfortunately, Erasmus had a great many other ideas, all of which he crammed between the covers of *Zoonomia*. The book sold well, but to a particularly bemused population. Indeed, the word "darwinizing" was coined, meaning to indulge in far-fetched and speculative thinking. (So, when I darwinize in this book, please remember that I am emulating Erasmus and not his more sobersided grandson.) Still, Erasmus Darwin was astute and prophetic, as is evidenced by his poem "The Temple of Nature":

---

he met enthusiasts of the "fancy." Darwin sat in the corner, not contributing to the conversation but intent on every word. The Pigeon People were tolerant of Darwin, complimented by his attention and interest. There was no denying he was odd, though, quiet and preoccupied. He seemed to be wrestling with something; there seemed to be a great weight upon him. The townspeople knew he was sickly— often his face would be covered with patches of red, raw skin, and he was winded by the slightest exertion—but they sensed a more profound malaise. So they answered his questions about pigeons, as though that could help. Darwin himself seemed to think it might, because he asked his questions with urgency, even desperation. He wrote down their answers and then returned silently home.

4   This was the very word that Charles wrote on the title pages of his secret note-books, "Zoonomia."

Organic life beneath the shoreless waves
Was born and nurs'd in oceans pearly caves;
First forms minute, unseen by spheric glass,
Move on the mud, or pierce the watery mass.
These as successive generations bloom,
New powers acquire and larger limbs assume;
Whence countless groups of vegetation spring
And breathing realms of fir and feet and wing.

Other pioneers of the field include the impoverished French aristocrat Jean-Baptiste Pierre Antoine de Monet, Chevalier de Lamarck (1744–1829). Lamarck very clearly saw nature's continuum from microbe to man. Indeed, he discounted any seemingly large gaps in the chain of being with the rejoinder that the link had simply not yet been found. Changes in specific structure corresponded to changes in condition and habit; so, for example, the giraffe's long neck was produced by the creature's practice of stretching and craning its head upwards to devour foliage. Again, this is pretty sensible stuff. Lamarck's downfall was to believe that characteristics acquired within a parent's lifetime would be passed on to the offspring. The aforementioned hypothetical giraffe could, by constant straining at the highest branches, lengthen its own neck by a fraction of an inch; according to Lamarck, this fraction would be inherited by the giraffe's issue. This is wrong-headed, I guess (the blacksmith's children are not born with bigger arms than other kids), but not entirely mad (the blacksmith's children, it seems to me, do tend to be rather beefy little porkers). Yet "Lamarckism" is to biology what "flat-earthism" is to geology. (And, ironically, Lamarck invented that word "biology.") The theory's current reputation might have much to do with Paul Kammerer and the scandal of the midwife toads,[5] and more recently Lamarckism was tainted by association with Trofim Lysenko and his pseudo-science "Michurinism."[6] But even Lamarck's contemporaries thought he was so full of hooey that he smelt from the next town. (And, in those days, long before Mendel the Monk learned from his peas the surprisingly mathematical nature of inheritance, people had no really good reason to disbelieve Lamarck.) Lamarck, like Erasmus Darwin, was an unabashed and fearless speculator, but for some reason the populace was not amused. This may have been due to the weather forecasts he published annually, which were reliable only to the extent that they were utterly and absolutely wrong.

So people were thinking about this stuff. There was a best-selling book entitled *Vestiges of the Natural History of Creation*, published in 1823, which made a number of statements that we can identify as "evolutionary." Mankind, claimed *Vestiges*, was descended from a giant frog. Well, um, perhaps. Yellow creatures, maintained *Vestiges*, are evil; is not the tiger the most fearsome creature in the jungle? The book was filled with such iffiness—the notion of "spontaneous generation" figured large—but its author was not, after all, a naturalist or man of science.

---

5 In the 1920s, Kammerer managed, through control of the laboratory environment, to get the toads to generate "nuptial pads," roughed growths on their feet that would aid mating in wet conditions. When nuptial pads were seen in the subsequent generation—despite the toads being born and raised in dryness—it seemed evidence of Lamarckism. However, the pads were discovered to be nothing more than ink injected subcutaneously. Kammerer committed suicide, although there is compelling evidence that he was not the culprit.

6 Trofim Lysenko had many odd ideas, all of which appealed to Stalin. Lysenko equated his own brand of Lamarckism with Marxism, and made grandiose claims about enhanced crop yields and larger cattle, improvements in one generation appearing in the next. In order to support these claims, Lysenko was forced to suppress both experimental research and experimental researchers.

His name was Robert Chambers (1802–1871), and he was a journalist and publisher. *Vestiges* was written with his brother William, and published anonymously. Although there was no explanation for the mechanics of evolution given, *Vestiges* clearly and unabashedly announced its operation: "It might have been seen, ere man existed, that a remarkable creature was coming upon the earth." The Chambers brothers also emphasized, repeatedly, the importance of random variation. This may have had something to do with the fact that both Robert and William had six fingers on each hand.

Another pioneer was Lord Monboddo (1714–1799), a Scottish jurist, amateur natural historian and linguist. Monboddo was, admittedly, a little eccentric; once, while he was visiting the King's Bench in London, the hall began to collapse, fixtures plummeting from the walls and ceiling. Judges and lawyers panicked and ran pell-mell, fleeing for the exits. Lord Monboddo sat very still, watching all the commotion. "I thought it was an annual ceremony," he replied when asked why he'd remained so imperturbed, "with which, being an alien, I had nothing to do."

Anyway, it was Lord Monboddo's notion—mentioned in his six-volume *On the Origin and Progress of Language*—that humankind was descended from the apes. Monboddo claimed that our tailbone was a vestige of this ancestry. "It is a pity to see Lord Monboddo publish such notions," stated Monboddo's contemporary Dr. Johnson. "There would be little in a fool doing it; we should only laugh. But when a wise man does it we are sorry."

I don't mean to imply that thinking about the question of specific variation was the purview of eccentrics. It may seem difficult to escape that conclusion, but I can assure you that many reasonable men of science were grappling with the question. Charles Lyell (1797–1875), for example, was a cautious and circumspect man who had originally studied for a career in the law. It was his training to marshal evidence and present it clearly, and in his book *The Principles of Geology* he makes a cogent case on two important fronts: (1) that the earth is of an awesome age, vastly older than had been thought; and (2) that for much of its history there has been a succession of species. Lyell recognized many of the determinants—geographical, even what we would today call ecological—and he hovered around the mystery of Natural Selection without placing his finger squarely upon it.

For that Insight was to be Darwin's.[7]

Charles Darwin realized that the force was *competition from within the species itself.* This thought was inspired by Thomas Malthus (1766–1834), whose "Essay on the Principle of Population" argued that the population has a tendency to increase faster than its means of subsistence. The phrase "struggle for existence" became a key component of the theory, as did another phrase, one not original to Darwin, but one that he liked the sound of, "the survival of the fittest."[8]

I was looking at a magazine one day (this was *Newsweek*, for the week of May 6, 1996) when my eye was caught by a particular item. My eye was caught, I'll admit, because there was a picture of a very attractive woman, indeed, a former Playmate of the Year. The accompanying article began this way:

> You gotta feel sorry for the male contestants on MTV's Darwinian dating game, "Singled Out." Of the 50 guys who start on every show, only one finishes.

---

7   Charles Darwin carried the first volume of *The Principles of Geology* on board the *Beagle.* The second volume reached him during the voyage.

8   The phrase was actually coined by one Herbert Spencer. It was first pointed out to Charles by young Alfred Russel Wallace, the collector from Malay.

Now, the notion that this process is "Darwinian" is one of the reasons that the Theory of Evolution is still encountering resistance, even by many people who accept it as fact. We don't like to believe that we have become the cultivated people we are through a barbaric process, that our ancestors routinely clubbed one another over the head until only one, thick-skulled and woozy, was left standing.

But the process need not be depicted as so very brutal. The basic mechanism is *adaptation*, and it works this way. The parents both contribute DNA, which combines into what might be viewed as a genetic recipe for the next generation. Now variations, mutations, are going to be introduced, perhaps because of an outside source (radiation, maybe), perhaps because DNA replicates itself, over and over again, and from time to time it's going to get itself slightly wrong. Some of these mutations are going to be disadvantageous, in which case the creature in question will likely die soon and that will be the end of that. Or the mutation may make no difference at all to the creature. But in some small percentage, the mutation will prove beneficial. And the portion of the population that possesses the mutation will have an advantage over the portion of the population that lacks it. They will accordingly fare better, and over time—and Darwin's Theory of Evolution is best understood if one can conceive of great tracts of time—the mutation will establish itself as the norm. Evolution has taken place.

Let us consider some buffaloes that live in Africa, of which there are two sorts, the field buffalo and the forest buffalo. The main difference is in the distance between horns, the forking; the field buffalo possesses big things that coil off lazily to either side, giving it a headspan of three-plus feet. The forest buffalo has a much tighter set, shooting forward from its forehead.

According to the Theory of Evolution, at one point there

was likely just one sort, what we might call the all-terrain buffalo. And there was, because of the vagaries of DNA replication, some variation in horn formation. Now, usually there is a geographic factor involved; for whatever reason, some of the all-terrain buffaloes were forced to seek permanent habitat in the forest. What I'm saying is that a smaller, tighter horn formation gave the owner a *slight* advantage—in terms of mobility through the trees, of being slightly less conspicuous, etc., etc. (The etc., etc., means "I've thought of two, now it's your turn.") Over time the mutation established itself, and we were on the road to speciation, dividing the herd of all-terrain buffaloes into the types we have today. This is at odds with the popular conception of Evolution, which would have it that all the buffaloes with big wide horns got pronged between the trees and perished there.

So there is the science, in a cracked nutshell. Why then the Great Squabble? *It's not as if*, as Old Man Cooper used to say, *you're losing money on the deal.*

The answer is that there was, in Darwin's time, a general belief in something variously called "the Chain of Being" or "the Scale of Life" or some other combination of those words. Ironically, a popular graphic depiction of the Chain of Being looks much like a high-school textbook representation of Evolution: a succession of creatures, starting very small in the left-hand corner, progress in size and complexity until there strides a naked man. But there is a subtle but very significant difference: in the Chain of Life there is no suggestion of movement, growth or development. It is meant to portray immutability. Indeed, the Chain of Being represents a view of life as egocentric as the notion that the earth is the centre of the universe. According to this view, when God created the species, he set them down upon the world with especial care, in a certain order of importance and dominance, and at the very top is Homo sapiens.

When Darwin made the Scale of Being a continuum, he made it fluid and hard to handle. God didn't do His creating with care at all, it was suddenly claimed, he did it in a slip-shod, half-baked way, and left everything in a state of flux. Why would He do such a thing? The unsettling answer is, in a cracked nutshell, He wouldn't, unless He didn't exist at all.

My father has long held out Charles Darwin as an example. But of what, of what, has been my question. It was here that I thought I had found an answer, looking at this brave and star-tling assertion of godlessness. Because Charles Darwin had no personal stake in this (or so I thought); he had no reason to want to make everyone suddenly cast a tiny glance upwards and gather their collars together. Indeed, Darwin was, at least to begin with, a religious man.[9] He had considered the ministry as a career choice; mind you, it was a common enough calling for young men like Charles, fairly well-heeled and -schooled.

My father has always advocated fearless exploration in the muddy fields of Knowledge. I was taught that knowledge, any knowledge, was good, and that you shouldn't worry about dirty-ing your shoes in the getting of it. I'm trying to think of an example of my father illustrating this in his professional life. (Indeed, I'm sitting in my kitchen in the dead of night, sipping what I hope is the last in a series of beers, trying to think of an example.) I know shamefully little about his career. He originally went to university to be a geologist, he told me one

9 "Whilst on board the *Beagle* I was quite orthodox and I remember being heartily laughed at by several of the officers ... for quoting the Bible as an unanswerable authority on some point of morality. I suppose it was the novelty of the argument that amused them."

time.[10] He was going to be a geologist, so in love was he with sticking his hands into the belly of the earth and pulling out whatever his huge fingers might wrap around. But he took psychology as an elective and misunderstood the purpose of a reading list he was handed. Reading the books was optional, but my father thought it compulsory, so he read every book on the list and as a result did fabulously well in psychology. So he made psych his major and ended up with the best B.A. of his class. (My mother ended up with the best B.A. of her class, too, at the same university. I ended up with no B.A. at all, which perhaps flies in the face of Evolutionary Theory.) He went on to attain his doctorate, although he took a year off after his M.A. to go to Saskatchewan, where he could instruct at the university with that degree. This is why my brother Tony was born in that chilly city, a circumstance I always counted as improbable and semi-romantic. My father's main career has been that of teacher, a professor first at the University of Toronto and then at York. He was so profoundly a teacher that when he moved out to the country—having remarried after my mother's death in 1969—the locals usually referred to him in that manner, as "the Teacher." He has a distinctly professorial air; his forehead is scored on either side by deep diagonals, evidence of long and arduous ratiocination. When I was a small boy, he told me these were duelling scars, and it is only now I realize the degree to which he wasn't joking, that he had spent long nights staring out the window, grappling with bogies in the fields of knowledge. My father has also done some private practice, largely with stutterers. I am therefore well-trained in

---

10 It's interesting—at least to me—that Darwin, like my father, originally wanted to be a geologist. As the *Beagle* neared the Encantadas, Charles exalted, "I look forward to the Galápagos with more interest than any other part of the voyage. They abound with volcanoes and, I should hope, contain Tertiary strata!"

dealing with stutterers. *Never complete sentences for them,* I was instructed, *just wait.* So many times I would be called away from the table, only to pluck up the receiver and receive the most profound of silences. I would sigh and, in those pre-microwave days, mourn the loss of a hot dinner. My father has also done research; he was one of the first people to investigate what are now referred to as "biological clocks," and someone told me that his name is attached to a paper which attempts to link frequency of stutters with particular phonics. My source told me the ultimate conclusion was that there were no sounds that had a significantly greater frequency, and counted the exercise as a failure. But from what I understand, the conclusion my father came to, near the end of his career, is that stuttering isn't that big a problem (provided everyone else has a little time on their hands), so the results of his experiments likely didn't bother him.

For a time during my childhood, my father, who back then was referred to as looking like Victor Mature, became a mainstay on local television. Whenever they needed a psychological type, they tended to engage him. I remember one show; the topic was astrology. The host demanded of my father, "Would you be prepared to believe that the stars influence our behaviour?"

"Yes," my father responded.

"Can you give us some instances where this seems to be the case?"

"No," said my father. "But I'd be prepared to believe it."

Maybe that's my example. Perhaps my father hadn't risked much—although many people don't enjoy looking a little foolish on television—but my father seemed to be saying, *There is no field of knowledge too mucky for me.*

My father used Charles Darwin (so goes this theory) to illustrate this point, because Charles pursued his quest knowing full well that he could end up destroying God.

Four

Our rooms aboard the *Corinthian* were adjacent and shared a common washroom. My father had a room all to himself, Carson and I the other. They were basically closets with coarsely blanketed berths in them, right-angled to each other and bunked. Carson immediately claimed the upper, climbing the little ladder, assuming a pose of cross-legged serenity and staring down upon me as I tried to stow luggage. There was a small cupboard tucked away into the corner, which I wouldn't have noticed were it not for the fact that the sea swell had thrown open the cupboard door and was banging it against the far wall. I began to unload the gear carefully, trying to assign specific locales for T-shirts, shorts, bathing suits, snorkelling gear, medicines and underwear, although finally I just threw everything into the cupboard and shouldered the door shut. The child's mother, I knew, would have maintained method and order, even if it meant taking articles of clothing and folding them in half eight times. I thought I was doing well in freeing up some space for dirty laundry, practically a whole shelf, maybe four or five square inches, although I could have anticipated that by the end of the trip I'd be selecting clothes from there as much as from anywhere else.

Carson descended the ladder and entered the washroom. A moment later I heard a low, doom-laden moan. "Uh-oh."

I entered the washroom, washcloset we might call it, to find Carson staring forlornly into the toilet bowl. She indicated a small sign mounted on the wall, instructing passengers to put toilet paper into the trash basket nearby, not into the toilet itself. Carson pointed to where a small piece of tissue floated, soggy and ghostlike. "What's going to happen?" asked Carson, meaning, *Is the ship going to explode or merely sink?*

I do not know from whence this comes, this dour blackness. Carson is cheerful enough, much liked and admired by her classmates and teachers. She is also constantly afflicted by misgivings and worriments, and has been since birth, or so it seems. In the months just before our departure, Carson had even fallen into one or two true, adult-strength depressions. Once, as the Canadian winter night fell at four o'clock in the afternoon, she lay on her bed and sighed deeply. "I hate it," she said to me, "when the sun goes down." This might have been SAD, Seasonal Affective Disorder, or whatever that is, because the winter of '95–96 had been long and cruel. But it may have been because often the world seems heartless and malevolent. The world is spinning madly, and any little thing could add crazy English to the big ball and shoot it off into oblivion. This is why she stared into the toilet bowl and felt deeply sickened and troubled.

Then it was time to go receive our instructions and meet the captain, crew and guides. Carson looked at me and smiled grimly, brave in the face of her own doom.

I knocked on the washroom door that connected to my father's room. He opened it up, showing that he'd already organized and stowed. I was impressed. Mind you, he had a whole empty bunk to work with, and had laid out his belongings there with apparent care: a plastic Ziploc bag full of tissues, a couple of novels, a sketchbook and drawing pencil. I was a little surprised to see the sketchbook. Funny as it might seem, I was aware that there was a graphically artistic bent to many members of the family, but not that it extended to my father. He hadn't even brought along a camera, claiming that it never occurred to him to either take pictures or look at them afterwards.

My father is a tall man, half a foot taller than I. He has thick hair that flows back from his brow; white now, of course, and grey for years, ever since I can remember. He wears spectacles and favours one ear, often repositioning himself so that he might hear better. This is performed either grudgingly or eagerly, depending on the nature of what is being said. If someone is dispensing instruction or practical information, my father brings the better ear forward somewhat irritably. If ideas are floating in the air, my father waves the ear about like a butterfly collector's net.

When I was growing up, and my father was always either going to or returning from the university, he affected a bow tie, which enhanced a scholarly mien. Now that he is retired, he dresses for comfort. For the journey to the Galápagos he wore a modified safari outfit, a ventilated shirt and matching shorts. He plucked his Panama hat from the top bunk and screwed it down upon his head.

We descended into the dining room—quite a large thing, the capaciousness of the dining room being one of the *Corinthian's* big selling points—and were introduced to the crew and guides. The purser, Judy, pulled a microphone from the wall and pressed it to her face, where it squealed and squawked. You might wonder what the microphone was doing on the wall. Well, on a ship, quite a few things are on the wall. This has to do with the economizing of space, and also with the fact that if things weren't attached to the wall they would be driven into your face and ears. The *Corinthian* was by all accounts a stable craft, but in the week to come there would be many times when one was set upon by invisible football hooligans. One would be mashed up against closed doors or suddenly doubled over the railing (and the railing corresponded to a place on the anatomy where most people don't double easily), and then anything that wasn't attached would be sucked up in a little whirling vortex and fired toward one's face. Mind you, there was always the possibility of reprieve, because the *Corinthian*, having to'ed, would next fro, so the projectiles would suddenly reverse, and one would be pulled up and propelled forward so that one could smash one's face into *them*.

So this is why the microphone was on the wall. Judy tore it from there, eagerly held it to her lips and said, "Goodahevenin-ladiesandgennelmen. Justsoyoonow, sorryforifyour-late, *bud* you-shoonow, SAETASAN, deyare *now*thintodowithus."

My father held his hand behind his good ear and turned as though it were a miniature satellite dish and he was searching for optimum reception. His brow knitted and furrowed, his eyes locked in a perpetual wince, and his mouth fashioned into a strange twisted shape, a shape you could recreate by taking an old hound dog and making him sit under a hot sun for a few hours. "What?" he demanded loudly, although he didn't direct this at Judy the Purser. He had already decided that he and Judy would never communicate, so he said, "What?" in my general direction, or "What?" to some people close by, who had assumed bogus expressions of comprehension, or "What?" to his granddaughter, working on the theory that she owned the freshest ears.

"Oh," said Carson, "she says hi."

"Oh," said my father, relaxing momentarily, throwing himself back in his seat.

Judy raised her arm and cocked her wrist like a leggy game-show assistant, and people dressed in white materialized behind her. I will mention now that almost everyone dressed in white down in the Encantadas. The difference between passengers and crew is that the latter were crisply uniformed. The passengers tended to wear looser-fitting clothes, but white was definitely the colour of choice. Judy recommended her announcement, causing my father to throw himself forward so that he could fix his elbow and arm, the base of his manual hearing aid, on the table. As Judy babbled, people would step forward from the line-up behind. A tall man, his upper lip decorated with a bristly black moustache, bowed slightly and then turned and left the room altogether.

"Who was that?" demanded my father.

"The captain," Carson replied, a little wearily.

More of the crew stepped forward. I was not sure what their functions were, although one I discovered to be the navigator, because he was often spotted thereafter standing in the lounge area on the middecks staring at a map suspended there. When passengers wandered by and demanded clarification or explanation of the *Corinthian's* path, this young man would grin and fix the tip of his finger to the glass face. He would draw long smears around and about the islands. We met the ship's doctor, an alarmingly young man with a gourdlike physique. We were introduced to our waiters, a group which included Hugo; the reason I single him out is that he usually served our little table of three. He also functioned as the bartender topside, so my father and I got to know him pretty well. Then the guides stepped forward, Maria, Orlando and young Carlos.

Maria started the slide show, directing a shaft of mote-filled light at a screen set up at the front of the dining room. We saw two strange birds stacked like flapjacks. "These are blue-footed boobies," she told us, "and they are having fun."

My father stood up and marched out of the room, leaving behind the impression that he had the daintiest of sensibilities and wouldn't tolerate such off-colour frivolity. I knew that he had heard none of it. My daughter (who likely knew this as well) dealt him a withering scowl and returned her attention to Maria. Even though she found the slide show as boring as eternity, she folded her hands neatly upon her lap and listened with impressive concentration.

There was, I should mention, a little uneasiness between my father and my daughter.

You'll recall that we waited at the Quito airport for quite a long while. Most of it was spent in the departure lounge, although before that we'd been waiting in the airport proper, which is divided in two. This may have represented a division between domestic and international flights. It may have been a case of an addition being added to an existing, no longer adequate, facility. I'm not sure. At any rate, it was necessary to physically leave one in order to get into the other, which is what we had done earlier that morning. The older, domestic building was alarmingly active, swarming with people frantic to get to the Galápagos Islands. Ecuadorians didn't swarm; they lounged around, half-grinning as though remembering good jokes, or, more infuriatingly, lining up without being told to, moving as one, rising without benefit of broadcast announcement to form an orderly queue in front of an old wooden door that was not labelled in any manner whatsoever. The door would open and they would disappear. This caused the tourists to hum and bristle, because it was almost certain that these people were boarding planes, even though no plane was operating according to schedule as far as we knew. We could see no planes taking off, but often we could hear distant mechanical drones. This section of the airport was also filled with children. The older ones would offer to do things for you in exchange for a few hundred sucres. I'm not being coy here; they weren't alluding to sexual favours, they were offering help and assistance, although everyone seemed to be able to handle the primary activity—waiting for something to happen—pretty much single-handedly. The younger children merely came and asked for money. My father turned out to be a soft touch, which, I'll admit, surprised me a bit. It's not that I thought him hardhearted, but I thought he was logical—intellectual—enough to know that handing out sucres was like throwing a few grains of sand down a near-bottomless abyss in the hope of filling it up. But when approached he would dig into his pockets; and when approached by a girl no older than Carson who was already saddled with the care of an infant, he not only dug into his own pockets, he borrowed a few thousand sucres from me.

So we'd left this part of the airport and wandered over to the other building, which was a lot emptier and quieter. We sat down on some plastic seats and went about our own business and distractions. My daughter fished around in her bag until she found some book on the subject of dogs. (You shall hear my daughter further on the subject of dogs.) I resumed my research on the Galápagos Islands, rereading the section in the traveller's guide on how to get there, which was turning out to be nowhere near as easy as I'd thought. My father immediately went to sleep for a little while. Then I began to worry that in our absence they'd loaded up the plane bound for the Encantadas and sent it on its way, so I roused everyone and suggested we go back to the frenzied building. I gathered up bags, we walked outside and through the other doors—a process that occupied maybe forty seconds—and then Carson said, "Oh-oh. I left my bag back there."

I threw down the other luggage and dashed back. It was gone, of course, and probably had been the instant after we'd left. Feeling rather useless, I prowled around the building for a minute or two. It was possible that whoever had taken the bag had peeked inside—seen dog and colouring books, pens and pencil crayons, rulers and erasers, asthma medicine and a puffer, sunblock, enough lint to gag a moose—and abandoned the thing. But it was gone, of course it was gone, because there was poverty enough down there to give even lint some value. (I phoned home sometime later that morning and told my wife about the mishap. "Did you check the Lost and Found?" she asked. Pretty Canadian, eh? They don't have a Lost and Found at the Quito airport.)

But what happened was, my daughter began to wonder what was keeping me, because she was expecting me back almost instantly, her bag held aloft, proudly reclaimed.

My father sighed and answered, "He's looking for your bag. You shouldn't have left it behind," or some words to that effect; I wasn't there, after all, and I've heard conflicting reports. My daughter reports that the words were full of blame and rebuke, which I doubt very much. But he can be very imposing and grave, my father, and I believe he scared the shit of Carson. I been there before.

When the slide show ended, I told Carson it was time to go to bed. She fled the dining room eagerly, which will give you some indication as to just how dull she'd found the entertainment. In the tiny washroom she brushed her teeth dutifully. Not only did she put toilet paper into the plastic wastebasket, I think she folded it carefully. Then she ran up the ladder to her top bunk and crawled under the grey blanket.

"You know Alan's dog?" she demanded.

"I don't want to talk about dogs."

"No, no. But you know Alan's dog?"

"Yes."

"Is that as big as it's going to get?"

"Yes."

"Can you pick it up?"

"I've told you before ..."

Before I get into the relatively complicated answer to the "Can you pick it up?" inquiry, I might as well explain what's going on. Because it's going to be going on a lot. Carson has an ability—it may well be a curse, the future shall tell—to fixate on one notion, idea or desire. To the exclusion of all else, and for all time. This notion, the longing for a dog, could not be quelled or sated.

Not even, I should mention, by the acquisition of a dog. Back home waited a creature named Zoë, a curious interbreeding of the Labrador and the Jack Russell terrier. How we acquired this dog is: one day I came home to find Carson and her mother talking in hushed tones, their heads inclined toward each other and almost touching. My wife looked at me and said, "We're thinking seriously about a dog." Carson's face was transformed by happiness.

So a dog was got, a family pet, except it was really more like a furry parasitic twin for yours truly, a drooling little adorer who skidded and slipped in my wake. My wife didn't exactly care for the beast, due to Zoë's propensity for devouring huge chunks of the universe. And Carson soured because the dog was slightly too big, and nervous, to be hefted up and toted around. She still liked the dog, even loved it, but Zoë could never be "her" dog.

So I sighed and said, "You *could*, you would be able to, pick up many dogs. But that doesn't mean that the dogs would like it. Why do you want to pick up dogs all the time?"

Carson shrugged, pulled up the covers. She closed her eyes and fell gently to sleep.

Five

The Encantadas were first spied by the Incan King
Tupac Yupanqui. I will state that as fact even though it is more
like fable. Actually, as long as I'm reporting fable, I should get
it right. The Galápagos were first spied by Antarqui, Tupac
Yupanqui's personal necromancer, who, possessing the ability of
flight, acted on a hunch of his master's and sortied out over the
waters. He flew back and said that the strange islands Tupac
Yupanqui had dreamt about were indeed there. So Tupac
Yupanqui ventured far out into "Mama Cocha"—"the Mother
of All Lagoons"—and returned with tales of islands of fire.
Tupac's tale must be taken with a grain of salt (it is said that
he returned with much gold and silver, which is hard to come
by on the Encantadas), but he got the "islands of fire" part right.
Because the Galápagos were spit out of the sea, the oldest a
mere seven million years ago, a trice in geological time. They
are the summits of huge volcanoes that rise as much as ten
thousand feet from the ocean floor.

There are five major islands, eleven smaller ones, and some
fifty islets. There are also many huge monoliths thrown up out

of the water, pointed pieces of rock that look like the fingers of drowning giants.

The first authenticated sighting of the Galápagos Islands was made in 1535 by Tomás de Berlanga, the Bishop of Castilla de Oro, as Panama was then known. He hadn't intended to make the sighting. His ship had been carried there, transported via a vexing combination of strong currents and windlessness. It was the Bishop who first saw the strange life-forms ("Nothing but seals, and turtles, and such big tortoises that each could carry a man on top of itself, and many iguanas that are like serpents"). It was the Bishop who noticed that the islands seemed to appear and disappear, were draped and made naked by cloaks of mist, and he gave them their best name, Las Islas Encantadas.

Some years later, Abraham Ortelius, the famous Flemish cartographer, chose the Bishop's other appellation, the one that means "tortoise." Although if you want to be a hopelessly annoying pedant (and who, in his or her heart of hearts, doesn't?), you should insist that the word means "saddle" and only refers to the carapaced beasts by analogy; in his *Orbis Terrarum*, Ortelius drew in the tiny dots and labelled them the Isolas de Galápagos.

Next came the pirates and the buccaneers. And this in some way fed my desire as a boy to go to the Galápagos Islands, to play upon the same field as cutthroats. I don't know exactly when I made the connection. I never read anything then about, for example, Woodes Rogers and his pitiless pillaging of Guayaquil. The Galápagos is where he brought his loot, and no doubt some of it lies buried still, 'neath a cairn of clinkers. (Woodes Rogers was not charmed by the Encantadas, finding "nothing but loose rocks, like Cynders, very rotten and heavy, and the earth so parch'd that it will not bear a Man, but break into Holes under his feet.")

I certainly didn't know, until recently, about William Dampier and the Merry Boys. Dampier's portrait hangs in the British National Portrait Gallery; underneath it, a mounted plaque announces proudly, "Pirate & Hydrographer." Dampier was both a buccaneer and a quester after knowledge. He journeyed around the world, mapping out his meanderings, recording his thoughts and observations in *A New Voyage Round the World*, sketching the animals and birds and describing their habits; the anaconda, wrote Dampier, lives in deep pools and oftimes "flourishes its tail" out of the water in order to lasso passersby. It could well have been Dampier of whom Loren Eisley was thinking when he wrote that the Galápagos Islands "belong less on the genuine equator and rather more on the latitudes of literature and science."

Dampier and the Merry Boys once took over a Danish slaver that held forty guns and sixty black women. Being scoundrels and gallowsbirds, they promptly renamed the ship "The Bachelor's Delight." They then captured three Spanish boats carrying timber, flour and eight tons of quince marmalade.

The Merry Boys beat it to the Galápagos.

William Ambrose Cowley (the main Merry Boy) was responsible for giving the islands their English names, chiefly honouring English officials (like George Monck, Duke of Albemarle) stationed at Nassau and Bermuda, who had been obligingly lax in their exacting of the laws.

"And between York and Albemarle's island lieth a small one," he wrote in his journal, "which my Fancy led me to call Cowley's Inchanted Island!"

I knew none of this as a lad. I was sufficiently staid and bookish to associate the Encantadas—intellectually, that is—with Charles Darwin. But I knew intuitively, whenever I first saw a photograph of the isles, that pirates had been there.

For one thing, it's the perfect place. Pirates, I imagined with all the romance a child can summon, were so fundamentally at odds with the world that only a pile of black rock could serve as a home. They had removed themselves from humankind, and now could only feel kinship with the boulder-burdened tortoises, the iguanas with the rotted, beshat hides. And all around, the sea, with its sad lullaby of freedom.

Where does a child get ideas like this? Why, from the Don Mills Odeon, of course, on Saturday afternoons. The Don Mills Odeon was a squat, bunkerlike building sitting adjacent to the Don Mills Plaza. (This would have been in Don Mills, a suburb of Toronto.) It didn't look like a movie theatre, and perhaps was never intended to be one. Certainly as soon as we grew older and moved away with our regular custom, the Odeon abruptly ceased being a cinema and became a succession of things.

We congregated there on Saturday afternoons, arriving at one o'clock. The manager didn't open the doors until 1:30, but we gathered early, forming a small herd in the parking lot and consuming cigarettes with precocious fervour. Cigarette smoking was so common that it conferred no coolness; instead we attempted to raise our status via the butt flick, snapping the spent smoke off the thumb with the middle finger, hoping for a graceful arc and maximum hang time.

This half hour was not spent in organizing a queue and lining up before the box office. It was instead given over to an inspection and analysis of the posters on either side of the glass doorway. The one on the left announced the first feature, as I remember, the one on the right the second bill. Admission was fifty cents, although simply mentioning that fact makes me feel, now, decrepit and gaga, as though the projectionist turned a crank and a humpbacked piano player rattled and tinkled over in the corner.

I should try to locate the manager of the Don Mills Odeon and thank him for these posters. It seems remarkable enough that he bothered to acquire movies for these Saturday matinees (there was an adult feature that changed every couple of weeks), but to get the posters and hang them up in those fancy glass display cases was really above and beyond the call. They tended to be paintings, artistic renderings, back then, rather than photographs, and more often than not featured women who were on the verge of losing their clothing. Either the garments were about to slip from their shoulders or else they had been largely consumed by giant moths or rats or something and were pictured just before the instant of final disintegration.

We would look at the posters, file away mental images for the night, and discuss the nature of the upcoming fare. Often the genre was science fiction, movies produced by people whose grasp of science was considerably less sure than our own. Westerns were frequent, of course, and World War II movies. There were quite a few historical dramas, although they were enacted by the same men as in the World War II movies, wearing different costumes. But my favourites were the pirate movies. For one thing, the women in the pirate movies were always the nearest to nakedness (having only a loose blousey thing and a small piece of material serving as a crude skirt to lose) and, moreover, were complicit in their own mysterious denuding, usually knuckling their hands on their hips and rearing back with laughter, which you had to know shook free their breasts in the next (sadly unpictured) instant. The men lacked body parts. Eyes and legs, mostly; sometimes a hand had been replaced by a golden hook. Despite this, the men, too, were pictured laughing, or at least flashing a brilliant white smile, because they knew that in the next instant, the blouse was about to be laughed away from the woman's breasts, technically, her *heaving bosom*.

I was not so naive as all that; I knew something was awry. I knew, for instance, that the pirates' teeth would not be brilliantly white, because teeth brushing would have been the first thing to go. These men and women had made a decision. They eschewed toothbrushes, combs and all vegetable matter.

They had embraced evil.

After Carson fell asleep, that first night aboard the *Corinthian*, I reeled out onto the gangway and fell up the stairs to the Jacuzzi deck. Many plastic chairs and tables were set up, and Hugo, the somewhat doleful bartender, sat behind a curved bar. He had a solitary customer, my father, who sat drinking a beer and watching the swallow-tailed gulls.

My father fell in love instantly with these gulls, which are reputed to be the most beautiful in the world. (They were introduced to the Old World in 1939, fetched back aboard the French frigate *Venus*, which I think is a lovely touch.) They have, of course, a prominently forked tail arrangement, hence the name, although they are remarkable for more than that. These are the only gulls in the world that feed nocturnally.

As the birds flew beneath the moon, immediately beside the ship, often just a few feet away from us, light reflected from their white breasts—light from the *Corinthian*, light from the stars and moon—and bounced like a ball upon the surface of the water. And light, as you know, is the Great Bait, so little fishies struggled upwards like crippled pilgrims. The gulls—their bright red eye rings somehow enhancing night vision, their eyes themselves incandescent and glowing—would dive suddenly, making the merest of splashes, and the fishes would be food. The swallow-tailed gulls hunted with determination (silent except for a clicking sound which may, scientists postulate, enable them to echolocate), but they seemed far more like angels than vampires.

My father watched the gulls with a wide smile playing upon his face. He made a soft, tired sound, "Ah-ha ...," as if recuperating from a bout of high hilarity. My father had his hand wrapped around a can of Club, the beer of Ecuador, and seemed at home in the world.

We began to talk, focussing our visual attention upon the gulls. I told how Carson seemed to feel that a sheet of single-ply was going to bring an end to all life as we know it. "But," I concluded, "I suppose I was like that. I guess I used to worry about things a lot. I was a worrywart."

"I wouldn't say you were a worrywart," said my father. "You were more conflicted."

"Hmm?"

"You were kind of a strange kid," my father remarked emphatically. "Even when you were very young, I'd see you sitting over in a corner brooding."

"Hmmm."

"You seemed to be torn between two courses of action. You'd sit there thinking very hard about which to pursue."

I had been, I suddenly remembered (at least, my mind suddenly clouded with hazy recollection), considering becoming a pirate, a vicious man who lacked body parts and spent his time in the company of women wearing exploding clothes. I would embrace absolute evil and throw away my toothbrush.

But—the current staining and decay of my teeth notwithstanding—I turned away from evil. And then I remembered why.

One day we raged out of the Don Mills Odeon, a whirling clutch of windbreakered hellions, for this was the fall. The day was Remembrance. They had granted us leave from school, so we had gone to the movie theatre. The posters on either side of the doorways proclaimed a wondrous rarity: a double bill of pirate

fare. Two women stood, hands buckled on hips frozen mid-gyra-
tion, raven-haired women about to laugh and loose their bosoms.
The pirates lurked in the background, all eye patches and jerry-
rigged prostheses. I can remember none of the plot details from
the films. There was a keel-hauling, that much I recall, because
throughout my childhood I was mildly obsessed with this inhu-
mane punishment, where the offending pirate was tethered and
dragged from port to starboard across the bottom of the ship. I
was mildly obsessed with it because I couldn't see why it was
such a big deal, why the sinful sailor was always reeled up close
to death. Many times I would hold my breath for the duration
of the punishment's portrayal, and while I might be red-faced at
the end, I was never blue-. So if not lack of air, what was the
ordeal? The keel itself loomed large for a while, and I imagined
it was honed to razor-sharpness. But if that were the case, I reasoned—all this reasoning was going on when I should have been
learning, for example, the nine times table, which still vexes
me—then the miscreant buccaneer would be fetched up nearly
halved, not simply gasping for breath and wincing from unevi-
dent injury, other than a few smears and dabs of stage blood.

Then a friend set me straight. It was the barnacles. The barnacles clung to the bottom of the boat, and they scraped and
tore at the pirate as he was dragged beneath the sea. This had
the ring of authenticity. The barnacles likely bit savagely, too,
I speculated, and raked with their blood-tipped talons.[1]

---

[1] Charles Darwin, needing to establish himself as a "specific Naturalist," a fellow who
had grappled with thorny questions of taxonomy, undertook, in 1846, an exhaus-
tive study of barnacles. He began by examining some peculiar specimens he'd found
on the shores of Chile; eight years and four thick volumes later, Darwin had sorted
out the whole barnacles thing as well as it could be sorted out.
    Charles discovered something quite peculiar, whilst poking about at a species he
dubbed *Ibla cumingii. Ibla* was, like most barnacles, hermaphroditic; then Darwin

About half a mile down the road from the Don Mills Odeon, and across a field from my house, was the Church; the three buildings formed the points of a triangle. Much of the field was put to good use by the city; there was a baseball diamond year-round, and, in the winter, workers would drop off enormous stacks of lumber that were transformed into a skating rink— magically, I often imagined, as I had never witnessed the nocturnal construction. The Church sat in its own little corner, and the ground around it was ruled by weeds. We children believed that the weeds covered consecrated ground. "A graveyard," we whispered to each other.

One day the Church Elders (I had never seen any, but imagined them to be ancient and wrinkled beyond the point of being recognizable as human) decided to use a portion of the field for automobile parking. In preparation, bulldozers razed the land just beside the holy building, pushing two huge ridges of dirt to either side of a barren pebbled expanse.

Two pirate movies plus day parole from school had driven us into a state of high restlessness. We fled to the field beside the Church and divided into two camps. On what basis the segregation was made, I couldn't say; we had a gang, but it was a curiously fluid one, always dividing and mutating. I guess this was because there were no rival gangs, so if we wanted violence and excitement we had to do it ourselves. The two sub-gangs, having rapidly become bitter enemies, having exchanged insults

---

discovered that some tiny "parasites" were, in fact, males, functional and rudimentary ones, a head attached to an "enormous coiled penis." He saw that many barnacles shared this oddity, a combination of hermaphroditism and sexuality as we understand it (aside from the "enormous coiled penis" stuff). He wondered what in the world was going on until he realized that he was looking at *transformation*, that these creatures were, in an evolutionary way, discarding one sexual method for another.

and threats, crouched behind the small dirt mountains and awaited the commencement of hostilities.

I appraised our gang. It consisted of myself, my younger brother Joel and four or five rankers of international reknown. A ranker might be defined as a creature inhabiting the lower rungs of the status ladder. I was the coolest guy on the gang, which meant that we were doomed, that a swift and merciful annihilation was the best we could hope for.

The first few projectiles were clods of dirt, lobbed high so that, upon landing, they would produce satisfying poofs and miniature mushroom clouds. But then a stone was fired. It's likely that it was thrown in some innocence, that one of us picked up a dirt-encrusted rock and was as startled as anyone to see the shell fall away, leaving behind a prehistoric bullet. The stone made no satisying poof as it landed; it made a dull sound, *thwock*, that was nonetheless very alarming. The little hillocks abounded with stones, so we gathered them up and began pitching them across the way with zeal and enthusiasm. Things had escalated in very short order. We were now engaged in serious hostilities, and along with the stones flew some very rancorous insults.

I was delighted with the proceedings, because I was still intoxicated with the pirate films, and I knew this was how god-lessness must feel. This was freedom. I threw stones with force and precision—not hitting anyone, mind you, just missing them, sending a stone hurtling by a wind-roughened cheek, leaving behind a slash of ruddiness. And I would stand fully erect to throw, a display of high recklessness, but I existed in a state of godless grace. Either the stones were flying well wide or else I would twist and contort my chubby body, snapping it out of harm's way. I was somehow made giddy by the fact that I was behaving this way on consecrated ground, and I repeated to myself the most chilling of the rumours we spread, that the erst-while graveyard beneath my feet was the final resting place exclusively for children who had died in the act of being born.

As I crouched down to gather up more ammunition, I saw Joel, a far more natural buccaneer than I, leap wildly to his feet (he couldn't do much without it being done wildly) and receive a stone to the forehead. To my eyes it seemed to drill a hole in his brow, and suddenly blood was pouring, thick red stuff that in seconds had moved beyond his brow, covered his eyes, and stained the whole of his freckled face. He stumbled over the brink of the hillock, his arms describing the wide frantic arcs of a blind man, his feet failing to make purchase on the clods of dirt. He was issuing low moans between a litany of forbidden words.

I peeled off my windbreaker and covered my younger brother's entire head with it, which I thought might help, which at least hid this hideous sight from view, the sight of Joel blinded by blood, probably mortally wounded. And I was sore afraid. If I myself had received the stone, I don't know that it would have had much of an effect. It seemed much more retributive that my brother should receive the stone. A truly earnest blackmailer will threaten the family of his victim, after all.

I recall arriving home with my brother from the hillocks in the churchyard, my jacket, blotchy now with blood, still wrapped around his head. My mother shrieked once and then got down to business, conscripting Mr. Bailey next door to drive us to the hospital. Mr. Bailey was concerned about his uphol-stery, but finally and reluctantly agreed. We three sat in the back seat, my mother cradling my brother, me staring out the window. My mother never asked what happened. Which is just as well, because the only answer I could have given is, "God got mad at us."

I date my belief in the Almighty from that moment, but partly because my memory isn't very reliable on anything that happened prior. I suspect that something within me had always believed, just as a boy believes in Santa Claus or the infallibility of professional athletes. Perhaps I was born with a belief in the Deity the way that some kids are born with little teeth. Or perhaps (who knows) I was born with a belief in God because my spirit had only just been shuttled out of Heaven, or some glorious waiting room for souls, and placed into a pale and pudgy little body. (I heard a story not long ago, one that I was quite taken with, about a three-year-old grabbing hold of a newborn baby and demanding, "What's Heaven like? I can't remember.")

After the incident, I demanded that I be allowed to attend Sunday school. I wanted to know Him. (Also, evil is like any kind of intoxicant; it's not so easy as simply turning your back on it. You need to fill in the emptiness, and I suppose I recognized Sunday school as a kind of support group. I imagined that all the attendees would be sullen little blighters who'd thought too much about the sea.) My parents concurred without a lot of comment or interest. My mother regarded the Sabbath as a day for the ingestion of a novel, the thicker the better. She would take her position upon the living room sofa sometime around nine in the morning. At three or four in the afternoon she would close the book and see about dinner. My mother could read five hundred, six hundred pages in a sitting. If this talent is genetically encoded, I didn't get the right stuff. I am a plodder, like my father, who would spend his Sundays in the den, slowly working through thick, scientifical tomes.

There had been, in fact, a certain amount of attention paid to my spiritual needs. For one thing, I had been given a godfather, Howard Roseborough, who was a professor of economics at Harvard. (In many photographs of my earliest days I am wearing a little Harvard sweatshirt with the words "LOVE ME" stitched onto the back.) I have heard that Howard Roseborough took my spiritual education seriously, or at least, had every intention of doing so once I became fully sentient. Unfortunately, he died, leaving me tutorless. (Perhaps it is this man—whom I can't in all honesty claim to remember—who inculcated my belief.) I had also been baptized, but such is the secular nature of the clan that I didn't discover this until I was perhaps eighteen years old. I didn't know until that time that I was Anglican, which came as a pleasant surprise. Anglicans conduct themselves with some pomp and circumstance, after all, and sometimes their churches are filled with beautiful, if slightly dour, music. Before that I considered myself United, a much blander sect. I thought that because the Church across the field was United, and it was there that I took myself, having turned away from the Dark Side.

I will tell you another story about churches here, a story from the trip to the Encantadas, although not from the actual cruise through the archipelago. That journey was book-ended by two nights and one full day in Quito. It's an impressive city, nestled in the Andes and watched over by the Wingèd Madonna, La Virgen de Quito. Quito is quiet and frenetic both, and sometimes in the morning it is enveloped in cloud. We stayed in the New City, but took a bus tour into the Old. This is where the Spaniards built their cathedrals, and they are improbably magnificent. It was a Sunday, so our tour trickled into the cathedrals, past the huge inner doors (which appeared to be rendered out of solid gold and precious stones) to find the pews filled with Indians. They stared straight ahead at the priest and paid us no attention. They sat there—above them flew angels festooned with priceless jewels—in clothes with frayed cuffs and missing buttons. I was a bit uncomfortable to be interfering with their worship, so I concentrated on a study of stuff that was suspended on the walls. There was quite a bit; several glass-covered boxes contained statuettes of the Wingèd Madonna, as though she were a lepidopteran specimen. Carson followed the tour group obediently, and when the guide stopped to explain something in a barely hushed whisper she would press into the group so as to better hear his words. She gave every indication of being extremely interested, but I recognized that her boredom was thus vast and profound if she was reduced to listening to the tour guide for diversion. (Although, this guide, Rodney, was quite knowledgeable and entertaining. He was also something of a nationalist, at least, a spokesman for South America generally. "What happened in 1492?" he demanded rhetorically, placing two fingertips together. "The Union of the Two Worlds.") My father clasped his hands behind his back like a member of the Royal Family and inspected odd and small things. The tiles, for example, or curious carpenter's joints. He wore a profound scowl.

Sometime between cathedrals, my daughter wondered what this *Catholic* business was all about. You might think me remiss in my spiritual guidance here, but remember that I didn't even know I was Anglican until I was fully grown. Carson was Nothing, but that's why we were there in the first place, so that she could make His acquaintance.

"Well, Catholics believe in Jesus Christ."

"I believe in Jesus Christ," she spoke up excitedly. "I believe that He was God."

"Yeah," I nodded. "Catholics *really, really* believe in Jesus Christ."

I was heartened by my daughter's enthusiasm, and confident that when she saw wondrous and astounding things upon the

Galápagos Islands God would fill her heart and she would be whole and happy.

At the next cathedral—they populate the Old City of Quito like Fotomats, huge cavernous churches made with such squandermania that their construction today would be inconceivable—my father hung near the back, allowing the Indians to pray in peace, allowing the rest of the tour group to sweep forward with their videocams purring softly.

I gesticulated vaguely at the surroundings. "Magnificent, isn't it?"

My father nodded, but with no enthusiasm. "Poor Indian bastards," he muttered, and then he abruptly turned and left the cathedral.

I don't think he meant the ones who were sitting in the pews, he meant the ones who had died lugging all the glittering ornamentation through the mountains. It is, I saw suddenly, hard to worship a God that would exact that kind of tribute.

Mind you, *men* had done these things. God was not in the cathedrals, only his false representatives. I knew where God was: hiding behind the black volcanic mountains in the Enchanted Isles.

We drank beer aboard the *Corinthian* as we ventured forth to meet Him.

I suppose I should tell you that, as well as introducing my daughter to God, I was thinking that He and my father should get reacquainted. (If, indeed, they'd ever met.) My father had, two years previous, suffered a heart attack, not a particularly vicious one, but one that greatly alarmed the family. He was now in fine health, due to a change in diet that—as far as I could determine from watching him eat in the days to come—involved a total eschewing of maraschino cherries.

My father took a sip of his cerveza and turned again to watch the swallow-tailed gulls hover in the slip-stream, their red-ringed eyes aimed and steadied at the roiling water glowing about the ship's belly. There were no islands around us now, only sea and more sea, but the gulls were unconcerned, willing to stay with us until we circled the world or reached its abrupt end. The gulls were willing to fly forever into the night, and it was this more than anything else that pleased my father.

Eventually, though, we rose drowsily and bounced along the railings, down the staircases and into our little rooms.

I lay down upon my berth and was soon wide awake.

Six

The passengers aboard the *Corinthian* were divided into three groups: the Boobies, the Albatrosses and the Cormorants. Carson, my father and I were Cormorants, which meant that the Cormorants were the best. The main reason for the division was to facilitate transportation to the islands. This was done by means of Zodiacs, motorized inner tubes with high opinions of themselves. Most of the passengers referred to these craft as *pangas*, and rapidly became adept at their boarding. After breakfast, one would repair to the pitching closet for teeth brushing and failed experiments in bowel voiding. Well, I don't know if that was what *one* would do, that's what *I* would do. I suspect most other people as well, because there was this sticky technical problem: you couldn't go to the washroom on the Galápagos. You couldn't go in a literal sense, because there were no washrooms, and you couldn't go in the more figurative sense, because they wouldn't let you. It was strictly forbidden throughout the archipelago, except in, you know, designated areas. Seems a bit prissy considering the islands were once the haunt of cutthroats, but there is the danger of unwittingly depositing bacteria or even, after an evening of too many cervezas, alien life-forms upon the Encantadas. When I reported this news to my father, that the rules forbade washroom-going and that it would best be done prior to leaping into the panga, his eyes rounded with alarm. "But that's not my time," he whispered. Exactly. No one's time is five minutes before you have to leap into a panga. Anyway, in the midst of the teeth brushing, etc., the piped-in music would abruptly disappear and Judy the Purser would holler at you over the intercom. Truth to be told, she wasn't hollering, but she was possessed of ratchety vocal cords, and the effect could be very alarming. (Mind you, she might have been trying to aid all the passengers with their experiments in bowel voiding.) "Good morning, ladies and gentlemen," she'd begin, making it all one heavily accented word, "it's already eight o'clock in the morning ..." She used this idiom all the time, even at wake-up. "Goomorninladiesan-gennelmen," Judy would say, "it's already seven o'clock in the morning ..." This always sounded accusatory, as though Judy were disgusted that we lazy people had wasted so much of the day. So, Judy would give us the schedule for departure, say, Cormorants first, Boobies next, finally Albatrosses. The passengers would then file toward the stern, prepared for the excursion. Everyone had knapsacks jammed with water bottles, sunscreen and towels. Everyone wore sunglasses, sun hats and an assortment of cameras as jewellery. Everyone wore white clothes, so as to deflect the sun's heat and vicious rays.

Which reminds me. When, exactly, did the sun turn vicious? As I mentioned, the fare at the Don Mills Odeon often included science fiction movies, and I vaguely recall one that had to do with a sun turned spoiled and petulant, choosing to roast the planets in its system rather than simply keep them toasty. The people in the film lived under darkened bubbles, huge sunglass lenses. They wore white clothes, white hats and elaborate zinc nose-coats. Further details are lost; I remember mostly that we laughed at this film, we jeered with high hilarity, all of us little children who found nothing far-fetched about giant moths or monsters made from stuff lying about the kitchen.

Carson wouldn't have found anything funny about that movie. Indeed, she viewed the sun as a familiar threat, a schoolyard bully who had to be appeased through a continual dousing of unguents and lotion. And I was always slapping these preparations on, because I couldn't even imagine the greeting I would get if I returned home with a sunburnt child.

There was a rack and a clothesline at the stern of the ship, upon which hung a number of blue life jackets, what my fishing friends and I call "Personal Flotation Devices," which makes them sound like more fun than they actually are. The passengers would don these—my daughter always managed to find a PFD fashioned for a giant, my father a tiny one, so that he appeared to be struggling to dress in a bow tie—and then line up for panga loading.

Panga loading is more strenuous than you might think. The Zodiac pulls up alongside the ship, near where a gateway in the railing allows one a free step into the rubber craft. Unfortunately, that step is about six feet straight down. Sailors and guides are always at hand; those on the ship hold onto your elbows, judging the rhythm of the water's pitch and roll, waiting for that moment when a swell brings the panga a few precious inches closer to the deck. They then propel you into the empty air. Sailors and guides aboard the panga catch hold of your upper arms. You are supposed to take hold of their upper arms, too, you are supposed to execute what looks like a secret fraternity double handshake, and while you're doing that, you step gingerly onto the slick, rounded side of the panga. All this while weighted down by knapsacks and cameras. But, as I said, we all became very adept at this stunt, those of us who survived the first two or three loadings.

The first excursion was to Gardner Bay, on Hood Island, or Española. This was a "wet" landing, as opposed to a "dry." Or—another way of looking at it—"death by drowning," the sailor's great fear, as opposed to a more civilized passing ashore. No, no. It's true that we passengers feared these wet landings for a day or two, until we realized that the term only signified a drop as near the beach as possible. The water that one stepped into was typically only a few inches deep. Then you could calmly and easily walk ashore, after being scuppered and doused by the enormous wave that you failed to see coming from behind.

Sea lions lounged upon the beach at Gardner Bay. They are great loungers, surely the finest in nature. Sea lions can lounge even as briny surf shakes them like a landlady who's finally had enough. Many were well up on the strand, catching a tan; others were snugged between black rocks, searching for shade. Some were rolled onto their backs, their flippers folded across their chest. The air was filled with hoary snores and the satisfied chewing sound that comes from successful repositioning.

As we approached them, a few of the creatures deigned to open an eye. They watched only as long as it took to identify what kind of beast we were. *The two-legged thing*, they noted, *that doesn't go to the washroom.* The sea lions then closed their eyes, not caring. They gave the impression that they wouldn't care if we were mutated land sharks, amphetamine-crazed and armed with chain saws.

The Cormorants' guide was a young man named Carlos Jurado. His background was in marine biology, and he did wear a pair of round, wire-rimmed glasses that lent him a scholarly air. But that was about all that lent him a scholarly air. He tended to go about with a muscular, top-heavy lope, and his customary outfit consisted of a pair of white shorts and a T-shirt bearing the emblem of the Charles Darwin Research Station. He spoke English well, betrayed only occasionally by idiosyncratic pronunciations; "moanth," said Carlos, for "month," that sort of thing.

I will tell you something interesting. I actually heard it from Carlos, under these very circumstances that I am describing, but I'm writing the book, and I shall report all the interesting things myself. Only sea lions, and not seals, are able to push themselves up onto their front flippers, which are like strangely elongated hands, with long, thin bamboo shoots for "fingers" that run beneath the rubbery blades. These odd appendages bend nearish the middle. A seal's flippers don't; they are more properly and functionally flippers, which means that a seal is better in the water than a sea lion, but more awkward upon the shore. You see the implication, of course, which struck me immediately. The trained "seals" in circuses—who rear up onto their fore-flippers constantly to catch balls upon their glistening noses—are really trained *sea lions*.

The Cormorants began what was, essentially, a walk down the strand of but a few hundred yards. The sand was studded occasionally by large chunks of black rock. These were typically festooned with Sally Lightfoot crabs, which are odd creatures, bright orange and deepest black, and eerily transparent. When I was a child I used to assemble plastic models, but unlike my friends, I disdained tiny automobiles and airplanes. My favourites were kits labelled "The Visible Man," "The Visible Dog," etc., which had transparent outer shells and showed the interior workings with sometimes off-putting clarity. The Sally

Lightfoot crabs looked for all the world like animate models from this series.

The Cormorants went into photographic mode, evidencing individual methods and aesthetics. One man, Alan, favoured close-up work, and was always determined to get as near as possible to the subject. Another, Bud, favoured compositional artistry. He would first frame the black rock and then direct his wife Carol behind it, there to drive little Sally Lightfoot crabs up the side of their little mountain. Bud would photograph them as they claimed the summit, their claws just clacking over the edge.

The most elaborate of the photographic equipment was owned by the most elderly of the photographers. I shall call him Mr. B., because the portrait I will draw is not the most flattering, and I suspect that Mr. B. was involved with either organized crime or the motion picture industry. Either way, he could have me snuffed with an inaudible pop of his brittle fingers, so "Mr. B." he shall remain. Mr. B.'s wealth was vast and apparent. He wore a short-sleeved, short-pant-legged robin's-egg blue leisure suit that set off his tan; Mr. B.'s tan was so deep and burnished that it shamed his jewellery, which was all solid gold.

Where Mr. B. was adorned with ostentation and excess, his Wondercam was a triumph of resourceful engineering. It was a sleek black box with curious appendages, robotic arms that threw out thick beams of light. Mr. B. seemed to have undertaken the recording of his every single waking moment. He wandered about with the Wondercam perpetually screwed over his eyeball. He continued to chant by way of explanation, and although he didn't seem to be speaking overly loudly, his words managed to shatter any silence that might exist. Mr. B.'s voice could be heard for yards around, so we all grew familiar quickly with his commentary, which had a sameness. Stumbling upon a sea lion, Mr. B. would press buttons and the Wondercam would send up a light whirring sound. "And here he is in all his glory," Mr. B. would vociferate with all the enthusiasm of a coroner, "a seal."

The creature would look up at Mr. B., dark lids bisecting large round eyes, and yawn hugely.

That the creatures in the Galápagos are oddly placid in the presence of human beings has been remarked upon many times. Even the Bishop of Castilla de Oro noted it: "The same conditions prevailed as on the first [island]; many seals, turtles, iguanas, tortoises, many birds like those of Spain, but so silly they do not know how to flee, and many were caught in the hand." I don't know if Antarqui came back to deliver the same observation, but I think it entirely likely that the island creatures were unfazed even in the face of a flying necromancer. The most wary are the marine iguanas, and they are wary only to the extent that upon a human approach they will set their limbs into curiously slow motion, their cursed hide wrinkling like fabric, and clear the path. This has the air of politeness, the beasts trying to compensate for their grotesquerie with immaculate manners. Birds, for the most part—I'm bolting ahead, as you see; we haven't actually met any birds at this point in the story, they remain graceful slashes in the sky—are indifferent. They care about mating, with a resolute single-mindedness, and in the wake of that they care about tending of the nest. They don't care about human beings loaded with camera equipment.

Young sea lions are the most interactive. A pup might wake up, pop open his eyes, and notice a human being nearby. A somewhat addled grin will lace the youngster's face and he'll flip over, approaching eagerly with a front-loaded waddle. Human beings tend to scatter at that point, because the animals are clearly capable of, if not intent on, mischief. I did witness, later that afternoon, a remarkable, though certainly not rare, moment. One of the Ecuadorian sailors stood upon a small rock, holding a rope attached to a panga, which bobbed and buffeted in the shallows. Suddenly a head popped up beside the rock, a blunted doglike head slashed with a Looney Tunes grin. The sea lion nipped the sailor's big toe, which caused the sailor to leap skyward with a panicked squawk. The sea lion, patently pleased with itself, nodded at the assembled island-goers and disappeared abruptly. This familiarity—as you can see, it has already bred contempt—is most manifest when one is swimming.

After our stroll along the beach that morning, the passengers from the *Corinthian* went swimming. We donned snorkels and masks and waded into the surf. I myself donned snorkel and goggles, prescription no less, and splashed about the area. I was determined to see as many fish as I could, a grudging substitution for catching them, which they wouldn't allow me to do. Picture me splashing about, a pale man from Canada, my own hoary breath amplified and broadcast by the tube sticking out of the water. Suddenly there is a muffled shriek and the pale Canadian begins a strenuous crawl toward shore at a speed that is in line to beat the Olympic record. The explanation: the sudden sighting of a sea lion snout, of a size to suggest that the creature was nearby; in this case, a few fractions of an inch away. And the beast seemed to be saying, "Hey. Are those things *prescription?*" I got used to this attention from young sea lions, over time, although I was never entirely comfortable with it. I simply ignored them, and continued to swim, aware that the sea lions often accompanied me, describing ornate curlicues and figure eights about my far less graceful form. And I enjoyed watching the sea lions interact with other swimmers. As the Corinthians paddled about, staring downwards, dozens of sea lions would sometimes appear, flanking the bathers and idling gleefully. "Okay, people," they seemed to be saying, "just what is it we're looking for?"

Boring of us, the animals would cavort with each other. That word, "cavort," should simply have as its dictionary entry "*See* sea lion." Sea lions are nature's great cavorters. They flounder and gambol, often in pairs, executing airborne manoeuvres for the sheer athletic exhilaration of it. They slice through the water so quickly that they seem to create draught, and their buddies follow behind, sucked into the draught, whiskers folded back by the force. Even a solitary sea lion is an accomplished cavorter. I have seen one play an energetic game of solitaire catch, dropping a stick from just beneath the ocean's surface, circling downward and opening up its maw in time to receive it again.

Carlos did tell us that if a bull approached—the bull would be recognizable by the fact that he'd be much larger than these teen-agers—we should exercise caution. If the bull should bark, we would be well-advised to demur and swim away, indicating no intention of mating with any of the creature's harem. But Galápagos tour operators have lost no customers to these behemoths, and I'm sure that there have been at least one or two inebriated tourists who probably *did* want to mate with some of the cows. Not only that, we were told not to be alarmed if we should happen to see a shark. "The Galápagos shark," said Orlando, another of the guides, "is a very friendly shark."

I never saw a shark, but again, I heard not a single story about a snorkeller or diver being consumed by one. I did hear about a drunken passenger on one of the cruise ships going overboard while proposing a toast, disappearing into the squid-ink black sea, so it's not as if we didn't exchange such stories. I have to assume that death by animal ingestion doesn't occur. Even the Galápagos *predators*, therefore, are strangely placid. So we have to wonder what in the world is going on.

One theory has it that because most Galápagon residents existed for millennia without predators, the trait of wariness was never genetically reinforced. The expression used by the writer David Quammen—who admittedly has a lot more on the scientific ball than I—is "ecologically naive." While I might accept this about some of the creatures—the uncomely marine iguana, for example, would seem to have no enemies (nor friends either, mind you)—it doesn't ring true for sea lions, because white-tipped reef sharks have long lurked just outside the bays and inlets. As a species, the Galápagos sea lions have had plenty long enough to figure out that a certain percentage of the population is going to be gobbled up.

I prefer to look at things this way. The question is not why the creatures that dwell upon the Encantadas are so tame; the question is, why is every other living creature so skittish? We are all wee tim'rous beasties, and human beings are becoming the most tim'rous of them all. We're afraid of the *sun*, for goodness' sake; we tremble upon its rise and try to placate it with ointment and balm.

I suppose this might provide a clear model for evolution in action. If we conceive of a range of behaviour from temerity to timidity (and imagine, what's more, that that behaviour is controlled by a specific gene), then creatures tending toward the timid end will tend to survive to adulthood because they've been hiding. Creatures on the other end of the scale will have been (at least, will stand a far greater chance of being) gobbled up. The population will tend toward timidity, and soon—has this day already come?—everything will be timid. We are not looking at the survival of the fittest, we are looking at the survival of the faint-hearted. "The meek shall inherit the earth" turns out to be a scientific truism.

The day might come when a genetic mutation will cause a Galápagos sea lion to pause at the water's brink and stare out toward the horizon. "Geez, I dunno," he'll mutter, as all of his playmates waddle into the sea. "Seems a little, um, *cold.*" And in a few generations we shall see the sea lions pressed between the rocks, their flippers over their eyes, their glistening bodies all a-tremble. Until then, we have to admire the way they've got things worked out. As long as everyone goes in, as long as it's a huge and all-encompassing Cavort, everything will be fine. Certainly, they shall lose some pups to sharks, but that is going to happen anyway; that is not something that need either influence, or be influenced by, behaviour.

Despite which, I kept coating Carson's body with sunblock. I wasn't perhaps quite as maniacal as her mother, who sometimes seems intent on applying a layer to the kid's tongue. But I slathered it on, and when the first panga came, I pushed people aside and put Carson on it, even though the panga was supposed to be for Albatrosses. We hurried back to the safety of the *Corinthian.*

Seven

After lunch aboard the ship, and a quick nap, during which I managed to field Carson's questions about the size and tote-ability of various breeds of dogs without waking up, the Cormorants once more leapt into the panga and were transported to shore. We landed at a new location on Hood Island, Punta Suarez, where we were scheduled to see some very exotic birdlife, namely, the blue-footed booby. This is a bird that Dr. Moody had made much mention of, offering a lot of footage of the species' intricate mating ritual. It's not really intricate so much as, well, goofy. (As is the bird itself; its appellation was bequeathed by the buccaneers, not given to sensitivity about appearances, "boobie" coming from the Spanish "*bobo*," for clown.) Basically, the booby flaps his wings at a female and picks up and displays his blue feet, emphasizing their very blueness. The female judges this attribute, and—I think more often than not—shakes her slightly silly-looking head and wanders away. Actually, I'm being unfair to the ritual, which can possess an undeniable beauty. If the female finds the male's blue feet attractive, she shows him that hers, too, are blue, and then the two bow, like strangers at a country dance, before "sky pointing," stretching their necks upward to see whose beak can get closest to heaven. This raises the momentous subject of Sexual Selection, which we shall discuss in more detail when we meet the frigatebird.

We are, at any rate, past all that on the blue-footed booberie. Couples have been established, and nests have been set up, which the birds seem to do wherever they happen to be standing at the time of their meeting. They don't actually build nests so much as plan them out, scratching out the property lines. They etch with guano a square yard or so, and it is within that box on the ground that they lay their eggs. (Blue-footed boobies sometimes toy with a symbolic twig, pushing it back and forth like newlyweds deciding where to put the settee.) So upon the island were thousands and thousands of these little boxes, a suburban subdivision of boobies. A path, eight feet wide and delineated on either side with crude white stakes, was constructed through the middle, and upon this path we were instructed to march. Carlos would snap at us when we ventured off, albeit with a patina of politeness. "Mr. Quarrington! Please!" he'd shout. "Mr. Perdomini! The path, the path, if you would." In defence of Cormorants, I will say that the stakes were sometimes infrequent, and it's not as if the boobies themselves differentiated between the path and the fields of nests. Many stood upon the path, suspended above their eggs, staring at us as we approached with a kind of addled transfixion on their faces. The Cormorants, especially the more avid amateur photographers, withdrew their gear from Gore-Tex camera bags stealthily (force of habit, I think), deftly popping off lens caps. Most cameras were burdened with attachments of focal prodigiousness, gigantic telescoping zooms. They would hoist these and aim them at blue-footed boobies, who regarded the lenses warily, particularly as they tended to knock them about the head.

Mr. B. immediately turned on his Wondercam. "Here he is in all his glory," he intoned. "The blue-boobed footy."

The sky was without cloud, and the island was without vegetation, other than small emaciated shrubs that struggled out of the rock and achieved a mean height of a foot or two. What the island lacked, therefore, was shade. We tourists, white-clad and perpetually suckling at our water bottles, began the trek with energy and enthusiasm. The first twenty blue-footed boobies were wondrous and astounding, even if they only squatted on their eggs and looked stupefied. (Lacking "brood pouches," the birds actually incubate the eggs with their feet, and often appear to be hiding something somewhat sheepishly.) The next few score were slightly less wondrous and astounding, although this may have had something to do with the rather mundane parenting arrangements the boobies have made. Both male and female do child-care duty, tending to the nest while the mate looks for food, so there are always birds on the ground looking bored and vaguely pissed off. The creatures would often tilt their heads backwards and search the sky, and I'm sure that if they'd had wristwatches they would have been checking them every couple of minutes. (In the interest of fairness, I'll mention that the female does get the short end—as the eggs hatch she'll manoeuvre them to the top of her feet, and there the chicks will remain, often for as long as a month.) The next few hundred blue-footed boobies were hardly wondrous and astounding at all. I concentrated on making sure Carson was hydrated and shielded from mighty Sol. (My father, wisely, had remained aboard the Corinthian.) I lurched over the hardscrabble ground, alarming blue-footed boobies, although not to the extent that they would actually move out of my way. They preferred to confront danger by opening their perfectly round eyes even further; they have tiny dots in the centre, and these would dilate fractionally, or seem to. The female has a larger dot than the male, which is a bit of free-floating scientific arcana I relate to portray my state of mind at that moment. Thoughts, facts and notions came freely and unaccompanied; i.e., I had already spent too long in the sun, and we were just commencing what I came to think of as the Death March.

My half-baked musings turned to things biblical. As we trudged along, frying beneath the equatorial sun, snippets of the Good Book's poetry came to me unbidden: "Thou hast walked up and down in the midst of the stones of fire." Our ordeal began to take on a timelessness, a hopelessness, so that one felt the need for a spiritual shield or guide—preferably in the form of a big illustrated edition that could be hoisted up over one's head for shade. But perhaps the biggest reason for my scriptural frame of mind was this deceptively lightweight fact, which actually enkindled a brushfire of rumination: there is no mention of the blue-footed booby in the Bible.

Before I get into the strenuous biblical scholasticism required to fully unravel and elucidate that last observation, I need to say a few things in my own defence. You see, I'm a late starter in this field. Many people in our culture are spoon-fed the Bible from infancy. The family next door even had verse readings before the evening meal. A few times I was invited to dine with them, and it was with bafflement that I listened to these odd snippets. I think in retrospect that they were probably working their way through the entire volume, because sometimes the selection would be pretty good, full of swords and assorted slewings, and sometimes it would be an endless threnody spoken in a strange tongue. But I don't believe the father ever announced,

"Here is this evening's Bible reading," because the truth of the matter is, when I first attended Sunday school at the Church, I didn't really know what the Bible was. I was vastly ignorant, and most Sunday School teachers never think to conduct little refresher courses reminding their charges just what the Bible is, just who Jesus was. I'd heard of Jesus enough to know only that he was male, but in my imagination he became, like all important people, a young boy, maybe ten years old. And so this song I learned—"Yes, Jesus loves me, yes, Jesus loves me ..."—became a plaintive love ballad (I knew about plaintive love ballads; my house was empty of religion but rang with folk song) sung by a young girl. I had no problem adopting her voice: "Yes, Jesus loves me, the Bible tells me so." Hmmm. Now that was a poser. I tossed around the notion that "the Bible" was the nickname for a gabby little matchmaker ("The Bible says that Linda Corcoran thinks you're cute") but discounted that as too silly, which is really going some, because here is what I finally came up with. (Remember, please, I was just a little boy.) My house was nestled in amongst ravines and pathways, and at the end of the one that wandered westward stood the Water Tower. It was brilliantly white and could have starred in many a matinee at the Don Mills Odeon, seeming at the same time constructed and organic. At the top, two hundred feet in the air, was the reservoir, a fantastically oversized mushroom cap. The cap was supported by eight Doric columns, and the whole thing was connected by cabling, guy wires and ladders. The Water Tower assumed huge importance in my personal mythology, and I guess still does. (I once knew a woman, and she had occasion to give me her address over the telephone. My hand started to tremble. "But you must live underneath the Water Tower," I gasped. "Yes," she answered. "It's the Mother Ship.") So I ideated the Bible as a water tower, and imparted to it the ability to tell people things by imagining a band of flashing lights such as move across theatre marquees on Broadway. "YES! JESUS LOVES YOU!!" the lights on the towering Bible said, and the little girl's heart was made whole and happy.

Still, as misguided as this was, at least I imagined *something*. At least I applied my tiny mind to the unriddling of mystery, unlike my fellow Sunday school students. One lad I remember in particular, a little boy of whom I was always suspicious owing to his preternatural ability to keep his hair neat. Having neat hair was bad enough. Worse, this boy was proud and vain about it, and would often remove a little comb and mirror from the inside pocket of his jacket. Oh, yes, he wore a suit. I believe he owned at least two, one a dark blue, the other beige and flecked with little beads of colour. Regardless of which he wore, the lapel always bore a series of tiny bars, each suspended below the other and connected with fine silver chain. If you got close—really close—you'd see that the bars were individually inscribed: *Three Months, Six Months, One Year, Two Years*. These were, you see, decorations for Sunday school attendance, and I was greatly taken with them. And you'd think, wouldn't you, that I would be able to earn at least the three-month medal, although this was not the case. Every third week or so, it would prove impossible for me to attend. My father would need to go into work, say, and he would take my younger brother and me with him. We would drive down to the university and go into a quaint brick computer. It looked like a quaint brick house but was actually a computer, and as my father wandered around trying to make the house function, my brother and I would invent and play a series of games that all involved missiles and rockets. We would play these in the bowels of the computer, as the house heaved and sighed and clicked its way through calculations, and every so often we would lose sight of our projectiles and the house would shudder and, as we say these days, crash. So I could earn no attendance medals. However—and my bitterness over this has not abated a bit—*it's not as though the boy with the neat hair attended every week, either.*

He would often be away, and for no particularly good reason. His family owned a huge motoring sedan, and the father would routinely herd his brood into the cavernous back seat and tour the countryside. The little boy would then turn up the following Sunday with a note, which he would hand the Sunday school teacher. (I am vague here because the teachers changed often.) The teacher of the moment would amend the attendance record and the boy would be headed toward a new bar.

If this boy could get a note because his family had gone on a drive, I reasoned, I should be able to get a note because I'd had to accompany my father on a trip to the big brick computer. However, I failed to negotiate this. Oh, I might have squeezed one or two out of my mother, but my mother was often distracted and otherwise involved, devouring books or chatting on the telephone. It was sometimes hard for me to get a note justifying an absence from *school*. My mother seemed not to understand why I couldn't simply write one myself, seeing as I knew as well as anyone that, the day previous, my skin had erupted with boils and my tongue had swollen until it was the size of a ham. When finally prevailed upon, my mother would take up a pen and a blank piece of writing paper and inscribe, in a beautiful hand, the following words: "Please excuse Paul's absence from school, as he was ill." She would date and sign the note, and if you took a ruler you would see that the lines were all true and evenly spaced, as though she'd been working on lined paper. But, as I say, it was hard work getting these notes, especially for Sunday school, which no one in my family, save me, counted as worthwhile.

Particularly my father. He wasn't much of a note-writer to begin with, and the notes he did scrawl were almost illegible and filled with excess information: "Paul did not attend school yesterday as he was diarrhetic." I knew he'd never produce any Sunday school notes, so I simply went back to the church basement after a week's absence, and I sat there ashamed and silent, as though I'd missed school the week before because I'd been on a junket to Vegas.

I know that many people are soured on organized religion because of more lofty complaints, but the inequity of this situation eventually hit home. The boy with the perfect attendance record didn't really give a shit about God, if you want to know the truth. He could care less about the Commandments. I'm sure the boy felt, in his shrivelled heart of hearts, that if the Almighty ever did haul his ass onto the heavenly carpet and begin a Divine arraignment, he would simply reach into his back pocket and remove a neatly folded note. I, on the other hand, was doing my best to be pious and saintly. Still, I had a vision of the afterlife, of walking down the cloudy white corridors toward the Great Throne, of hearing a voice of Infinite majesty intone, "Hey, kid. Where's your attendance bars?"

Carson was undaunted by the Death March. She tramped along, pausing only when I commanded her to do so for ointment application. She would obey and then tramp off again. Her enthusiasm was dampened somewhat by the fact that she saw nothing whatever extraordinary about blue-footed boobies. They were certainly nothing compared to that most wondrous of creations, *Canis familiaris*.

Occasionally Carson would pause and allow me to stagger near. "Can I ask you a question?" she would ask.

"Is it about dogs?"

"Yes."

"I don't want to talk about dogs."

"We're not going to talk about them. I just have one question that I want to ask you."

"But it's about dogs."

"Yes."

"If I answered a question about dogs, then we would be talking about dogs."

"But it wouldn't be talking. It would just be you saying yes or no."

"Okay."

"Can I have another dog?"

"No."

We came over a rise and the ground now levelled off; apparently the island was a truncated volcano, topped off by a plain of black rock. There were more tiny bushes, bonzai'd by cruelty and nature's starvation, popping out of crevices, grasping at rootholds. Crowding the plateau, like conventioneers at an ice breaker, were blue-footed boobies.

The Cormorants regarded the birds with patent disinterest. Someone wearily raised a camera and clicked the shutter. Mr. B. commenced whirring and muttered, "And here he is in all blah-blah-blah ..."

Across the black plain lay the ocean, which looked endless and verdant. (You see that I was now suffering calenture, the fever that afflicts sailors and makes the ocean appear as Elysian Fields.) A spray of water repeatedly spouted behind the cliff faces, and I imagined that a whale was parked just over the edge, nestled in the rocks below and happily tooting through its blowhole. I began to stumble toward it, although this caused Carlos to grab my arm in an all-too-stern manner.

"Stay on the pathway, Mr. Quarrington."

I waved toward the happy whale, hidden though it was. I opened my mouth to explain my intention of bathing in the cool mist of its spray, but my tongue was too swollen for speech.

"Anyway," said Carlos, turning me about, facing me at another small barren rise, "we're going this way."

"Whey?"

"Hmmm?"

"Wha oher dere?"

"What's over there?" repeated Carlos. "Why, the booberie!"

I am getting nearer the rigorous biblical scholasticism mentioned earlier, but am not quite through excusing myself. I am largely self-taught in these matters, having abandoned, quite early on, the established Church. You see, the lapel of my Sunday school blazer, naked and unadorned, soon acquired a kind of obscenity. The little boy with the perfect hair could not approach any nearer than twenty feet without a sneer fashioning his upper lip. The other children, although lacking his long chain of hardware, all had a bar or two, and were therefore quick with snotty glances and the tsking of tongues. The Sunday school teachers themselves had no respect for me, although this might have had as much to do with my wondering aloud if anyone had ever fallen off the Bible, and if so, did they live or die?

I eventually grasped the fact that the Bible was a book. That was something I understood. Every room back home was filled with books, although there was no Bible. The closest thing to a Bible was a massive tome bound in black leather. The cover was intricately tooled; someone had carved the letter "Q" so that the family's initial, ivy-wrapped and intricate, occupied the spine of this volume. I know now that the leather cover was a gift to my parents, and that my father had merely attached it to the book that it best fit. But these little accidents have their repercussions, and I think it still affects me today that the book that seemed most like the Bible was entitled *The History and Social Influence of the Potato.*

I left the Church (although I would continue to write "United" on any form that asked my religion, not yet clued in to the fact that I had been baptized an Anglican), but I saved up my paper route money and purchased a Bible.

Over the years I've owned several Bibles, and own several today, a couple of which are currently littered about my feet. I use them chiefly as reference tools, seeking out little pieces of poetry to plug up the holes in my often slipshod work.

The King James version is not actually my favourite version of the biblical creation story. I don't like its tendency to use words like "firmament," which has always sounded a little like a trade name to me. I keep expecting to see:

And God made the firmament™ and divided the waters.

Much nicer, for my taste, is the New Jerusalem Bible, which uses the more poetical "vault."

God said, "Let there be a vault in the waters to divide the waters in two." And so it was.

The blue-footed booby is not mentioned by name in either book. Here is the King James account of the origin of species:

God said, "Let the earth produce every kind of living creature: cattle, reptiles, and every kind of wild beast." And so it was. God made every kind of wild beast, every kind of cattle, and every kind of land reptile.

That last qualifier, "land" before "reptile," seems a little awkward, unless we are to understand that God therefore went out of His way not to create the marine iguana. This recounting is, all in all, a thoroughly unsatisfying explanation for what we're now calling biodiversity. What about beetles? One out of every four living creatures is a beetle, so why doesn't the Bible report that God made beetles, and then threw in some cattle and creeping things, and decided at the last moment to create the human, a rare and specialized creature designed to fill a particular niche?

Of course, most would have it that this biblical section should not be taken literally. Perhaps it simply *can't* be, except by scholars and linguists; the rest of us can never know what the original writer or writers said or meant. My New Jerusalem Bible is at odds with the King James version, for example; it replaces the mundane if precise phrase "land reptile" with the far more eloquent "creeping thing." That would mean that God did create the marine iguana. Indeed, the implication is that the iguana was one of the first things out of the box.

Of course, those who believe in the literal truth of Genesis make good use of the vagueness of the assertion that God made every kind of living creature. Indeed, the name of our landing site, "Punta Suarez," has special import, because Francisco Suarez, a Spanish Jesuit who lived in the sixteenth century, was as responsible as anyone for the Doctrine of Special Creation, which holds that God knew exactly what He was doing. God created species, He rendered them carefully and made them immutable. Moreover, He set them down in precise places and locales and bade them stay put. So, according to Francisco Suarez's theory, at some point God decided that what the planet needed was a bird with blue feet and glazed eyes. So He created these birds and in His wisdom put them on various remote islands where other creatures were not likely to trip over them.

What is most important and implicit in Special Creation is the idea that God made humans, that He conceived of us and pieced us together carefully and put us here so that we could manage things for Him.

This is the loudest of the squabbles, the Creationists versus the Neo-Darwinists. If you thought that this was all settled long ago, think again. "A district in Georgia recently endorsed the teachings of Creationism," reports the *New York Times*, "which holds that all life forms, including humans, were fully formed by a Creator and did not evolve." This is dated March 5, 1996. A full one hundred and thirty-seven years after the first Great Squabble, they're still at it. There's more, taken from the same clipping. The Tennessee state legislature considered permitting school boards to dismiss teachers who present evolution as a fact rather than a theory of human origin. Alabama approved a disclaimer, to be placed in biology texts, calling evolution only "a controversial theory." I often wonder at the energy and determination of these arguments, as Genesis can clearly be appreciated for its poetical content—"And the spirit of God moved upon the face of the waters"—and is particularly prone to attacks of schoolboy logic. But many emulate mad Captain FitzRoy. "Here is the truth," they intone, holding the big book aloft. "Here in the Bible, not in the mouth of that evil snake in the grass."

There are some peoples who would not have been rattled by Darwin's Insight, cultures that seem to have easily grasped the basics of evolution, even if they messed up a bit on the particulars. The creation story of the Ainu of northern Japan has it that in the beginning there was nothing but mud. The Creator sent down a little bird who beat frantically at the mud with its wings, somehow summoning forth life. This story may show the Ainu to be standing rather shakily on scientific ground, but they intuited the notion of special change; they believe that the creatures who crawled out of the primordial ooze transmutated over time. For example, the Ainu believe that humankind, being somewhat hairy, descended from the polar bear.

That's kind of an intriguing notion, isn't it? If it weren't taught in schoolbooks, I wonder if the notion of the monkey as our progenitor would be so obvious. If evolution had come down another pathway, perhaps we would be short-legged creatures who lumber about devouring things and scratching our backs on trees. Which is, come to think, exactly what I am. Hmmmm ...

(Actually, many scientists wonder not why we're so hairy, rather why we're so un-. After all, we are primates, big monkeys or little apes depending on how you see things. Our genetic make-up is so similar to the chimpanzee's—we share about 98.2 per cent of our genetic sequences—that some claim we do not even deserve our own genus. This seems like an appropriate time—at least, I don't see much chance of it ever coming up again—to mention the following theory. Some folks believe that humankind actually began to evolve into the water. We were in the midst of becoming aquatic mammals—and losing our body hair in the name of aquadynamics—when something happened to direct us back the other way, back onto the lichen-covered rocks. Perhaps a portion of the population remained in the sea—this isn't part of the original theory, which gets its supporters in enough academic trouble without any such weird corollaries—which would lend considerable credence to the legends of the Lost City of Atlantis.)

Those of you who read my books (and by the way, Christmas dinner is at my house this year) will know that I have a particular fascination for the Dogon tribe of Mali. These are the people who worship the Dog Star Sirius, and have for centuries. They also worship, or at least acknowledge, Sirius's companion star. The significance here is that western astronomers didn't even see the companion star until the middle of the twentieth century. The Dogons have a perfectly reasonable explanation for this knowledge: the people from the Dog Star visited and told them all about it.

Here is what the Dogons believe: in the beginning were two sets of twins, each of them androgynous. From these four descend all of humankind, so that every brother is in a sense parent to his sister's offspring, every sister to her brother's.

This is sufficiently confusing as to have its basis in scientific fact. Perhaps the visitors from the Dog Star Sirius lectured the Dogons on genetics, and this is their version. It's significant, for example, that the Dogons begin with two sets of twins for a total of four, because the essential stuffs of DNA are four nucleotides: adenine, guanine, thymine and cytosine. And the idea of twinning has resonance because these align themselves only in a prescribed manner, the purines with pyrimidines: adenine to thymine, guanine to cytosine. That never varies.[1] Four nucleotides aligning themselves in sets of twins—which indeed sounds very much like the Dogon version of things—can write enough code (do the math, which is beyond me, and think about the possibilities) to account for all the life on our little blue stone.

Getting back to creation myths, here's another that appeals to me. The spirit Tangaroa, according to the Samoans, roamed

---

1 Actually, though, for the Theory of Evolution to work, it has to vary sometimes. There are occasional shifts in the positions of the hydrogen atoms responsible for the bonding, and a modified purine may link with a pyrimidine. This "tautomeric shift" results in, you guessed it, mutations.

about in space, the eternal void. But He stopped once, and a rock appeared, so Tangaroa told that rock to split apart, which it did, and then those rocks split, and so on. Then those rocks began to talk to each other, and so came into being many things: water and the sky, certainly, but also concepts like male/femaleness, ideas like height and time, intangibles such as thought and will. Tangaroa told the biggest rock that spirit, thought, will and heart would come together to form human beings. And then Tangaroa left, abandoning His creation for all time.

The Bible would make more sense, somehow, if it ended this abruptly; if, at the end of the Book of Genesis, God saw that His work was good and left for parts unknown. But the Christian God is eternal and omnipresent. Despite claims of immutability, He changes character throughout the Bible. He becomes vengeful and petulant; often He is more destroyer than creator, and *that* God must be persuaded by prayer and placated by hymn. Believers seem to do this willingly enough, without particular complaint, because to many the earth is but a way station. Those who are most insistent about the truth in the Book of Genesis are often the most fanciful in describing the Heavenly Kingdom.

I have a notion that *genesis* is not at the heart of the matter. I think that what's really at issue is revelation, the promise of eternal bliss. Charles Darwin, in a circuitous way, closed the door to Paradise. Only a God capable of the sort of construction and forethought implied by the Book of Genesis would be capable of making our Heaven. And by the beginning of the eighteenth century, Heaven had become a very complicated place; according to Swedenborg, it had cities, complete with avenues, gardens, parks and other "splendid places." (Swedenborg was in a position to know, seeing as he visited Heaven frequently.[2]) Neo-Darwinism has it that the earth exists only by chance. What are the odds, then, of that sort of Heaven? Mighty damn long.

Even as a small boy, I found notions of celestial bliss somehow uncompelling. Perhaps I had an intuition of severe overcrowding; perhaps it seemed obvious from the get-go that I had my work cut out for me just to make it through the Presentlife, let alone worry about the After-. I also never really believed that the here and now was so very sad. I wondered if something very near heaven might not exist on this little blue planet. My thoughts then, as now, are a little muddled. But I think I learned a lesson, there on Hood Island, from the mighty albatross.

Carlos squinted, capped his hand on his brow to shade his eyes, and got visibly excited. "Look," he said, shooting a forefinger with precision. "On that cliff over there." Carlos meant a cliff that seemed to be half a mile away, seen across a stretch of ocean formed by a huge bite in the topography. "An albatross." The Cormorants dutifully executed the manual visor, and those with binoculars—those with binoculars and strength enough after the trek—hoisted them to their eyes.

I stood on the outside of the group, close to the brink. Though I was squinting, this was evidence more of irritation than of any desire to see an albatross. And because I wasn't concentrated on albatross-spotting, I was the only one who noticed a prehistoric creature, his beak fashioned to equip the bird with a sardonic grin, flap by about ten feet away. I

---

2 I recall my father playing for me a tape when I was a young lad, a recording of an interview that he'd conducted with a man suffering from delirium tremens. This man, like Emanuel Swedenborg, claimed to have visited Heaven. "What was Heaven like?" asked my father, on the tape. "Heaven," the man responded, "was one of the nicest places I've ever seen."

suspected it was an albatross, but I was also seized by the notion that it might be some sort of pterodactyl or a creature escaped from the set of a Japanese horror movie, so I said nothing. Meanwhile the Cormorants were demanding, "Where? Where?" and Carlos was giving rather detailed instructions: "You can see over there a small shrub about just near the top of the cliff."

"And there in all its glory," intoned Mr. B., his voice as flat and otherwoldy as a druid's, "a small shrub." But his camera was circling, a confused and frustrated predator.

"Where is it?" asked the Cormorants, and quiet Mr. Perdomini said, "There."

Mr. Perdomini was a young Italian man who said virtually nothing. These were perhaps the first volunteered words I'd heard him utter. Like most of the passengers I put this down to his knowing very little English, but I'd also seen him addressed in his native tongue, and his usual response was a small smile, a quiet shrug. Mr. Perdomini was very neat and organized. He often worked in a small journal, writing in a cramped hand, leaning back in a deck chair to suck on the pen cap as he considered what might come next. On the side of his neck Mr. Perdomini wore a large circular bandage, modern medicine against seasickness. He seemed to be a birder by avocation, concentrating on them during the tours, often referring to brightly coloured books, the plates picturing feathered fliers. And he demonstrated now that he had developed a birder's finely tuned powers of observation, for it was he who saw the albatross sitting on the ground about twenty feet away.

The bird twisted its head and fanned its magnificent wings. Albatrosses have the greatest wingspan in the animal kingdom, up to twelve feet. They are overburdened by aviatory power. This bird was likely returning to its birthplace after no less than two years away. (This was the first albatross spotted on Hood, the world's only breeding ground, that year; Carlos made especial note of this for the Charles Darwin Research Station, taking out a small book and inscribing the date.) "Man," I supposed the bird was saying, because he looked both sheepish and exhausted, "did I take a wrong turn."

Dr. Moody had shown film footage of the albatross (the one that we were staring at now was a waved albatross, much smaller than the wandering albatross), and Moody himself, certainly no stranger to God's glories, seemed slightly stunned at the two-year sojourn. Of course, the birds do often settle their weary butts upon the face of the waters. They do linger around ships, perching on the masts and evidencing a great reluctance to leave. (This accounts for the creature's significance in folklore, the burden that cannot be relieved.) But they are two years away from home. For an albatross those years must acquire the weight and solidity of existence—like the Death March, like our own lives—and when he finally crashes upon the bush-spattered cliffside, it must seem like Heaven indeed.

Eight

During the night, the *Corinthian* moved. Sometime around midnight, the belly of the boat shuddered and engines started to whine. Winches squealed as the anchor was hoisted. Sailors scurried to and fro, pausing outside the porthole to our sleeping chambers so that they might holler at one another. Carson managed to sleep through all this. I didn't.

Neither could I sleep when we were underway. This had to do with the pitch and roll of the *Corinthian*. It didn't induce seasickness, but it physically prevented slumber. On a pitch I would roll forward and the blinds would smack me in the face. On a roll I would pitch backwards and almost spill out of the berth, saving myself only by clutching desperately at the mattress.

Denied sleep, I spent hours mulling, searching for Insight. Eventually the pitch and roll of the *Corinthian* sent me into a grateful half-slumber and I experienced odd dreams.

I dreamt that I raised myself up on one elbow and leant over the side of my berth. I reached downward and took hold of the brass handle there, pulling outwards. A drawer opened beneath me; I could see black earth. Incandescent worms roiled, tying themselves into complicated knots, impossible to undo.

The next morning, we leapt into the panga and blasted across to Floreana Island. My father had joined us for this expedition, not worried by the tales of suffering related by the survivors of the Death March. Indeed, the Cormorants were uniformly refreshed and reinvigorated, with the exception of yours truly. It was a wet landing, so we struggled up on shore and then sat down to dry off our feet, wipe sand away and put on shoes. I selected a black rock as my seat, turned around and aimed my keester at it. My daughter nodded vaguely in its direction. "Are you going to sit down there?"

"Yeah," I said, descending.

"There's a iguana there."

I spun around and saw the creature snugged into the crannies. Although it's hard to justify a complete failure to spot a three-foot lizard at close quarters, let me try to explain. A marine iguana is "ectothermic," which means that its body temperature is not constant and must be adjusted by what the literature calls "postural changes." For this reason, iguanas are often standing in the sun, warming up; every so often they'll puff out huge clouds of steam as the sea water they sucked in along with their daily Ulva heats up. At noon they'll all turn and face the sun, minimizing body-surface contact with the rays. To cool down they'll position themselves in the sea breeze or, if possible, find a shadowy nook. And when they've found a good position, they keep it with a profound stillness.

These marine iguanas are very dark—like much of the volcanic rock that litters the archipelago—and they are decorated with irregular shingles of disparate dull hue, so that they seem lichen-covered. Or afflicted with psoriasis. Or, it so often seemed to me, accursed. So, although scientific thinking may have it that they are merely avoiding the cruel sunlight, I believe they are cowering between rocks, finding refuge in eroded recesses, out of a very deep sense of shame.

(Carson proved very adept at spotting them. A small wall of black rock would present itself, a dozen rocks tumbled together by time. Carson would look at it for a second or two and say, "Seven." A careful recount would appear to contradict her. "Six," I would say, until my daughter pointed out the lizard squeezed vertically into a shadowed crevice.

(This talent was soon noticed by the other Cormorants. One couple, Peter and Carmen, seemed especially delighted by it. "Carson," Peter would call, "come up here and spot marine iguanas." Carson would move toward the front of the pack and assume a stance like Cortés regarding the Pacific. "There's one," she'd say. She soon developed a sense of pride in this, and before long was showing off, assuming the stance, pointing to a rock face seventy feet away, nonchalantly mentioning the lizard there. Sometimes even our guide Carlos would squint and shake his head. "There's no iguana there, Carson," he'd say. She'd run over and virtually yank the beast out of its nook. Except that Carlos would stop her, as it was illegal to grab and yank the wildlife upon the Isolas de Galápagos.)

Floreana—one of the four islands that Darwin walked upon —is undeniably a beautiful place. The other islands can assume a kind of beauty, but only with an energetic assist from the beholder, who is forced to find aesthetics in the austerity of black rock. Floreana, remarkably for the Galápagos, achieves lushness. The profile of the island is informed by a mountain, although this mountain looks like it was sketched by a four-year-old child. It is a huge rounded hump, as symmetrical and curved as a croquet hoop. Trees stud the summit, simple sparse trees that, again, are positioned as a child might draw them, evenly spaced and protruding only from the line of the silhouette, the meeting of mountain and sky.

The beach at Punta Cormorant, where we landed, is an odd colour, olive green, because of volcanic crystals of magnesium, iron and olivine. Behind the beach is a drapery of plant life, palo santo trees and beach morning glories; there is the greyish ground cover called *Tiquilia*, there is a little yellow flower named muyuyo. My father immediately started pulling ferns and tiny blossoms out of the ground, lifting them to his nose and inhaling lustily, as though he'd been experiencing a kind of deprivation. He came up beside me and opened his hand to reveal a few green tatters.

"Hmm," said I.

"It looks like purslane, doesn't it?"

"It sure does." All right, I admit I had no idea. But my father seemed convinced, which was good enough for me. This was his bailiwick, after all. Things botanical had absorbed most of his interest for years. More than once he gave his vocation to the other passengers as "Gardener." So I was willing to agree that whatever he held in his hand looked like purslane, although I had no idea why this should be noteworthy.

We were led through a forest of lichen-draped *Scalesia villosa* on a pathway, narrow and paved with cinder chips. Hidden in there was a huge brackish lagoon, which doesn't sound all that appealing except that standing in it was a stand of flamingos. Not just any flamingos, either, but pink flamingos. To paraphrase the coroner, my favourite Munchkin, they were not just merely pink, but really quite sincerely pink. The flamingos on Floreana are actually said to be the pinkest in the world.

Mr. B. was beside himself, lifting the Wondercam and wandering into the lagoon, dampening his pale blue knee socks.

"And here they are in all their glory," he droned, which of course had the effect of lifting the entire flock into the air. They cruised a few hundred yards to the far end of the lagoon and settled down gently.

Murmuring darkly under our collective breath, we left, taking another pathway through the forest of palo santo trees. In doing so, the Cormorants from the *Corinthian* almost collided with some other group from some other ship, who were tramping along on their way to see the flamingos that Mr. B. had frightened away. The two groups shuffled like a deck of cards. Neither group acknowledged that the other was there.

"I want another dog," proclaimed a voice from behind me.

"You have a dog."

"But I can't pick her up."

"So what?"

"Zoë is your dog. I want my own dog."

"Zoë can be your dog. She wants to be your dog. She doesn't always enjoy being my dog, I can guarantee you that."

"But I can't pick her up."

"We can't get another dog just so you'll be able to pick it up."

"Mommy said I could have another dog when I'm twelve."

"She did?"

"She did."

"Well, wait until you're twelve, then."

"How about when I'm eleven?"

"Look, it's not an *age* thing. It doesn't have to do with the number of years you've been alive. It has to do with maturity and responsibility."

"I'm responsible."

I shook my head with weary exasperation, because Carson assumed no responsibility for the care and upkeep of Zoë. I was the one who walked after the little arfer and collected her shit in plastic bags. I was the one who stepped, freshly woken and bathrobed, into her puddles of vomit. I was Alpha Dog; I lectured Zoë sternly when she ate Persian rugs and family heirlooms.

Actually, it was while walking Zoë that I noticed the door in my Toronto neighbourhood that said "Galápagos." The houses on our street back onto an alleyway, which we share with the backs of the houses on the street to the north. It was one of these houses, I noticed while walking around the block, waiting for Zoë to hunker and drop a log, that was adorned with the single word "Galápagos." That fact had, indeed, informed my decision to pitch the idea to the Publisher. It is one thing to have a vague notion, to wave at television sets late at night and make giddy proclamations. Which is to say, I am constantly stating publicly that I'm going to do things that I will never do, haven't the slightest intention of doing. So it might have been with the Galápagos idea, except this door, so close, shoved the whole thing into the realm of destiny. Somebody or something clearly wanted me to make the journey.

There is a beach in the middle of the world, with sand as fine as flour, where people gather from all over the world to hear a tale of mystery. They may have been lured by the prospect of glimpsing giant sea turtles, but often these behemoths are mere shadows in the water many yards out. So instead of photographing the creature, the people make a careful appraisal of its nest—a crater perhaps ten feet across, with tractor-tire marks leading down to the water—and then simply stand on the beach. Their guides step forward and announce, "Now I'll tell you about the human history of Floreana."

There have actually been a few attempts to settle the island the English call Charles. In 1832, when Ecuador laid claim to the archipelago, a General Villamil arrived, hoping to colonize, bringing with him eighty convicts whose sentences had been commuted from death. The General then went about naming things, as men are wont to do: the island he called Floreana, after Flores, the president of Ecuador. The bay they abided he called Asilo de la Paz, Asylum of Peace. Before long, of course, the convicts were running amok. Those who survived were removed and scattered over the rest of the islands. There was another colonization attempt made in 1870, again with convicts, again in the Asilo de la Paz. They planted citrus fruit, coffee and tobacco. Unfortunately, the settlers soon divided into two distinct camps, and then the two distinct camps went at each other (as distinct camps are wont to do). Hardly anyone survived, but their cows and pigs carried on their work, gobbling up the plants and then dropping the seeds across the whole of the island. So, despite the failure of people to actually inhabit it, Floreana was indeed becoming sort of a paradise: an island where coffee and tobacco plants grew wild. However, another attempt made in 1927 by some Norwegians hoping to start a canned fish factory likewise failed.

But the particular human history that people find so fascinating—the story all the guides tell when the turtles have gone back to the sea—has to with Dr. Ritter and the Empress of Floreana.

When the Empress first arrived on the island—at Asilo de la Paz—she laid claim only to the title "Baroness." She was an attractive woman, youthful and blonde, and had arrived upon the shores of Floreana with two young men in tow: a dark surly sort named Robert Philipson, and a more chatty Aryan man named Lorenz. She came to Floreana with a lot of bathtubs and a grand vision—to build a huge luxury hotel where rich people, when world-weary, would come seeking rejuvenation. She would call this dream palace "Hacienda Paradiso."

(I heard this story from Carlos, there on the shores of Floreana, but I have to admit, I didn't pay a lot of attention. I spent most of my time preventing Carson's hat from flying off her head, standing behind her and smacking down lightly on the crown whenever I heard the telltale flutter. It was hot that day, but the wind was howling, making everyone's white clothes flutter and smack. Besides head-wear governance, my main source of distraction was trying to glimpse turtles riding the pounding surf. Occasionally, I was successful. Every once in a while the rolling of the surface would fashion a lens out of the water, and for a brief moment a round shape beneath was brought into clarity and focus. The turtles fanned their flippers, treading water. They stared at the beach and looked bored. They had heard the story too many times.

(It doesn't matter that I didn't pay keen attention; the Floreana story can be read in at least three books. By the way, in case you're wondering, my father didn't pay attention either. He waded into the surf—one hand resting on top of his head to prevent his Panama from becoming airborne—and stared at the horizon. He seemed to be looking for whales.[1])

Floreana was not quite deserted at the time of the Baroness's arrival. There was a German family, the Wittmers, which numbered four: Heinz; his wife Margret; their sickly son Rolf; and a newborn baby. The Wittmers were attracted to Floreana chiefly because of a book that was very famous in the 1920s, *Galápagos: World's End*, written by William Beebe. Beebe, a world-reknowned naturalist, explorer and author, had visited the Encantadas, retracing Darwin's steps. Indeed, the popularity of

---

1   Whales are interesting. They are in a sense the largest example of Paley's hypothetical watch, because there are no clear evolutionary ancestors for them, no proto- or mini-whales. They seem to have been popped into the waters by the Almighty.

the Galápagos as a tourist attraction today has much to do with Beebe's book; prior to that, I take it, the archipelago was as obscure as it had been throughout history, a footnote merely. When the Wittmers arrived on the island they found two other residents: Dr. Friedrich Karl Ritter and his companion Dore Strauch Koerwin.

Dr. Ritter was a strange little dude. A photograph shows him as short and stocky, his body impressively muscled. Ritter stands shirtless; his belt can't prevent his trousers from riding very low on his hips. (Beside him, her arm curled around his waist and cupping a bulging oblique, Dore appears gaunt, and regards the camera's eye with wariness tinged with mischief, if you'll buy that particular combination.) Ritter had been a dentist in his former life and, knowing that good care was going to be hard to find on Floreana, came up with a novel idea. He and Dore both had all of their teeth pulled. They then commissioned the assemblage of a set of dentures rendered out of stainless steel. In case you suspect I've blundered syntactically, let me make this perfectly clear—they had a set of dentures made, which they then shared.

Ritter had also read *Galápagos: World's End*, but what he loved was the notion of emptiness, vacancy, that Beebe described so well. Ritter was not there seeking Eden, he was there because he wanted not much to do with the human race. He maintained a kind of terse civility with the Wittmers, who were, after all, German. Occasionally he would share his philosophy with them. It had something to do with vegetarianism, that's as much as they could fathom. Ritter was generally aloof and sometimes displayed a remarkable and alarming temper, but he was not without his good points. When Margret Wittmer went into labour Ritter arrived with furious industry, helping Margret with a difficult delivery.

So everyone lived in harmony that was only slightly wonky, Ritter and Dore sounding sharp and off-key. Then the Baroness arrived, with her airs and affectations and two young men. (Actually, when she first arrived, there was an additional Ecuadorian fellow named Valdivieso, who stayed only a few weeks and then left.) The Baroness immediately displayed what we might call antisocial behaviour. For example, it had become established practice, started by the buccaneers many years before, for passing ships to drop off mail and goods sent by sea at a particular location on the island, which accordingly had been dubbed Post Office Bay. (Sailors also picked up mail from the bay and posted it when they reached their destination. This was the only means of communication available to Floreanians.) The Baroness showed an alarming propensity for helping herself to whatever was left at Post Office Bay. When confronted, she would deny the accusation with all the guilelessness that bred-in-the-bone eccentricity can provide. Other examples of her oddness are less perfidious. She often went about with no clothes on, for example. This upset Dore, even though Dr. Ritter's own philosophy had something to do with nudism.

The particular squabbles that afflicted this handful of people aren't really all that important. They were mostly enjoined between the Baroness and Dr. Ritter; the Wittmers tried not to take sides. Dr. Ritter, iconoclast and maverick, was likely especially rankled when the Baroness elevated herself to the station of Empress. Adding to the ill feeling on Floreana was the fact that there had been something of a swing in the Empress's affections and preferences. When she arrived it was clear that she favoured Lorenz, but as time went on (and as Lorenz, not taking to the conditions and climate, grew emaciated and sickly), the Empress became much more drawn to Philipson.

One day Lorenz presented himself at the cave of the Wittmers, distraught and suicidal. They let him stay for a few days, although they were fearful that the Empress might exact revenge for this bit of collusion. (The Empress, it should be noted, had guns, had even shot a visitor in the stomach; she claimed, with eerie dispassion, that it had been an accident.) When the Empress presented herself, however, she seemed calm enough; and oddly, she announced that a ship had arrived and had agreed to take Philipson and her away from Floreana.

Then the two disappeared. They were never seen again.

But no one had seen a ship anchored in the Asilo de la Paz. No mail had been left or taken at Post Office Bay. And no one on the island was talking much about it. If the Baroness and Philipson were murdered, as many suspect, who was the culprit?

Lorenz, his health worsening, his behaviour erratic and in-formed by black moods, determined to get off Floreana. He convinced a passing sailor to take him away; the man was reluctant, but finally agreed to take Lorenz only as far as Santa Cruz. Any greater journey would be hazardous, he told Lorenz, as his craft was old and unseaworthy.

Months later the two were found on the island of Marchena, almost due north and far beyond Santa Cruz, the fat island in the centre of the archipelago. They had floundered and ship-wrecked. For the most part, the islands in the Galápagos are inhospitable; there is little to eat and absolutely nothing to drink. Lorenz had died a horrible death.

As did Dr. Ritter, who died from eating tainted chicken meat. This was suspicious beyond the fact that Ritter was an avowed vegetarian. He'd known the meat was bad, and so had boiled it, which really should have made it palatable. And Dore had eaten the same meat with no ill effect.

Dr. Ritter died in a rage even greater than had informed his life. Margret Wittmer was present at his passing, and noted that he stared at Dore with undisguised hatred burning in his eyes. Then he turned toward Margret and folded his hands together briefly, a mute plea for forgiveness.

Forgiveness for what? many wonder. Perhaps for killing the Empress and her lover ...?

One day, making my usual rounds with Zoë, I knocked upon the door marked "Galápagos." It was answered by a tall woman with a lovely face that had been only slightly worn by time and cigarettes. She pointed out that I hadn't really needed to knock, seeing as this was a place of business: she gesticulated at all the stickers on her window, as many certifications and validations as a travel agent is capable of accumulating. I followed her into the place, removing my boots in the foyer, because despite her denials, this was obviously her home. For one thing, there was a rug on the floor, which business people tend to avoid due to the slushiness of Toronto winters. Plus there was *colour*, which business people tend to avoid in general. Toronto business people in particular. The city is my home, and not without its charms, but on its worst days (which generally inform the winter, which in fact makes up much of the year), it can be a grey and dismal place. Torontonians tend to reflect this in their interior decorating, favouring beiges and off-whites. We prize serviceability in the furnishings, because after a few weeks of winter, we want only to sit down. We do our work on square tables and lie down upon square beds; our windows frost up so that no sunlight can enter, and what little colour there was inside our domiciles and places of business is thence lost for another season.

Ingrid's place wasn't like this. There were bright blankets

upon the wall, and tiny edifices containing hundreds of tiny carved, smiling people. Outside her back door—and this I know because her back door is near mine, separated by our tiny back yards and a dogleg—someone has painted a mural on one of the walls, a strange surrealistic thing that pictures a beach and a huge shell, neatly bisected as in a medical illustration, so that one can look inside. A dozen exotic fish swim around in there, evenly spaced and orderly.

Ingrid Versteeg was born in Holland, where her father was a lawyer in the diplomatic corps. Her family lived briefly in Switzerland and France, but her father, consternated by the dreadful war that had just taken place in Europe, decided to seek other climes. Mr. Versteeg selected Canada as their destination; first the city of Montreal, then, and most lastingly, the town of Almonte, which lies just outside the national capital.

Ingrid herself wandered further as she reached early adulthood, and in her mid-twenties wound up residing in Quito, officially papered and sanctioned to dwell in Ecuador. A friend of hers, a young woman with a great interest in nature and photography, came to visit from Boston, and it was the friend's idea to visit the Encantadas. "It had never occurred to me," Ingrid says. "It never occurred to anyone living in Ecuador."

There were, in the sixties, two ways of getting there. The American military used the island of Baltra, just to the north of Santa Cruz, as a strategic base from which to patrol the Panama Canal, so it was sometimes possible to cross over aboard what was called a logistical flight. The only other way was on an infrequent charter. "It cost something like fifty or sixty American dollars," Ingrid recalls. "That was an enormous amount of money back then." I have described the modern-day airport on San Cristóbal as primitive, but I guess I've just been spoilt. When Ingrid landed on Baltra she found the most rudimentary of places; there was a runway, an observation tower and a small shack. From there she and her friend hired a small fishing boat to take them across to Santa Cruz. "And I mean a fishing boat," Ingrid iterates. "It was full of fish, it stank of fish." The transit took something like eight hours. Check the map at the front of the book, which I browbeat the Publisher into providing. The distance looks to be the size of a synapse, but between the islands the sea is wild and treacherous. Ingrid and her friend finally arrived in Academy Bay, where they boarded at the home of Gus Angermeyer, who has achieved a measure of fame as the "Iguana Man"—David Quammen recounts a visit to Angermeyer in *The Song of the Dodo*, a book you want to read anyway—which means that there were a lot of marine iguanas around. Marine iguanas are not the best emissaries for a region's fauna. Still, Ingrid and her friend began to explore the area, chartering tiny stinking fishing boats to take them from isle to islet to isle. "And back then, it's not as if there were guides. We had our books and we would stare at these strange creatures and then look them up." Many of Ingrid's sentences share this beginning: "And back then, they didn't have ..." One thing they didn't have, she pointed out, was PABA. For a while they hooked up with a third adventurer to defray the cost of chartering fishing boats, a Scottish fellow with flaming red hair. Before long, his skin made his hair look dull by comparison. Ingrid and her friend wrapped the man up in toilet paper ("which we'd brought with us," Ingrid points out) so that he would not be further damaged. "People quite often got third-degree burns," Ingrid recalls. "It was quite a serious problem." So that was the Galápagos experience thirty years ago. "It was quite horrible," Ingrid says. "I thought it was terrific."

Ingrid found herself visiting the Encantadas more and more. When a friend in Ecuador bought a travel agency, Ingrid began to specialize in the Galápagos, knowing first-hand which fishing craft were the least malodorous. Cruise ships began to plow the swells; Ingrid began to book passage on them.

She returned to Canada in the early eighties and set up her own travel agency, although she has continued to visit the Galápagos and is now married to a very pleasant Ecuadorian fellow named Francisco.

All of which makes Ingrid a good person to question about the unsolved mysteries on the isle of Floreana. For one thing, she still sees Margret Wittmer. "She has her house on Black Beach," Ingrid tells me. "She has a little shop in her house where she sells some things, mostly her book.[2] The farm is still a going concern. She raises a lot of potatoes. Every time she sees me, she wants to discuss the price of a sack of potatoes." Mrs. Wittmer also identifies herself, for the benefit of tourists, as the postmaster. They bring their cards and letters to her, and she makes a grand show of stamping them at her table; she then goes and deposits them in the barrel at Post Office Bay.

And what does Ingrid think went on at Floreana?

"Well, I think you have to understand that these people were perhaps not the most normal to begin with. There was *nothing* there. I can't even imagine the trip from San Cristóbal to Floreana back then. When the Wittmers first made it, they were in something barely larger than a dinghy, with all of their possessions piled up around them. It was madness, really."

And the underlying cause of all the trouble, in Ingrid's opinion?

---

2 Margret Wittmer's book is entitled *Floreana*. Dore Strauch Koerwin's version of events, *Satan Came to Eden*, is currently out of print.

"Envy for other people's possessions. You know, you're on this island where no one really has anything. And you start thinking, *Hmm, that's a nice shiny pot.* Or you see that the other person has real white sugar. Or real cloth to make a real dress."

And, I wonder, does Ingrid have any insight into who may have been behind the disappearances and poisoning?

"Oh," say Ingrid Versteeg, "Mrs. Wittmer knows a lot more than she's saying."

All of which I suppose forces us to consider the failure of humankind to live in Paradise.

It's what follows the creation story in the Bible, after all. Adam and Eve had to leave the Garden. Our ancestor Cain had to move to the east of Eden, and that's where we've been abiding ever since. We are incapable of living in Paradise, due to our own natures. Some would have it that this is precisely why we need a God; that without the Heavenly Father, too many people would conclude the universe was informed by anarchy and lawlessness. What's stopping anyone, in a Godless world, from doing whatever they want?

Well, what is stopping anyone anyway? I mean, where is the evidence that anyone has stopped? We are not behaving at all admirably, and I don't think that a long list of examples is required. We are like children left alone in a big house. It's getting close to midnight and we're running wild, destroying furniture and eating everything in the kitchen. The pious believe that God is going to come home any time, that He will swing open the door and stomp into the foyer, His arms crossed and His brow furrowed. The pious hope that when this happens they are in the act of cleaning up, that by this He will be appeased.

What would happen, do you think, if we discovered that He was not coming home at all? Would we destroy the house? It's possible. It's also possible that we would eventually tire of our mutual frenzy. We might realize that we should clean up, restock the larder and make the beds, because no one else is going to.

CHAPTER

Nine

One of the most famous quotes concerning the Galápagos
is this:

> Little but reptile life is here found: tortoises, lizards, immense
> spiders, snakes and the strangest anomaly of outlandish
> Nature, the aguano. No voice, no low, no howl is heard; the
> chief sound of life here is a hiss.

It was written by Herman Melville, who had visited the Encantadas at the age of twenty-two, a young sailor aboard the American whaler *Acushnet*.

The circumstances under which Herman wrote these lines I
shall relate, because he wrote them at a specific stage in his
career, and I think a lot about career. Specifically, a writer's
career, because I've got one (*knock wood, stroke the bunny paw,
call my agent*). At least today I do. My career has its ups and
downs; it's rarely hale, often sickly. I sit up nights with my
career; I take my career out and buy it drinks. Sometimes I have
a vision of my career hooked up to life support systems, pale
and motionless within an oxygen tent; I pull the plug.

Herman Melville's career was remarkable, as rare and unexampled as a vermilion flycatcher, which we shall be attempting to spot in a chapter or two. After spending much of his youth and early manhood riding the briny, Melville settled down at age twenty-six to begin a career as a man of letters. His first book, *Typee*, was based on his experiences at sea. It was a popular success, and Herman (no doubt thinking, *Hey, that was easy*) followed up with another salty yarn, *Omoo*, which was another smash. The first remarkable thing about Melville's career is the astonishing productivity. This is hard to believe, especially for me and all of my writing friends, but over the course of six years, Melville produced seven long, dense novels. What my writerly friends and I have no trouble believing is that each book sold more poorly than the preceding. *Moby-Dick* was pretty much a dismal failure. Herman then did what many a writer does; he wrote a dark, troubling and intensely personal book. *Pierre, or, The Ambiguities*—I can imagine Melville's publisher pursing his lips at the title, wondering wistfully if he couldn't maybe come up with another catchy zinger, like *Opee*—sold only a handful of copies, and there was the bright young flame all but extinguished. Melville was broke, married and a father. He knew of no other way to make a living (other than returning to sea, and I'm certain that the notion occurred to him; I'm sure he sat up nights staring out his window and feeling the roll of the ocean in his belly), so he wrote a couple of long pieces for *Putnams' Monthly*, one of which was entitled *The Encantadas, or, Enchanted Isles*.[1]

---

1   Melville didn't actually write the pieces *for Putnam's*. He'd received a three-hundred-dollar advance from *Harper's*, the publishers of *Moby-Dick*, to write a novel based on his adventures tortoise-hunting. He couldn't, finally, assemble the pieces into a long cohesive narrative, so he ordered them as ten sketches and sold them to *Putnam's* under a pseudonym, "Salvator Tarnmoor."

"Take five-and-twenty heaps of cinders dumped here and there in an outside city lot," it begins, and it doesn't cheer up.

I recognize the mood. It doesn't take much failure to fill a body with bile. And, although I've heard alcoholism called "the writer's black lung disease," I suggest that a wet tooth is merely symptomatic, that the real illness is bitterness. For there is no way to avoid failure. A writer will erect a bench mark for success, one that reflects both artistry and popularity, and then subsequent books will fail to achieve it. Of course, there is always the chance that another book will "break out," as the publishers say (usually in the context of explaining my low advances, because I haven't done it yet), and achieve lucrative and lofty heights, but let's face it, the trend is more often downwards. And it is embittering because it rarely corresponds to a diminishing of talents. Writers tend to get better each time out. (Or do I sound like an aging ballplayer, excusing creaky knees with claims of enhanced wiliness and know-how?) Certainly Herman Melville did. He just went to new places in his heart and imagination. And when his readership rejected him, he took it personally.

Perhaps I read too much into the ninth sketch of *The Encantadas*—there are ten, roving from island to island like a cruise ship—which is entitled "Hood's Isle and the Hermit Oberlus." Oberlus, who proclaims a kingdom of one upon one of the islands, is a creature of manifest bitterness:

> His appearance, from all accounts, was that of the victim of some malignant sorceress; he seemed to have drunk of Circe's cup; beast-like, rags insufficient to hide his nakedness; his befreckled skin blistered by continual exposure to the sun; nose flat; countenance contorted, heavy, earthy; hair and beard unshorn, profuse, and of a fiery red. He struck strangers

much as if he were a volcanic creature thrown up by the same convulsion which exploded into sight the isle.

The tale has to do with Oberlus's great misanthropy, which is only tempered by the fact that there are rarely any people on the island, his constant companions the giant tortoises. When sailors venture ashore, looking for food and water, the vile Oberlus, armed with his blunderbuss, makes of them prisoners. Men die under his inhuman command. Oberlus ultimately steals a boat and sails off for Guayaquil. He leaves behind a note, an explanation, not a very credible one, for his dastardly conduct. And here is where I begin to suspect that the wretched Oberlus had a certain personal significance for Herman Melville, because the note showed that Oberlus was "an accomplished writer, and no mere boor; and what is more, was capable of the most tristful eloquence."

Melville was by all accounts now consumed by a monumental moodiness. He would be possessed by paroxysms of rage and then abruptly fall silent; silent he would remain for days. (Where have we heard about silence before: did Herman and Charles Darwin share the same post-Galápagon madness?) Melville's health deteriorated, he worried constantly about finances. Finally, at age forty-seven, Herman Melville decided to be done with writing as a career, and took a job in New York City as customs inspector. And, other than his family and fellow workers at the custom house, Melville decided to be done with the human race. Perhaps he had acquired, like Oberlus, "a pure animal scorn for all the rest of the universe."

Oh, except there was Nate Hawthorne living down the road. There is a suggestion here that Herman's hatred for humankind was not pure and unsullied, because he liked Hawthorne. Fawned over him, really, had nothing but guileless admiration for the author of *The Scarlet Letter* and other books that had sold tons and made Hawthorne a literary star of the first magnitude both here and abroad. It is hard for writers not to loathe literary stars of the first magnitude. I know I do. Well, I don't *loathe* them, perhaps, but when I'm invited to cocktail parties where literary stars are in attendance I spend a lot of time conceiving ways of making them stumble face first into the baba ghanouj. I delight in pointing out to other people that the zippers of the literary stars are unzipped, their brassiere straps showing, even when it's not true. I'm sure this seems very petty, but pettiness is one of the great symptoms of bitterness, isn't it, you obsess over the tiniest things, like Oberlus clutching his treasure of "degenerate potatoes and pumpkins." But listen to a writer's view of things (although I'm sure it holds for all professions; just make the appropriate substitutions). Granted that at some point during a writer's career, he or she has acquired a certain mastery over the words themselves—you'll grant me that, won't you, even though I myself seem intent on crafting a sentence of considerable awkwardness?—then popularity reflects more profound differences. The literary star of the first magnitude is more poetic than I. The literary star has more rarefied sensibilities. The literary star is *a better person*. And when you find yourself wanting on this level—an analogy might be a professional football player discovering that he only has one leg—it is hard to avoid bitterness. Herman Melville didn't. And although I'm sure there were many times when someone going through customs erupted with, "You're Herman Melville? I loved that whale thing!" he maintained his dark, incivil silence.

Questing for God is not undertaken lightly. Although I've given the impression that all this was mere happenstance and timing —the Publisher wanting another book, God bless him, my

daughter reaching an age I'd announced very arbitrarily, etc.—
I did have a very personal stake in this trip. I did not want
bitterness in my heart. I had not been entirely successful in
keeping it out.

Indeed, who am I kidding with this "Introduce my daughter
to—perhaps reacquaint my father with—God" business? They
were getting along quite well without Him. I was the one who
was suffering. Not howling, perhaps, not whimpering and sob-
bing, but the modern world doesn't seem the place for a good
old-fashioned spiritual collapse. Instead I can only relate a list
of small ailments and grievances. A tendency (on nights such
as this one) to filch more beers out of the veggie crisper than
is absolutely necessary. A case of careerism that flares up regularly. A kind of rabid psychosis that claims me whenever I'm
behind the wheel of an automobile, sending me snarling and
snapping throughout the city, damning everyone to hell.

It is this last symptom that worries me most, though on the
face of it it seems not so serious. But I guess it's like a cough
that won't die, nagging and persistent; each hack may be pain-
less enough, but after a year or two, one would have to conclude that something inside has gone very, very wrong. So I
worry about my short temper, even though each incident is
more or less trivial. Someone cuts me off, so I damn them to
hell. Someone fails to signal an upcoming left turn, so I damn
them to hell. I gesticulate and slaver, I nearly spontaneously
combust, I fall abruptly into a simmering silence.

When Carson was a baby, she would nap most easily in her
car seat, strapped in snugly and lulled by the hum and mechanical vibration. So from the ages of nothing through two years,
Carson was often in the car with me. One day her aunt
announced that she was going to drive Carson up north for the
weekend, generously giving my wife and me a couple of days of

relative quiet. The car seat was placed in her car; Carson was strapped in. They proceeded to drive. They weren't gone but a few minutes when two-year-old Carson turned to look out her window. A car drove up alongside and Carson gleefully shouted, "Hey, asshole!"

When I heard that story, I realized that I was a very sick man.

Doctors can't help with any of this, I knew instinctively. Only God.

I had another reason for seeking Him, for trying to espy His face, a professional one. God and literature are conflated in my mind. Why this is, I'm not sure. Perhaps because great books seem heavensent. Perhaps because I know that each novel is a puny but very valiant attempt at godlike behaviour. Perhaps because there is no difference between the finest poetry and the most transcendant mysticism. Perhaps because of writers like Thomas Merton, who are able to enter the realm of the spirit and come away with fine, lucid prose. Perhaps because of more secular writers, like John Steinbeck, whose every passage, it seems to me, peals with religiousity and faith. It once occurred to me that literature—all art, really—is either talking to people about God, or talking to God about people.

So when His presence is unclear in the writer's heart, the quality of the work suffers. This was happening to me, and the condition was exacerbated by a bout of careerism, which meant that sales were way, way down.

I will acknowledge a curiously quaint aspect to my quest. Surely, the sensible among you argue, you're not looking for *God*, which is to say, a white-robed long-bearded patriarch. I mean (again I paraphrase the sensible) most of us are past that; we're willing to acknowledge the presence of a certain *force*—

Oh, force, schmorce. Everybody knows there's a force. Acknowledging a force is, you'll excuse me, a useless, almost cowardly, act. *Name it*, that's what I say. Investigate its properties.

Look for signs of intelligence. Forethought.

Design.

That's the God I'm looking for. I don't demand the white beard or robe, although they'd be nice, but I want evidence of judgement, farsightedness and mercy.

I should address another point that might be raised by the sensible: Why assume a gender? Why couldn't your God be a woman?

Well, because She'd probably be doing a much better job.

I should tell you this about Herman Melville. He returned each evening to his apartment in New York City, and when the sun was safely tucked away and the moon in ascendance, he took himself to his writing desk and dipped the nib in black. He wrote poetry mostly ("Skimming lightly, wheeling still / The swallows fly low"), but from time to time would turn his hand to something slightly more substantial. I imagine him sitting beside the window in New York City, staring through the frosted pane and somehow espying the Encantadas.

When he died, in 1891, the *New York Times* had this to say:

> There has died and been buried in this city, during the past week, a man who is so little known, even by name, to the generation now in the vigor of life that only one newspaper contained an obituary account of him, and this was but of three or four lines. Yet forty years ago the appearance of a new book by Herman Melville was esteemed a literary event …

Years later, they found a manuscript in an old trunk, such as might contain a sailor's kit. (I made up that detail, about the sailor's kit, but I feel its poetic qualities more than compensate for whatever it lacks in veracity.) *Billy Budd, Foretopman* was first published in 1924, thirty-odd years after its composition, and is the greatest novella ever written. And even if you take issue with that statement, let's name it that in honour of Melville's victory over bitterness.

The little book revolves around a moral dilemma; it examines, in great and meticulous detail, the workings of the human heart. Briefly, the novella relates the story of Billy Budd, a young man who is pressed into service aboard the *Indomitable*. Budd, a beautiful and guileless young man (Billy, "in the nude, might have posed for a statue of young Adam before the fall"), becomes immensely popular with all of the sailors, with the exception of the master-at-arms, Claggart, who—although we are never sure exactly why—seems to have it in for Billy. And one day Claggart accuses Billy of fomenting ferment, that is, conspiring with some of the other sailors to rise up in mutiny against the wise, if somewhat pedantic, captain, "Starry" Vere. Vere believes none of it; he takes both Claggart and Budd into his quarters and asks the master-at-arms to make his accusation in the presence of the foretopman. When Claggart does so, Budd is speechless, literally and absolutely. Finding no words, Billy lashes out in violence and strikes Claggart dead. Vere recognizes both Billy's technical guilt and his moral innocence, and we watch the captain grapple with notions of duty and mercy. I won't tell you the ending, in case you've never read the book, but it ain't happy.

The story has personal resonance for me. (As soon as I drew near the Galápagos, things increasingly had personal resonance for me, as though the world were a piano, and all of the strings beginning to vibrate sympathetically.) Here's the description of the scene of accusation, wherein Billy Budd is rendered mute:

> Though at the time Captain Vere was quite ignorant of Billy's liability to vocal impediment, he now immediately divined it, since vividly Billy's aspect recalled to him that of a bright young schoolmate of his whom he had seen struck by much the same startling impotence in the act of eagerly rising in the class to be foremost in response to a testing question put to it by the master. Going close up to the young sailor, and laying a soothing hand on his shoulder, he said, "There is no hurry, my boy. Take your time, take your time."

Yes, Billy was a stutterer,[2] and Vere wise enough to realize that this was no great problem, provided everyone has the patience to wait for words. Indeed, there are many similarities between Captain Vere and my father. Like my father, Vere loved books, "never going to sea without a newly replenished library."
And like my father:

> Captain Vere, though practical enough upon occasion, would at times betray a certain dreaminess of mood. Standing alone on the weatherside of the greater deck, one hand holding the rigging, he would absently gaze off at the black sea.

My father did, indeed, do this quite often. He stood alone on the weatherside (I don't suppose he was making the distinction between weatherside and lee-, but wherever he chose to stand was where the wind chose to blow, forcing him to wave

---

2   As were, I've recently found out, both Erasmus Darwin and his grandson Charles. Charles stammered particularly on the first words of sentences.

and teeter like a very tall tree) of the greater deck (assuming that the greater deck is the one that has the lounge/bar/Jacuzzi, which has likely not changed since Melville's time), one hand holding the rigging (the other hand clutching rails or walls or passing crew members), and absently gazed off at the black sea.

After lunch on Wednesday, the captain fired up the *Corinthian* and headed toward the island of Santa Cruz. My father reeled up topside and assumed the Captain Vere position. He seemed to relish the time spent aboard the ship far more than he enjoyed any of the excursions to Darwin's islands. The reeling he executed was actually quite nimble; he took the small gangway steps two or three risers at a time.

My daughter and I followed him up, because we wanted to drink Coca-Cola in the hot midday sun.

My father clutched the railing and gazed upon the face of the waters. Suddenly he turned, a loopy grin breaking his face, and hollered at Carson and me. We couldn't actually hear what he was saying—the hot wind was whipping, and the howl was exacerbated by the fact that the *Corinthian* was underway—but we could see the excitement informing his eyes. So we got up from the plastic seats (pulling great slats of skin from our backs) and reeled over.

My father aimed one of his long crooked fingers. We saw nothing.

"Oh, yeah," said Carson, indulging her grandfather.

"Look!" my father insisted, loudly enough to shatter the wind. I followed his finger and saw, just beneath the surface, a chevron of greyish-blue rockets.

"Look!" I pressed the inside of my elbow against Carson's cheek and pointed, so that she might sight down my arm as though it were a rifle barrel.

"Oh, yeah," said Carson, indulging her old man.

But then the missiles launched themselves. With the synchronization of the Rockettes, five or six dolphins broke the surface of the water and drew a perfect arc in the sparkling daylight.

"Oh, yeah!" said Carson.

Before long other passengers were lined up against the railing—Cormorants, Albatrosses and Boobies—and pointing out dolphins to each other. This was easy sport, for there were many. The trick came in seeing how far away you could identify dolphins, because they dotted the water from the thin shadow of the ship to the horizon. Amazingly, the distant dolphins seemed just as involved in the play, the acrobatic escorting of the *Corinthian*, as the ones immediately beside the belly of the boat. Passengers began to scurry up and down, photographic equipment covering their faces like masks.

At the bow of the ship, where all three of us went, summoned by some palpable excitement coming from people draped over the railings, we looked straight down and saw a dolphin attaching himself like an animate figurehead, sitting just beneath the prow and keeping our speed and direction true and steady. "This way!" he seemed to be saying. "Follow me, you won't go wrong!"

And we were happy to do so, it seemed to me. I imagined the captain laying down his sextant, turning away from the compass and binnacle, dismissing his navigators with a little wave. "It's all right," he tells them. "We have a dolphin now."

My father, perhaps due to a stiffness of back, suddenly reared up from the railing. And then he reached out and placed one hand on his granddaughter's small shoulder, and one hand on mine.

Ten

Those who decried the Theory of Evolution by Means of Natural Selection had the Bible on their side, which claimed unequivocally that the Lord God fashioned the world and its occupants during one calendar week a few thousand years ago. Those who championed it had a couple of things going for them. For one, the Theory seemed to make sense. For another, people began to dig things out of the earth, ancient rocks with the ghostly vestiges of animals imprinted within. These fossils spoke volumes. They shouted silently that life was not always as we know it now, that there once were creatures both great and small whose like have not been seen for millennia.

A man named Philip Gosse didn't see this as any real problem. Gosse was both a zoologist and a man of profound religious conviction. In his book *Omphalos: An Attempt to Untie the Geological Knot* he unravelled the mystery with ease. God did indeed create the world a short while ago, Gosse claimed, but, being the very God that He is, he took care to fashion fossils, and all evidences of great age, in the same glorious instant. Gosse was confident that this would silence the Great Squabble, but such was not the case. Both sides had their problems with his theory; indeed, both sides claimed a rare common ground, finding Gosse's notions rather, well, silly.

Gosse was not a little undone by this failure, for he felt he'd grabbed hold of something there. Gosse sometimes gave the air of being privy to God's plan, as though he were already a lieutenant in the Heavenly Corps and the Almighty had called him in for strategy sessions. The Plymouth Brethren, of which he was an elder, a "Saint," were fundamentally devout and ostensibly modest. They rebuked him, their attitude being that God needed no such explanation or apologia. And the book cost Gosse some standing in the scientific community, too. He was hitherto well respected, the author of several fine works largely concerned with marine life. Truth to be told, Gosse would be well respected again, what with books like *Actinologia Britannica: A History of the British Sea Anemones and Corals*, but this period of his life, the one that saw *Omphalos* published and belittled, sorely tried his spirit. As his son Edmund wrote, "He could not recover from amazement at having offended everybody by an enterprise which had been undertaken in the cause of universal reconciliation."

The younger Gosse wrote this in a very famous little volume entitled *Father and Son*. The book details this relationship, from Edmund's birth until the time he leaves home in his mid-teens. For the first seven years of his existence, Edmund was reared mostly by his mother, an especially zealous woman, outdistancing even her husband on the fanaticism front. But she succumbed to breast cancer, and upon her deathbed made a request of her husband that he guide young Edmund into the light. So the boy's life becomes very odd, indeed. He is denied books and literature, offered only the Bible and febrifugal tracts with titles like *On the Pentateuch* and *The Javelin of Phineas*. (I got "febrifugal" from the very book I'm discussing. According to the *Oxford*

Concise Dictionary, it means "not likely to cause a fever of excitement." A useful word.) A kind of insipid bigotry is bred into the lad, directed sneeringly against "pedobaptists" and "the Popery." He battles internally with his own childlike instincts, and although these never give rise to the kind of outblown rebelliousness we'd expect today (his most daring and dastardly act was to nudge shut a door during his school days, locking the teacher into a closet for a few hours, a crime to which he all too readily confessed), *Father and Son* remains an eloquent testament to filial struggle.

I read the book with great interest, even though it would seem almost a mirror opposite to my experience. Whereas young Edmund Gosse snuck into the library and searched high and low for a book that wasn't about religion, I searched in vain for one that was. And if Gosse senior put blinkers on his son and directed him down a very narrow path, my own father allowed me too much freedom in the field. I often wished for some small indication from him that he felt I was on the right track, but it was hard to divine his opinions. Take the little silver attendance bars, of which he was disdainful; was this because their acquisition had nothing to do with enlightenment, or was it because enlightenment was not to be had within the walls of the Church?

Instead I got little stories about Charles Darwin. My father told me (when, I couldn't say, but if it's a story about Darwin, I know my father told me) that the reason for the fabled silence, the years that Darwin spent in Down House, apparently simply sitting on his Theory, was that Charles was doing battle with himself. Not spiritually—the truth of the matter is, his concerns were more for his wife Emma's religious beliefs than for his own—but intellectually. Darwin wanted no challenge to the Theory that he hadn't anticipated. He wanted to make sure he could slay all dragons, so he spent years summoning, then dispatching, them. He spent years, for example, determining to his own satisfaction that climate was not chiefly responsible for specific variation. This is, most evidently, the lesson my father meant me to learn. It is the notion of *thätige Skepsis*, the condition recommended by Thomas Huxley to the first readers of *The Origin*: a state of "doubt which so loves truth that it neither dares resting in doubt, nor extinguish itself by unjustified belief."

Now seems an appropriate time to mention that one argument against Darwin's (and Wallace's) Theory got away with its head only half cut off, and is still unleashed by Creationists. It has to do with those very fossils that Philip Gosse tried to explain away: the fossil record is incomplete. The argument goes that if Darwin were correct, rocks would tell the story from beginning to end and leave nothing out. Instead, there would seem to be huge gaps and leaps. Radically new specific forms are encrusted next to the old, as though transformation were instantaneous. And scientists hoping to bolster Darwin's argument searched in vain for the intermediaries: something that was neither reptile nor bird, but helpfully halfway between. Even Darwin had to admit that he was undone on this front: "The imperfection of the Geological Record," he wrote, "is one of the greatest difficulties."

I suppose that is another reason Philip Gosse's theories were not welcomed, because Creationists didn't want to explain away a piece of anti-evolutionary evidence. In the book *Father and Son* Father Gosse doesn't seem a particularly cruel man, but perhaps this failure to wed Religion and Science engendered bitterness. Perhaps the bitterness led to distance and distraction, subtle and surprising symptoms, but as particular to the disease as spots to measles. He was certainly insensitive to his son's needs, and though he was often well intentioned, he was a misguided and destructive father. Philip and Edmund "walked in opposite hemispheres of the soul," writes the son, "with the 'thick o' the world between us.' "

As I say, Edmund's experience and mine would seem to be contrary (although that phrase "the thick o' the world" has resonance for me), but there is one area where the two father-son relationships come together, namely, by the water. Edmund writes:

> It was down on the shore, tramping along the pebbled terraces of the beach, clambering over the great blocks of fallen conglomerate which broke the white curve with rufous promontories that jutted into the sea, or, finally, bending over those shallow tidal pools in the limestone rocks which were our proper hunting ground—it was in such circumstances as these that my Father became most easy, most happy, most human. That hard look across his brows, which it wearied me to see, the look that came from sleepless anxiety of conscience, faded away, and left the dark countenance still always stern indeed, but serene and unupbraiding.

As for myself, I cannot remember childhood and not think about the Pond.

On some Saturday and Sunday afternoons, when my father was not required to program the brick house downtown, he would load my younger brother and me into the red Edsel and drive to the Pond. For those readers who might be unfamiliar with Toronto, Ontario, allow me a few sentences by way of setup. The city is, essentially, slashed across its heart by a long ribbon of ravine. (It is also surrounded by woodlands, and I once heard a story that a Japanese urban planner had viewed Toronto from on high and remarked, "How splendid to have built such a huge city in a forest.") Near where I grew up, the ravine fattened into a series of parklands, the most famous of which is Edwards Gardens, a cultivated botanical paradise where young people marry and old people amble. To the south lies an area called Wilket Creek, and we would drive in the Edsel to a sign that announced that name, turn right and descend a long hill. My father would park the car in a gravelled lot, almost always deserted, and then the three of us would strike out through the bulrushes.

My brother Joel (who had survived the rock to the head without obvious ill effect) was keener than I. He owned a net, a small pocket of meshing attached to a wooden stick, which he used to catch specimens. Joel was always weighted down with glass jars, filling all of his pockets, even suspending three or four across his chest with string. He, being keen-eyed, would spot a likely specimen just feet from the parking lot. "*Danaus plexippus!*" he'd exclaim, disappearing into the vegetation. I would remain by my father's side, and we would continue toward the Pond.

It was, perhaps, a hundred feet across, and suspiciously circular. The water was still and brackish, often littered with candy wrappers and used condoms. (*What kind of candy*, I remember thinking, *comes in those things?*) My father would pause nearish the brink, take a look around, point out a red-winged blackbird sitting nearby. Then he would strike out into the Pond, setting his feet with not much care, acquiring a huge soaker in the process, although he rarely seemed to care. I myself hate soakers, my distaste for them is almost phobic, and I wonder if it is from the Pond that I acquired this, because it was next to impossible not to get one. The perimeter was soft and mushy, and although there was sometimes the appearance of solidity (in the fall, for example, there would be a blanket of russet leaves), your foot was usually sucked down into muck. Whilst the muck held your foot captive, the water would trickle in over the sides of your footgear, even if you were wearing black rubber knee-highs. As I say, my father rarely cared, although from time to time his face would collapse and set into miffed stone and he would say words that were forbidden to me. On a couple of occasions he became very upset and said words that were forbidden to pirates, but then he took a deep breath and continued with his pond investigation.

I'll briefly set out a little scene from the Pond, just so you get an idea of what was going on. My father and I are standing near the edge. Behind us there is much grunting and thrashing from the drab flora, which is my brother in pursuit of *Danaus plexippus*. My face is warped, as though by a funhouse mirror, by distaste, for, having received a soaker, I imagine all manner of creature to be nestled inside my boot. There are leeches in the Pond, and I'm certain that several of them have tumbled in and are currently gnawing through my sock. I'd take off my boot to check, except then I might stumble sideways, and then my naked foot would drive itself into the brown water, and the thought of that just barely beats out the thought of leeches presently residing inside my boot. My father, meanwhile, rolls up his shirtsleeve and thrusts it into the water. I manage to contain a moan of revulsion. "Aha!" my father exclaims suddenly, and his bushy eyebrows leap above the frames of his spectacles and he says, "Vot haf we here?" speaking in a stagy German accent. He stands up and holds his hand toward me. Contained in his palm is a tiny monster, a fish burdened with miniature arms and legs. Now I do not manage to contain my moan of revulsion. "Oooh," say I, "what's that?"

My father deals me a "What kind of kid are you?" look and holds the horrible mutant nearer. "It's a tadpole," he answers softly.

My brother then comes reeling out of the rushes, his net flipped and flapping, a butterfly caught in the bright white webbing. "*Danaus plexippus*," he tells us. He pauses for a minute to look into my father's hand. "*Rana catesbiana*," he says, then disappears.

I chose the example of mutating tadpoles for a specific reason, harking back to our scientific and historical investigation. Many people resisted Darwin's Theory of Evolution because there are aspects of it that seem, upon first blush, unreasonable. One being that a human being could be wrought, even over billions of years, out of a tiny speck of protoplasm. But this sort of trick is going on all the time, seemingly magical transformation. A fishy thing changes, almost before one's very eyes, certainly within three or four visits to the Pond, into a froggy thing. And as many have pointed out, why should we doubt that human beings were fashioned from microscopic bits of matter when it is a trick we have all pulled off, each and every one of us, starting off as motes in our mother's bellies?

When Anton van Leeuwenhoek (1632–1723) developed one of the earlier microscopes some three hundred years ago, I suppose that one of the first things he did was to whack off and have a look-see at the punk. That's rather a distasteful way of putting it, but you have to agree that the instinct is normal enough. I'm sure that men the world over, upon getting near that miraculous device or one of its antecedents, the conspicilium or the engyscope, closed the door, put up a sign reading HARD AT WORK—DO NOT DISTURB and started working on their trouser stays. Imagine their surprise when they saw little creatures swimming around.

"Animalcules," they called the little guys. They were tiny, tiny people, perfect in every way, possessed of all limbs and accoutrements. These animalcules needed only to be planted in the female womb and they would grow to a size of eight or so pounds, at which point they could be delivered unto the vale. Not only that, but each male animalcule came already loaded with other little animalcules, which could be fired into fertile wombs in years to come. Based on this theory, people even worked out the precise number of animalcules that Adam had in his belly when God set him down in the garden. And following this school of thought (which is known as "encasement"), all of those male animalcules would be useless without targets, so it was widely thought that Eve came equipped with all of the eggs necessary to produce the human race; like a large and seemingly endless babushka doll, Eve contained an estimated two hundred thousand million eggs.

If this, or even a more reasonable version of it that featured the fertilization of an egg by an agent which has pre-set properties or characteristics, were true, then evolution would not occur. There is no room for change. (Monstrous births and highly visible aberrations were thought to be the result of human/beast couplings, or else "prenatal impression"; therefore, the Alligator Man in early sideshows was created when his pregnant mother was startled by that same beast.) Darwin himself believed that the cells of the body threw off tiny particles, or "gemmules," which were gathered together in the sexual cells for transmission or reception. Each new being was created by a comingling of its parents' gemmules, which would result in "blended inheritance."

As Charles Darwin worked on his secret notebooks, his health worsened. His skin flamed up and broke apart. His lungs shuddered whenever they took in air, his heart pounded and echoed within his chest. His health deteriorated to the extent that he could only work for an hour or two a day. (Let's never mind the fact that if I manage an hour or two, I am damn proud and often treat myself to a beer as a reward.) Charles could cope, of course; his progress was deuced slow but steady enough, his home was comfortable and his family helped insofar as they were able. The thing that truly sickened him was to see evidence of the strange malady in his children. Annie suffered the most; she was regularly weakened, growing pale and labouring for breath.

The mystery of inheritance therefore tried Charles Darwin both personally and professionally. He felt he could make a convincing case that his Theory worked, but he couldn't explain *why* it worked. The operation that made the most common sense—blended inheritance, whereby a tall man and a short woman would produce a child of average height—actually worked *against* the Theory, pulling everything toward the norm, eradicating the spikes of eccentricity that poked evolution forward.

Fortunately, a quiet little prelate named Gregor Mendel was concerned with the question on the other side of the coin: not why offspring are *different* from the parents, why they are largely the same.

Gregor gave a talk in 1865 before the Brünn Society for the Study of Natural Science in Moravia; his topic, "Plant Hybridization." He explained that he had been doing some experiments with peas, and had come up with some very simple laws. For example, when purebred individuals exhibiting a pair of contrasted characters are crossed, the original types separate out in definite proportions in the second filial generation.

People came away confused.

"My time will come," said Mendel the Monk.

Which, indeed, it did, for the laws, when translated by scientists and school teachers, tell us how genetics work. Remember what you learned in grade ten science, which will do quite nicely for our purposes here. If each parent has a gene for both brown and blue eyes, then, in theory anyway, three out of four children will have brown eyes, because the gene for brown eyes is dominant, and only when the two recessive genes combine will they produce a blue-eyed child. Or something like that. Grade ten was a long time ago.

By the way, these days I live not far from the Pond. Indeed, I jog through a ravine that connects with Wilket Creek, and from time to time I will cross a stone bridge—it is abandoned and disused now, but I recall driving over it in the big red Edsel when a bright white line was painted down its middle—and I will follow my instincts and patchy memory. I cannot locate the Pond. I am tempted to lament its disappearance, but do you think ponds can disappear in a mere thirty years? I don't know, I'm asking. It's possible, I guess, but for some reason I prefer to think that I simply can't find the Pond, that the bulrushes have grown even higher and the surface is totally leaf-strewn. One day I will blunder on to it, the small and stagnant body of water where my father took me to search for Life.

Eleven

I suppose that underlying my decision to drag Carson to
the Encantadas was the notion that this was the grandest Pond
of all.

I am reminded, in writing the passages preceding, that my
enthusiasm for the Pond was, certainly at the time, not com-
mensurate with either my father's or my brother's. Some days
I'm sure I found it deadly boring, and would have much preferred remaining at home to watch hours of television: *Fury*, *Sky
King* and suchlike dramatic masterpieces, followed by wrestling,
Professional Canadian Wrestling, wherein people like Lord Athol
Layton, Sweet Daddy Siki and Whipper Billy Watson would
twist and thrash each other. I've no doubt that I squawked and
grumbled.

So I should have been more tolerant with young Carson, who
showed no signs of being lit up by the fires of wonder. It seemed
that she found the Galápagos no more remarkable than, oh,
Hamilton, Ontario, a city she visited many times because her
maternal grandparents lived there. She would look at Hamilton
with the same eyes. Not dull, that's not what I mean; her eyes

were actually quite active and lively, taking in the whole of that city's industrial oddness. Hamilton spit fire, was constructed of alien-looking spires and towers; Hamilton was black steel rib-boned and twisted into complicated knots, Hamilton was imposed on the heel of a great dark lake and stitched together with monstrous bridges. Carson, apperceiving this all, would push back into her car seat and demand that the cassette in the player be changed. Having seen Hamilton, Ontario, why should she find the Galápagos all that remarkable?

We went to the island of Santa Cruz, there to journey into the highlands.

We panga'd first to the docks in Puerto Ayora, a very strange town which we shall revisit in a later chapter. On this occasion we had no time for sightseeing, as we were delivered to an anti-quated bus and herded aboard by Carlos. My daughter and I sat in a seat near the back; my father lingered outside the bus doors until all of the tiny pews were filled. It looked at first as though he had no place to sit, but then he lucked out. Carlos reached toward the dashboard and pulled down what might have been a fire alarm but was in fact a rudimentary half-seat. My father settled himself onto it, crossed his arms and looked happy.

We began the journey up into the highlands. These are the hills that were once crawling with giant tortoises. The uplands held fresh water in small pockets and pools; the burdened crea-tures would struggle toward them, have their fill, turn around and start back down. Somewhere near bottom, I suspect, they would get thirsty once again and—heaving huge, world-weary sighs—turn around and start to reclimb.

The tortoises are not there now, at least, not so's you'd notice. Pirates and sailors clambered over the highlands too, many years ago, hauling off hundreds of tortoises. The animals were especially suited for the ship's larder. They tasted good and required little attention. They could be thrown into the hold and ignored; several weeks, even months later, the tortoises would be none the worse for their captivity.

The ecology on Santa Cruz has been futzed beyond repair, and not just by the removal of tortoises. Early settlers brought with them their household pets and livestock. Creatures—goats, dogs, cats—escaped into the highlands and turned feral, which, I was a little disappointed to learn from Carlos, simply means no longer domesticated. I'd had visions of goats with blood-tipped fangs, cats with their eyeballs glowing red with minatorial frenzy.

The settlers also ruined the place with vegetation, planting elephant grass and castor bean plants, which then claimed the island with the alacrity of the enchanted ivy that engulfed the castle wherein slumbered Sleeping Beauty.

Still the island goes on, and its English name, bestowed by Merry Boy William Cowley in one of his more poetic moods, reflects this tenacity—the island is called Indefatigable.

But it was hard to interest Carson in hundreds of tortoises that were no longer there, feral beasties that were not to be seen, and plants that vaulted skyward like blind basketball players. For a while I tried to show how, as we ascended, we passed through distinct zones, in terms of both vegetation and climate. But I myself found all that a little boring. It also lacks a big payoff, the kicker being that at the top it is always a little rainy. So it was into the drizzle, called *garua*, we were disgorged.

Mind you, there was up there a lushness, so rare on the Galápagos. There was plantlife—even flowers—so my father hiked about with a smile on his face, always many yards behind the rest of the Cormorants. Sometimes Carlos would herd us along pathways that were hacked through thick stands of scalesia trees. We would emerge into open ground, everyone except my father. I would turn back and locate him staring at a blossom or fern. I would have to take him by the arm and lead him back to the pack.

"Doesn't this look like purslane?" he might wonder aloud.

My daughter, on the other hand, placed herself in the vanguard, tramping along just behind Carlos. If something should happen to our guide—if he should be set upon by feral goats, maybe—Carson would be there to take his place. This is what I inferred from her single-mindedness, at any rate, for she seemed to have no purpose other than travel and relocation. There were, for her, no wonders in those highlands.

Not even the volcanic craters called Los Gemelos. There we stood upon the top of the island, and Carlos told us, "The craters are just over there." I eagerly traipsed forward a few yards. I parted some vegetation, took a big step and caught myself just before I walked into the abyss. The rest of the earth was suddenly a few hundred yards away. Everything else had been sucked down, in a huge and almost perfect circle.

Now *there* is a big difference between the Ecuadorian and the Canadian mind-set. If we northerners had such calderas—and we do have things like them, it's a huge country and there are several places where the pieces don't exactly fit together—we would erect huge Plexiglas barriers in front of them, and then safety fences to contain the Plexiglas barriers, then another fence to thwart people intent on suicide, and then we would line the perimeter with security guards.

We Canadians would also construct barriers around the Lava Tube, which is a gigantic wormhole, something like thirty feet in diameter, boring through the rock. It was formed by a huge river of molten lava; although Carlos lectured me on the precise process, I retained none of the science. I was too excited by the look of the Lava Tube, which seemed the kind of place where pirates would keep their treasure. Perhaps the Merry Boy with the best name—Basil Ringnose—had secreted some of the quince marmalade down there. I knew the chances of finding booty in a tourist attraction were low, but I pushed my fellow Cormorants aside, eagerly descending—the entrance to the Lava Tube is a rock-studded slope—and stumbled my way into the cool shadowed tunnel.

Carson joined me. Being seven years old and nimble, she was soon deep in the belly of the earth, sitting on a small jutting ledge high up the wall of the giant wormhole. She sat forward and cradled her head on her knuckles, the same attitude she would adopt on a subway train or settee. She patiently watched me work toward the light at the end of the Lava Tube.

One can't actually emerge at the other side, because the opening ends up being directly overhead. One can stand upon a rubbled cairn and receive the bright light (there are tiny flowers and mosses at your feet doing likewise), but lacking a superhuman vault, one is consigned to the umbrage of the Lava Tube. I took a few pictures and returned. Carson leapt down from her resting place and joined me, and although it made us both awkward and bashed up our elbows and knees, we left the Lava Tube hand in hand.

I have actually muddled up the sequence of events on Indefatigable. Between visits to these two geological attractions was part one of the hunt for the vermilion flycatcher. This is a somewhat rare bird, so elusive that the locals refer to it as "el brujo," the sorcerer. Carlos told us that we would be lucky Cormorants indeed if we could spot one. I took out my *Field Guide to Birds of the Galápagos* and spied the quarry. It was a smallish bird of a bright crimson hue. (You likely figured that out.) Part one of the hunt took us through a forest of tall trees, huge branches draped with moss. I had always assumed that my father was a fairly avid birder—indeed, I'm convinced that at one point in his life he was—but he seemed none too interested in the vermilion flycatcher. Instead of directing his gaze upwards, my father concentrated on the damp matting of the forest floor. He bent over, plucked something from it, and stuck it in my face. "What does this look like?"

"Um, purslane?"

"That's what I thought!"

Carson tramped along the pathways with her eyes in constant motion, as though she were wary of jaguar attack. The other Cormorants had pegged her as their best bet for vermilion flycatcher spotting, and she did her utmost to please. The forest was alive with birds—"There's a little yellow one!" Carson would point out, perhaps with a shade too much eagerness—but nothing that was tiny and red.

Part two of the hunt for the vermilion flycatcher took place on the bus. (By the way, the bus required that several of the huskier male Cormorants push it along the road before it coughed, sputtered and exploded into mechanical operation.) As we descended from the damp highlands, the road changed into one of a more commonplace rustic nature, the shoulders lined with dilapidated fencing containing fields and copses. And as we passed one of these copses, Carson remarked, "There's one."

The bus screeched to a halt and Cormorants alit in a frenzy; at least, the more prepared did. Many were caught unawares, and had to spend valuable moments fumbling with camera bags and lenses. Mr. B., of course, lived his life in a state of photographic readiness, his thin wattled neck perpetually bent by the Wondercam, so he was first off the bus. He stumbled toward the tree, essentially blinded by the technology stuck to his eyeball. "And here he is in all his glory," said Mr. B., "the venus flycatcher."

The tiny red bird seemed very vain indeed. He struck a pose and seemed, to my fanciful eyes, to be grinning. "Yes," he silently responded to Mr. B., "and all my glory is pretty fucking glorius." Far from flitting anxiously away, the vermilion flycatcher worked the photo op like a soap star in a shopping mall. "Let that lady in the back through. Okay, darling, snap away." Finally the bird disappeared, dancing back toward the highlands.

The Cormorants reboarded the bus, and I checked the field guide, pointing out the image of the bird to my daughter. "You see," I noted, "that was a male. Because the female, you see the female over here, the female is yellow."

"Yes," she said. "We've seen lots of those."

I was struck by this odd irony, that we had in fact seen a vermilion flycatcher, but were unaware of the fact because the female vermilion is a rather drab yellow. The kingdom is full of this sort of anomaly; for example, I understand that 5 per cent of red-footed boobies in the Galápagos Islands are white rather than the usual brown. Why this should be—other than to confuse birders—I couldn't say. I started thinking about taxonomy, and although my first thoughts were muddled, I sensed that there might be Insight to be had.

That evening, having put young Carson into bed, having read in the lower berth until I heard that deep rhythm of her slumber, I stumbled up the gangway to the Jacuzzi deck. My father sat there sipping his Club, staring at the lights of Puerto Ayora.

The harbour was crowded with ships at rest, all manner of sloops and yachts and seaworthy vessels. The *Corinthian*, being the largest there, sat well apart, bobbing in the ink-black sea.

"It's somewhat ironic," I said, gathering up a beer from sloe-eyed Hugo, "that we spent so much energy in pursuit of a bird we had already seen." I thought some kind of high-handed language might just tweak my little observation into the realm of Insight.

My father he nodded. "Castor beans," said he.

"Hmmm?"

"I was reminded when we saw those castor bean plants. My father, your grandfather, planted those in the back yard. He liked the way they'd grow so fast, you know. In a few weeks those plants would be towering over his head. He enjoyed that."

My father got up suddenly and lurched over to the railing, latching on and leaning over. This had nothing to do with seasickness, this was simply how one got about aboard the *Corinthian*, via the lurch. Sea legs have nothing to do with acquired steadiness, that's what I've decided; when you have sea legs you have rather abandoned yourself to chaos and perpetual lack of purchase. So my father lurched over to the railing to have a look-see at the ocean.

"Come here," he said.

I flung myself toward the starboard, clinging to the metal rail before I flipped over onto the lower decks.

"Look out there," my father gestured.

The light from the *Corinthian* cast a huge halo around the ship, twenty-five or thirty feet thick. Then it disappeared and left the sea to its darkness. And in that darkness, my father pointed out to me, were strange green shapes. They lurked beyond the light, incandescent and eerie, oddly geometrical shapes in oddly geometrical formations. These formations were forever shifting, the green shapes moving, very slowly, like chess pieces handled by an old man in an endless park, a man with nothing but time on his hands.

As we wondered about this strange sight, Carlos materialized beside us at the rail. Carlos was more interested in the sky, and held in his right hand a book about astronomy, but he looked down when we bade him, and he nodded. "The cow-nosed ray," he answered.

Some time later I went down to the pitching closet, peeled off my clothes and climbed aboard my bed. Before closing my eyes, I took out one of the field guides and flipped through to an illustration of this creature. It was alarmingly ugly. Rays are unsettling to begin with, given their very peculiar shape, which looks as though God had tried to grind them under heel and eased off at the last possible moment. These particular rays were uglier still, as the unimaginative name implies. Far from the blunted arrowhead design of their cousins, which at least lends them an air of logic and engineering, these rays were saddled with a schnozz, a proboscis.

Despite which, the dance that I had witnessed—for dance it was, a mating dance, two rays cut loose from the pack so that they might do-si-do in slo-mo, the others rearranging themselves to get a better view—was one of the more beautiful things I have ever seen. I let out a great sigh and felt myself on the verge of Insight. Then I tumbled down into a deep sleep.

Carson was born a full month before anyone expected her. As things turned out, she wasn't a full month premature. There had obviously been mathematical miscalculations somewhere along the line. Still, as the pediatrician who examined the newborn announced, "She's definitely premature. There are aspects to her that aren't as well developed as they should be." When we asked, "Like what?" the doctor, employing a remarkably ill-chosen phrase, confided, "Her brain." What he meant was, her instincts and reflexes. Even suckling did not come naturally to her. My wife struggled hard to breastfeed the infant, and by the time those two had it all worked out, they were pretty much a team. Carson, although she regards me with undeniable affection, has never been entirely certain where I fit into the picture.

Mind you, I have wondered about this myself. I'm a good parent, especially in the sense that there are practicalities I can realize, strategies that would not work without my participation. For example, I am a very dependable driver (despite the aforementioned fact that behind the wheel I am a blithering bedlamite, snapping and snarling at the cityfolk). When Carson was very young, it was I would rise with her at five in the morning to watch goddamn Barney through bleared eyes, my wife's slumber being profound. I cook the occasional meal, now that Carson is older I take her to and from school; in short, life at the household is improved by my presence.

But that still doesn't answer the basic question. I worry that I am facilitating Carson's passage through childhood rather than enriching it.

What, exactly, is a fellow to do?

My father (and, I think, fathers for generations before) have pondered this same question. My father's answer, which I see clearly now, was to expose my siblings and me to, well, all manner of things. He would take us to hockey games and operas. He would haul us down to Kensington Market, where I delighted in watching the rabbi first bless, then kill, an endless series of chickens. He would take us many times to the Pond, where we would search in the muck for tiny wonders.

For a few weeks in my childhood, my father even responded to my desire to go to church. But he did not go with me to the Donway United, no, he packed me instead into our blood-red Edsel and drove me to various and sundry houses of worship, a new one each Sunday. Much of this is dimmed in my memory, although the Buddhist Temple stands out with clarity. I remember, or am fairly certain I remember, everyone sharing a palpable serenity.

I see now that this has been my strategy, too. I am not as good at it as my father was; I am not as good at thinking of different places, and I am not as good at persuading my offspring to accompany me. Carson, once she reached a certain age, settled into a homey routine, preferring to remain inside to draw, watch television and play with stuffed toys. These are the things I did as a boy (although I never actually had much truck with stuffed toys), but somehow my father managed to drag me outside into the world. (I suspect this is because of my brother Joel, close to me in age, far away from me in temperament. I can't even summon a reasonable memory/imagining of Joel, as a small boy, watching a television or drawing a picture. I can summon a picture of him tearing through the side door of our house on Langbourne Crescent, colliding into the jambs with such force that his pants plummeted down and hobbled him, spilling him onto the driveway. I can see him leaping to his feet, gravel imbedded in his freckled face. "Let's go!")

I did manage, once, to convince my own little family to go on a birding expedition. I drove them to a ravine and we descended, clutching binoculars. Flannery, the little one, had a pair of binos rendered out of toilet paper rolls. Carson was quiet and preoccupied and lagged some distance behind. My family walked along the pathway for a long time and espied exactly nothing. As we neared the rise to the roadway, Flannery stopped and fastened her toilet paper rolls to her eyes. She began to emit a strange little sound. "Birtz! Birtz!" We stopped and tried to follow her gaze. "There's no birds there, Flann."

"Birtz."

"Yeah," said Carson. "There's birds there."

Sitting perhaps five feet away were two stout wood ducks. They appeared to be conducting a drug deal, and stared at us with undiluted maliciousness.

"Birtz," said Flann, quite proudly.

"I want to go home," said Carson.

Twelve

On Thursday morning, Carson woke up depressed and homesick. I was not surprised. Indeed, if I were a betting man, I'd have put a lot of money down that she would be. Actually, being a betting man, I should refashion the sentence. If I'd been able to find anyone willing to make book on the likelihood of my daughter's emotional crisis, I'd have put a lot of money down.

She woke up, glanced around the pitching closet rather dully, and then sighed. Judy the Purser hollered at her through the tin speaker in the ceiling, saying that it was already seven o'clock in the morning. I leapt from my berth spryly. "Breakfast!" I shouted, although the strange food was not likely to inspire my daughter, may even have contributed to her state of mind. For example, there was at breakfast a vat of purple gelatinous matter, its nature a subject of much debate. I ate a whole bowl of it one morning and am no closer to an answer. I was the only passenger to consume a whole bowl, most of the others preferring simply to spoon a bit onto their cereal or scrambled eggs. But I shouted "Breakfast!" and Carson sighed and told me she wasn't hungry.

"Right." I sat back down on my little cot. "Neither am I."

"I'm homesick," she said.

"Activity, that's what you need. Let's get up, get dressed, eat breakfast and jump in the panga."

"No," she said.

"Let's get up, get dressed and eat breakfast."

"No."

"Let's get up and get dressed."

"No."

"Let's get up."

"No," said Carson with finality.

I lay back down on my cot. My daughter can be obdurate about such matters. I'd recently experienced a bout of her agoraphobia in the city of Quito. After the rounds of cathedrals in the Old City, the three of us took a little bus tour a few miles outside town to the equatorial monument. There at the Mitad del Mundo Carson had straddled the world, placed one foot in the northern hemisphere and one in the southern. My father wandered about inspecting the flora.

(I found out later he'd also been sketching. I glanced at his drawings the next day, as we unloaded and unpacked in our tiny rooms aboard the *Corinthian*. On one page was a drawing of an ancient lady, her face aflow with wrinkles. Dark tears stained one cheek.

("Who's that?" I wondered.

("Didn't you see her?" demanded my father. "She had tears tattoo'd on her face. She smiled at me.")

You wonder how I occupied myself at the equatorial monument? Well, of course, being the scientific fellow you know me to be, I searched out a washroom and filled up the sink. Then I pulled the plug and watched what took place. Where I live, in frosty Toronto, the water would circle counterclockwise as it entered the pipe. I understood that an obscure writer living in, say, Melbourne, would see something quite different as he farted about with sink water; he would see the bowlful acquire a *clockwise* bias before it gurgled down the chute. This is called the Coriolis effect, and has to do with polarity and magnetic forces, so it has long brought up this question, at least to me—what would happen right on the equator? Well, the answer is that the water would go straight down. There you go. I suppose you might be suspicious of a middle-aged man who travels about the globe conducting grade-school scientific experiments, perhaps especially suspicious as most anyone else would have figured out that the water would go straight down. You're dealing with someone who just had to see it for himself.

At any rate, I had fun that morning in Quito, and I thought Carson did as well, but when we got back to the hotel she flopped onto her bed with some resolution, clutching the edge of the mattress as though fearful it might try to buck her off. "Let's get some lunch," I suggested.

"No."

I ended up going out for sandwiches and soft drinks. When I got back I told my daughter excitedly, "Carson, across the street is a city park. It is filled with such wonders as you cannot conceive. There is a huge playground. There are bands and musicians and artisans. There are magicians and acrobats. It is right now the most amazing place on the face of the planet. Let's go."

"No."

So I knew better, that morning in the Encantadas, to press her much about her refusal to leave the tiny room. When Judy the Purser screamed that the Cormorants should go and get in the pangas, Carson gave every impression that she hadn't heard her. Soon everyone was gone, leaving my daughter and me pretty much alone on the ship.

Actually, my father was up on the top deck, working once more in his sketchbook. He sketched the birds that encircled the *Corinthian*. These were mostly pelicans, not perhaps the most exciting birds in the world, certainly fairly common. My father hadn't been at all interested in the vermilion flycatcher, but he sketched pelicans in flight as though they possessed grace abounding.

My daughter listlessly thumbed through picture books, took valiant but short-lived stabs at chapter books, listened to the Walkman, and was determined to spend every moment of that beautiful day inside our pitching closet, as though she were conducting experiments in sensory deprivation.

Well, I had work to do anyway. Note-taking and research. The ship's library, a long bookcase in the main lounge zealously guarded by Judy the Purser, held a few items, and I persuaded her to open it up. She grabbed a key ring that flipped on her hip like a holster and tried about forty keys before she found one that turned the tumblers to the little brass stopper, allowing the glass door to slide open. When I made my selection she wrote down the name of the book in a ledger, and made me sign my name across from it. The book I selected was *Galápagos: World's End*, by William Beebe, the book that had inspired the Wittmer family to pack up their belongings and go to dwell in paradise. I took the book down to our room and began to read.

This is a delightful book, don't get me wrong, but I fell asleep within about twenty minutes—and this is less than an hour after eating breakfast—and dreamt an odd dream. I found myself on a shore littered with sea lions, their collective wheezes of satisfaction ringing with the power and resonance of a church organ. Crabs scuttled everywhere, some large and transparent, others tiny and almost invisible. The beach was ringed by black rock spat out of the centre of the earth, and marine iguanas claimed these as thrones and perches. The sky was blackened with bird life. Some had settled onto the land: frigatebirds with deflated pouches, boobies of all stripe (red-footed, blue-footed, masked). There were smaller birds, too, pipping about on the sand or in the small stand of saltbush. And I stood in the middle of all this, a notebook clutched between the fingers of my left hand. In my right hand I held a pen, although when I put it to paper it made no mark, merely scratched like a finger-nail on a slate. The pen was more properly a quill, I noticed, a feather that had fallen from heaven. Still, I had work to do and it was urgent, this is the feeling I remember from my dream; I continued to write, to try to write, looking at the wildlife and then tearing at the paper. I took an especial interest in the small birds, and it was their names I kept trying to inscribe.

Aristotle enumerated five hundred and forty species, and was pretty much the first human being to take an interest, at least, to take such an interest that he wrote down the names and tried to divide the creatures into categories. He constructed his own Scale of Being, using the large building blocks of logic. "By the possession of a soul, or an organic life with nutritive faculty, a plant is superior to a stone; by the possession of a soul or an organic life with sensitive, appetitive and motor facilities, an animal is superior to a plant; and by the addition of the intellectual faculty in his soul or organic life, man is supreme among animals." Aristotle made further divisions, differentiat-ing between those animals with blood and those without it. (Oysters, for example, had no blood, so far as Aristotle could tell.) He listed what he called "plant animals" (like jellyfish), which he felt were intermediate between the two kingdoms. Aristotle made much of what he called "vital heat." "The most perfect," he wrote, "are those which are hotter in their nature and have more moisture and are not earthy in their composition." Like his teacher Plato, Aristotle believed in an Ideal universe, the notion that there existed on some elevated plane a flawless exemplar of any creature (the Ideal Dog or Horse), and that what dwelt upon the earth were imperfect copies of it.

(I am drawn toward this thinking, only because it reminds me of my favourite childhood reading material, namely, any Superman comic book featuring stories from the Bizarro world. As I recall, the Bizarro world was contained within a bottle, a glass carboy, at the Fortress of Solitude; if I remember correctly it was the result of an early testing of Lex Luthor's duplicating ray. Whatever, the Bizarro world is peopled with very imperfect copies of Superman, Lois Lane, etc. I recall thinking, as a young pimpled lad, that our God may be a Lex Luthor type, a genius twisted by bitterness, and our universe nothing more than a failed experiment. I mention that I thought this as a very young man so that I won't have to admit I still occasionally think the notion has merit.)

The great hero of taxonomy, the science of classification, is, of course, Carl von Linné (1707–1778), better known by the Latinized version of his name, Carolus Linnaeus. His father was both a gardener and a priest; Carl exhibited little aptitude for the priesthood, but from a very early age he was interested in the plants. Carl was a believer in Natural Theology, the notion that the examination of nature would reveal God's order. He studied medicine at the University of Uppsala, but never practised it in any strict sense. Instead, in 1731, Linnaeus mounted a botanical expedition to Lapland.

I have an image in my mind of young Carl standing in the middle of a vast Laplandish tundra, surrounded by tiny plants and little furry animals. He picks up creatures and sits them beside others that look similar. He uproots flowerets and transplants them into family beds. Carl writes down names, based on a system that he himself invented. He did not invent, you know, the idea of calling things by a Latin name. People had been doing that for years, but without much forethought or reason, simply running together Latin descriptors until they thought the object had been sufficiently chanted into being. The brier rose, for example, was called (and this was by no means an agreed-upon designation) *Rosa sylvestris alba cum rubore, folio glabro*. Linnaeus first of all decided that the name should be much shorter, more concise. A binomial: *Rosa eglanteria*. He thought to group groups within groups, if you see what I mean, like huge abstract file folders. Therefore, the kingdom of *Animalia* contains the phylum *Chordata*, which contains the class *Mammalia*, which contains the order *Carnivora*, which contains the family *Felidae*, which contains the genus *Felis* and, finally, the species domestica. *Felis catus*, meow.

So Linnaeus cleared everything up for us, although it wasn't long before things got muddled again. This is from a huge book entitled *The Encyclopedia of Mammals*:

> Mammals themselves are part of a larger tetrapod group called the *Synapsida*. Synapsids make up one of the two largest groups of *amniota*. Not that all synapsids were mammals. A non-mammalian member of Synapsida is Thrinaxodon (a member of the group Therapsida, which contains Mammalia).

Hoo boy. And mammals, you know, mammals are easy. There are only something like 4,000 species, a mere pittance compared to some of the other phlya, like coleoptera (beetles), which has 290,000 named species (and that is likely only a very tiny fraction of the species that exist). People have identified over a million species in the kingdom *Animalia*, which probably ends up representing a very small percentage of life upon the little blue ball. Estimates of the total number of species of living things that dwell upon the earth run between 10 million on the low end and 100 million on the high.

It is this mess that we needed Darwin to make sense of. One of his qualifications for the job is that he understood Linnean classification—in his writings he uses it fluidly, even glibly:

> Under a piece of bark I found two *Carabi* (I forget which) and caught one in each hand, when lo and behold I saw a sacred *Panagoeus crux major*! I could not bear to give up either of the *Carabi*, and to lose *Panagoeus* was out of the question, so that in despair I gently seized one of the *Carabi* between my teeth.

And Darwin spent a long time wondering about the grey areas, why there were so many things in the natural kingdom that could not be fitted nicely either one place or another. Linnaeus thought his system would work because species were unchanging;[1] Darwin saw that the reason the system was bogging down was that species weren't unchanging at all, that they evolved and spilled over into each other, and only by understanding *that* process could we ever make sense of the world we inhabit.

Although I can't help thinking that we made our mistake long ago, that a basic assumption somewhere near the dawn of civilization would have spared us grief and hair-pulling. I'm wondering what would have happened if we'd always accepted (in

---

1   *Unitas in omni specie ordinum ducit*: "The invariability of species is the condition for order."

Erasmus Darwin's words) the notion of the "one living filament." There were people who opposed Linnaeus and his ideas—for example, that great German man of science, Johann Wolfgang von Goethe (1749–1832). If you don't consider Goethe a man of science, you should be advised that he himself did; he thought that his most significant contributions were made whilst tramping in the fields of Knowledge. His scientific work can be divided into two areas. One, as detailed in *Theory of Colours*, opposed the Newtonian school of thought; Goethe's thesis was that "colours are the deeds and the suffering of light." And Goethe likewise argued with classification cf. Linnaeus, in his book *The Metamorphosis of Plants*. Goethe posited the existence of the *Urpflanze*, or primal plant, and thought that all plants were transmutations thereof.

I see the sense in this line of thinking. Mind you, I seem to be congenitally incapable of identification. Despite being an avid angler, I am undone by the variations in the genus *Salmo*, or trout. I have laboriously book-learned certain reactions to the creatures at the end of my fly line, looking for large spots on their sides, checking for a vermicular pattern on their backs, but I have fished with people who, whilst they grapple with a distant flipper, casually spit out of the corner of their mouth, "Brown trout. Male." And I'm not just talking being taxonomically challenged as regards the natural world. I have a great deal of trouble distinguishing one make of car from another. I lament the near-extinction of the Volkswagen, because it gave me a small feeling of satisfaction to nail that one every time I saw it, the automotive Urpflanze. And when I was a teen-ager, a fifteen-year-old bluesman from the heart of Don Mills, my friends and I would go early to rock concerts, six and seven hours early, so that we could cluster around the front of the stage and identify the equipment being set up. "It's a Marshall," my friends would say as a large Naugahyde box was carted by, further confirming the classification with a series of numbers and a litany of specs. I found this all extremely boring, and was content enough with the much more generic "speaker box," even with the very broad "piece of musical equipment." Or definition according to function: "It's a big box for making loud music."

What Darwin told us, in essence, was that life has sprouted from a single seed, and all the variation we see is the result of adaptation as life manages to squeeze itself into the countless ecological niches that our little blue planet offers. The difference between a trout—any damn trout—and a horse is that a horse wouldn't fare too well in a river, even if the horse figured out that the easiest way to get food was to face upstream and snap up emerging insects. (It might make things easier for me, in the sense that, as I palmed my reel and listened to line disappear, I could casually mention, "Horse.") It seems to me if we take that lesson from the Theory of Evolution by Means of Natural Selection, our attitude perforce changes. I don't mean that we must therefore become overly tender and merciful, refusing to do harm to other living creatures. If anything, I see it as an invitation to really get in there and muck around. We can play the Game of Life, which involves both eating and, remember, being eaten. But there are many areas where we stand on really shaky moral ground. They've been doing experiments with the transplanting of baboon organs into human beings, and may be just on the verge of accomplishing the deed. Are we then to regard baboons merely as a pool of potential organ donors? Should we be allowed to help ourselves? Are we more entitled to a baboon's heart than the baboon in whose chest it already beats?

I myself can't conceive of a reasonable argument that we would be. No matter how eloquent, any answer would be predicated on an assumption of our *superiority*. The answer may even be predicated on an assumption of our *evolutionary superiority*, although that is a mistaken notion itself. There are certain areas of increased complexity on the bush of life. (It is best thought of as a bush. Dispense with notions of a treelike ascension toward the light; think in terms of sprawling directionless ground cover.[2]) But why is increased complexity any better? Because we, being fairly complex, say so.

I may be congenitally incapable of classification and identification. Still, you'd think I would have spotted at least *one* of Darwin's famous finches. There are thirteen species of them, you know, scattered over the archipelago, and the differences in beak size are a cornerstone of the Theory of Evolution by Means of Natural Selection, at least in the popular imagination. If you even flip through a copy of *The Origin of Species* you'll see that Charles was interested in many things and pulled examples from all across the face of the globe. The book is thick and jam-packed, and finches are actually not mentioned that much. The little birds are more significant to Neo-Darwinism than they were before, because scientists working with finches on the small Galápagon island of Daphne Major have now actually seen evolution take place. (Those of you who are interested can refer to the book *The Beak of the Finch*, written by Jonathan Weiner.) Prior to this, a big knock against the Theory was its theoretical nature—no one had ever seen it in operation, because it operates over great tracts of time.[3] This was

---

2 Or use Charles Darwin's wise analogy, coral, with "the base of branches dead, so that passages cannot be seen."

3 There was, as is frequently mentioned in books like this, the abrupt proliferation in the nineteenth century of moths with dark wings, hitherto rare, fluttering about England. This coincided with the building and operation of factories; the moths' coloration was changing as adaptation camouflaged them against the now soot-covered

another of the things that bothered Darwin, that proof for his theory seemed unattainable. But Peter and Rosemary Grant, along with their children and a series of graduate students from McGill University, spent years on the isle of Daphne Major, which sits, small and deserted and off the itineraries of cruise ships, in the centre of the Encantadas. The Grants measured the beaks of every finch they could, and recorded this information over successive generations. One year there was a severe drought, which destroyed much of the birds' food supply. Only the nuts with the thickest shells were available, and only the birds with the biggest, strongest beaks could crack them. I'm simplifying a great deal out of dullheadedness, but the point to be understood is that the Grants could afterwards point to the charts of beak measurements and indicate an unassailable increase in beak size in the generations following the drought.

But I saw no finches; I saw Galápagos doves. I say that because from time to time I saw a bird that I thought might be a finch, and should Carlos be nearby, I'd invariably let out a holler. "Hey, Carlos! What's that bird over there? Is that a finch?"

His responses came to have a predictable sameness. "That, Mr. Quarrington, is a Galápagos dove."[4]

"Oh."[5]

---

bark. This seemed fairly incontrovertible evidence of evolution—but it is not the same as actually *seeing* evolution taking place.

4 I vaguely recalled the Galápagos dove from the films shown in Dr. Moody's shadowy theatre. This is the bird that fakes injury, hurrying away from threats with a pronounced limp.

5 Charles Darwin had his own problems in this area. He wasn't sure that all of the finches he saw actually were finches—there was one creature he thought was a blackbird, and it took fairly intense perusal aboard the *Beagle* to convince himself otherwise.

This would be very excusable were it not for the fact that I was, for a time, an avid amateur birder. I once, having caused grievous injury to a little, and entirely innocent, fish, gave up the Art of the Angle. (Briefly. I fish once more; my solution was to improve my skills and techniques to the point where little fishes are much safer whenever I am upon the waters.) During the time I eschewed angling I took up birding as its substitute. Many of the pleasures are coincident (I got no break on that *up at dawn* thing), and little harm to a living creature is done. (I say "little harm" out of muted respect to those virulent naturalists who would claim that human beings, being large and oafish, cannot help but do harm whenever they go traipsing through the woods. Also, I guess we shouldn't discount the invasion of privacy issue.)

So I acquired a pair of binoculars and a Roger Tory Peterson and instead of walking to the river to fish, I simply walked to the river. I evidenced no talent as a birder, but I had evidenced no "talent" as a fisher, either, I simply enjoyed the discipline. More than enjoyed—craved it, needed it, whatever. Any sort of interaction with the world is preferable to none. Although I have yet to discover the joys of mycology (the gathering and subsequent serving to family members of poisonous mushrooms), I'm sure I could become addicted if it afforded me time in the wild. Which is to say, in the stilted poetry arising from my own past, *time near the Pond.*

The Argument from Design works on two levels, one small (examining the intricate construction and workings of the eye)[6]

---

6   Ah, the eye, the eye. Reverend Paley chose well when he selected the eye as his
     analogous object of examination. Anti-evolutionists were quick to point out what
     seems to be a logical inconsistency with Darwin's theory: how could an eye have
     developed through Natural Selection when anything less than an eye would have
     no apparent value? This is true of other things as well; wings, say. What good is

and the other grand. I recall sitting by the edge of Lake of the Woods, raised upon a throne rendered of rock a billion years old. Above me, the northern lights gambolled through the heavenly vault. I felt a certainty descend upon me, as well as a real, and very profound, contentment.

Sad-eyed Carson needed occupation and distraction. I believed that she needed time near the Pond. As she lay on her upper berth, dreaming of the slush-filled streets of her hometown, I had what amounted to an inspiration. "You should take up birding as a hobby," I said quietly.

Carson grunted. The grunt was shaded interrogatively.

"Think about this," I went on, encouraged, "you have a lot of the hard work done already."

"I do?" she asked warily. I've never known Carson not to be wary around proclamations of glad tidings.

"Sure. Look—you've seen a blue-footed booby, a red-footed booby, a vermilion flycatcher—"

She made no response to any of this. I played my trump card.

"You can use these binoculars."

"Can they be mine?"

"You can use them all the time."

"But will they be *my* binoculars?"

---

an appendage that is not quite a wing? But the eye always seems the strongest point of attack. "The eye to this day gives me a cold shudder," wrote Darwin. Still, when you think about it, a creature with not-quite-an-eye would still have an advantage over a creature with nothing-even-vaguely-resembling-an-eye. Also, the argument assumes a kind of God-granted perfection to our own organs of perception. But our eyes still have a ways to go, I think. They don't work well in the dark, for example, and we need to keep them shut for long periods of time. We have a narrow range of vision and our eyes require constant lubrication. (Which brings up another scientific question of the sort that really intrigues me: why don't we blink autonomously?)

Her enthusiasm, even if it was in the name of uncontested ownership, was gratifying. "Yes! They will be *your* binoculars!"

"Okay."

During the night we travelled to Genovesa—or Tower—Island. In doing so we crossed the equator. When a sailor crosses that magical line, there are certain things that must be done, gods that must be appeased, or else ill fortune is likely to come one's way. No one told us that, though, and as I say, the crossing took place in the middle of the night, as Carson and my father slumbered, as I clutched my mattress and tried to remain in my berth.

But the morning found us up and about with a new and rare enthusiasm. I was out of the sack even before Judy could holler at me through the yowling intercom. The three of us bolted down into the lounge and ate breakfast with vigour and gusto, three big bowlfuls of purple gelatinous goop. Then we stormed for the back of the *Corinthian* and dressed up in life jackets, adorned ourselves with water bottles, binos and cameras, anointed ourselves with sunscreen. The Cormorants leapt into the panga, and off it roared toward Tower Island.

Carson had leapt into the panga with the *Field Guide to the Birds of the Galápagos* clutched in her tiny hand. She sat on the craft's rubber side with *her* binoculars pressed into her eye sockets. In the back pocket of Carson's shorts there was a yellow piece of paper. This was a list, supplied by Carlos, of all the avian species that one could see in the Encantadas.

Mr. B. had his camera at the ready, clutched between palsied hands at chest level. I could see him wetting his lips, his little paean to glory already formed and waiting to be uttered. For we were on a birding quest, that morning; our aim was to panga about the bottom of the black cliffs of Tower for a time, in search of the famous equatorial penguin.

This is the most northern-dwelling penguin in the world. Its existence is another strike against the concept of Special Creation, at least an impudent contravention, for these penguins clearly had not stayed where they belonged (or, if you will, where God had put them). I imagine a clutch of penguins riding a huge iceberg, one that is snared by the Humboldt current, and drifting slowly away from the Land of Ice. The sun melts the iceberg daily, and before long the birds are jostling and elbowing each other to find room. Just as the ice disappears completely, the penguins take a little hop and find themselves on a strange black island. They look at each other for many long moments. "Okay," one asks, "who's got the sunblock?"

We puttered along in the cool shadows of the cliffs, but saw no equatorial penguins. "All right," said Carlos, waving toward Tower Island. "Maybe we'll see them afterwards."

Just then a little missile blew by, a foot or so beneath the surface, barely missing the prow of the panga. "Hold on," said Carlos. Two or three more bullet-shaped streaks blew by. It was as though we were being fired upon by some drunken submariner, for he could not seem to hit our boat, although he never missed by much. "Okay, okay," said Carlos, who was never a whit less excited than any of his Cormorants. "Where?" He stood up in the panga and looked about; he lifted his arm and pointed toward some rocks, a tiny mini-archipelago, a hundred feet away. "There."

We looked to where he pointed and saw the penguins pop out of the water. They shook as though dislodging water from their ears (do they even have them?) and then strutted about the few square feet of flatness afforded by the rocks. They all inclined slightly and set down their flippers with emphasis, which gave them a distinctly Napoleonic air, as if besiegement were at hand and strategies needed to be hatched.

The panga made for the birds.

Mr. B. started the Wondercam. "And here he is in all his glory," he chanted. The other Cormorants frowned at Mr. B., because he had managed to occupy, and block, the only vantage point. People bent awkwardly to shoot around him. One or two even took their photos from between his pale, trembling legs. The penguins looked up, took note of the paparazzi panga, and went back to their pup-pup-pupping ratiocinations.

Carson carefully took out her sheet of yellow paper, pulled a finger along the columns of black type. She did this for a long time, because, well, she was only seven, her reading skills were not all they could be. I pointed out the appropriate listing and Carson removed a pencil from her bag and made a small, neat check mark.

Carson still has the piece of paper. I'm bolting ahead in the story and writing of the present day, which is bitterly cold, being as it's the dead of winter. (It is not, however, the middle of the night; it's dawn. I tend to write about my father late at night, in the kitchen, and my daughter early in the morning, upstairs in my office. No, I don't get much sleep.)

Carson still has the piece of paper, and if she continues with birding as a hobby, she will be well appointed in later life. As I said before, she's got some of the really hard work done already. I helped her with that. There are few other instances in life when a parent can feel so certain and satisfied.

CHAPTER

Thirteen

The Prince Philip Steps, on the isle of Genovesa, were created when someone with far-reaching powers of conceptualization stared at the dark cliffside until he imagined that a staircase somehow existed within the carp. The Ecuadorian government (in a rare display of whimsical bureaucratic indulgence) added a wooden handrail, which was damn sporting of them. So what happens is, a panga sidles up to the rocks; passengers are discharged and must immediately begin the scramble up the scrabble.

My father, early out of the panga, made it with relative ease and spryness, although when he cleared the summit he stood amongst the frigates and boobies and puffed heavily.

We hiked through palo santo trees and witnessed the wonders of nature. Mind you, the Cormorants were, by this time, tiring of these wonders. It was hard to get excited about a booby that had evolved down a pathway allowing him to exchange blue feet for red. Many of the other birds were only interesting to very serious ornithologists, like Mr. Perdomini and my daughter. She now reared up to hike in his wake, both of them clutching their Tory Petersons. They pointed out storm petrels and lava gulls to each other.

"Do you own a dog?" Carson wondered.

Mr. Perdomini shrugged, as though admitting to owning something vaguely doglike.

"Look!" said Carson. "A frigatebird."

When you look at a frigatebird, you see the concept of Sexual Selection in action. Some of the adaptations that can be seen in nature—and the frigatebird's conjugal pouch is amongst the most vivid—have nothing to do with *survival*, per se; they neither enhance personal safety nor aid in the getting of food and the vanquishing of foe. They have everything to do with attracting a mate, thereby propagating the individual's specific type of DNA.

In many species, the male parades himself about and displays some characteristic that he feels is very compelling. Like bright blue feet. Or, in the case of the frigatebird, a huge red bag that balloons upon his chest, a crimson ball of air that shoves his head and long beak upwards. Staring up at the sky, burdened by this gular sack of sexual longing, the frigatebird flaps his wings and moans somewhat pitiably, hoping to attract a mate. That beak, by the way, takes a sharp turn downwards at the very end, and Carlos our guide reported that it was very possible for the male frigatebird to deflate his own pouch, inadvertently puncturing it on takeoff or landing, saddling the bird with a withered, empty bag and foredooming him to at least a season of celibacy.

I leave it to you to decide how at odds all this is with human behaviour. It may seem, on the surface, as though the female of our species does the displaying, but the model falls apart if we imagine it in its simplest form: a man, standing with arms crossed and lips pursed judiciously, watching a parade of women anxious to exhibit some portion of their anatomy either puffed up or brilliantly coloured. That model seems to work in the Playboy Mansion, but nowhere else that I can think of. It's better the other way round, isn't it, with the men jostling near the female judge, inflating conjugal pouches and shaking bright blue feet.

Which leads to a reflection on evolution, something that nearly qualifies as an Insight: in the movies we watched at the Don Mills Odeon, we often saw, in photographed representations of our collective future, people with huge heads, the cranium enlarged to accommodate the ever-growing brain. This, after all, makes sense in terms of the Theory of Evolution, because a bigger brain has its obvious advantages in terms of enhanced chances of survival (evading tax people, for example). But we can see that it doesn't really work, because it fails to take into account the importance of Sexual Selection. No woman is likely to select a Mr. Potatohead for a mate.

The issue of Sexual Selection did as much to alarm people as the impeachment of the Almighty. Much effort was put into proving it wrong. I cite as an example the Reverend John Thomas Gulick, who journeyed to Oahu and made a vast study of the "extremely local species of snails." His conclusions were at odds with Darwinism. You see, the shells of the mollusks the Reverend was studying were variously coloured—quite variously, too, stripes of blue or red or brown curling around them as on a barbershop pole—but not, Gulick wrote in his book *Evolution, Racial and Habitudinal*, for any reason having to do with sexual selection.

> Sexual selection is an incomplete explanation of divergence, even for higher animals; and in the case of creatures as low as mollusks it would seem to be entirely excluded from

having any effect in determining the diversity of colour in the different species. There is no reason to believe that differences of form and colour are capable of being at all observed by the sense with which they are endowed.

In other words, mollusks have no eyes, so what difference does it make what colour they are?

There are a couple of points to be made here. To begin with, the explanation for the different colours hasn't to do, as the Reverend supposed, with Sexual Selection. It has to do with not being eaten by the rather sharp-eyed birds hovering above; therefore, if mollusks in a grassy habitat managed to acquire green stripes, if those on rocks got brown, well, you see how nice everything would be.

But the Reverend missed this, and his explanation for the vivid mollusk colouring is, basically, that it makes them pleasing to look at. This notion had wide currency in the nineteenth century, that God made things beautiful chiefly for the aesthetic pleasure of human beings. *I* like the reasoning which has it that many things—mollusks amongst them—were beautiful long before humans were around to admire them, but the elegant simplicity of this thought didn't change as many minds as you'd think. It wouldn't have changed Dr. Moody's. He'd pick up those mollusks, members of the same genus, only yards apart geographically, yet so differently hued that they could be labelled Crayola-fashion. Who did this, Dr. Moody would wonder, and then the blinding smile would crack upon his face and he'd lift his eyes upward.

The other point is, I really wish Reverend Gulick had been more on the ball. I wish he'd examined those snails and had the great Insight, that Natural Selection is the most reasonable explanation. Those snails that didn't blend as well with their surroundings were gobbled up by birds. Those that matched better survived to pass on their genes for blue- or brownness. I'm suggesting that Gulick may even have been able to scoop or supplant Darwin, and the only reason I'm suggesting it is, wouldn't it be more pleasant for all of us avid amateur naturalists to go larking off to Hawaii to pay our homage? Similarly, Darwin would likely have drawn the same conclusions from this nicer archipelago. It is in the nature of islands—particularly oceanic ones, those never connected to the continents by land-bridges—to produce singularities in the flora and fauna. Darwin didn't need to see the Galápagos in order to have his Insight; the Galápagos had to be seen through his eyes.

It was decidedly prehistoric, there on Genovesa. The air was filled with the oddest of sounds: the blue-balled squawkings of frigatebirds, a rhythmic shoomping as the air was folded and whipped by their wings. There were squat trees everywhere, little cussers that just barely cleared banzai status. The frigate-birds perched on the branches, and the land in all directions bobbed with sexual frustration. The birds pointed their heads backwards and made pitiful sounds, gruffles and squawfs and suchlike, trying to find and force the word "please" out of long, pointed beaks.

As we headed back to the pangas, I mentioned that I found "frigatebird" an interesting name, and wondered what the connection was, bird-to-ship. Did the species prefer frigates as roosts over all other sorts of seacraft? Did they somehow resemble frigates?

Carlos began to tell me some rather interesting stuff, which I shall now relate to you as though I knew it all along. First, you should know what great fliers frigatebirds are, what wonderful soarers—they have been seen a mile high and a thousand miles from land. The nautical nature of their name is truly misleading, for frigatebirds, lacking waterproof feathers, never land in the sea. Instead—once they've slaked their awkward burden of desire—they abide mostly in the light-blue vault.

The birds have another name in English—man-o'-war—and both names likely arise from the fact that frigatebirds feed by harassing other birds midair (boobies, by and large) until the target coughs up whatever foodstuff it is carting in its beak. Frigatebirds are named, therefore, after the craft of pirates and plunderers.

I became much more fond of the creatures, knowing that.

We descended the Prince Philip Steps in an orderly fashion. When Carlos and the lead Cormorant reached the rocks below, however, they found that the Albatrosses, or maybe the Boobies, had commandeered the pangas, so we were forced to wait upon their return. Rather than climb back up to the summit, the Cormorants stayed where they were, in a single file that occupied the whole of the nonexistent stairway.

My daughter was down near the bottom, talking to Peter and Carmen. I couldn't hear her, other than the occasional word, but I could see her gesticulating in a gabby fashion. She'd cup her hands and then shape air as she explained something to Carmen (likely the perfect size for a dog, something that could fit inside an eggcup). Occasionally she'd thrust out an arm and run an index finger toward some black rock, pointing out an iguana or bird for Peter's benefit.

My father and I were up nearish the top, at a bend in the roughly hewn proceedings. Where my father stood there was even something that actually resembled a *step*, so he took the opportunity to sit down.

Just then some tourists, a German family, came rushing down the Prince Philip Steps in order to go swimming. The teen-aged girls came first. They didn't seem to apperceive the Cormorants as any great problem, and nimbly ran through us, knocking over only one or two of the very elderly. The parents made slower progress, plainly dismayed by the presence of people on the steps. I suppose I would have been, too. My father, still seated, glanced behind him and saw a German fellow waiting to get by. My father stood up and clutched the rock wall beside him. This plainly wasn't good enough for the other. "Excuse me," he said.

My father, I could tell, felt that he'd done plenty excusing already. "Go ahead," he said.

"Excuse me," repeated the German.

"Go ahead," repeated my father.

"Will you move?" demanded the German graciously.

"I'm not moving anywhere."

The eyebrows leapt high upon the fellow's forehead. "I have asked you to move!" he pointed out.

"And I have told you," returned my father, "that I am not moving fucking anywhere."

This fellow appeared to have studied English for the Indignant. "Really?!" he ejaculated, and he truly did, too. "The nerve of this fellow! Can you hear how he's speaking to me? What a rude chap he is!"

My father glowered, and blackness informed his face, sufficient to the task of propelling the German man by. Still, the man kept up his torrent of umbrage. "This fellow is most ill mannered!" he told anyone who would listen. No one would. *He may be rude*, was the feeling silently expressed by set mouths and slitted eyes, *but by god he's a Cormorant*. The German fellow pushed by me and then got stuck, aha, he ran smack into the back of Mr. B. "Excuse me!" the German tourist shouted, which had the effect of making Mr. B. do absolutely nothing.

The German fellow's energy flagged; he seemed all of a

sudden to understand and accept that he was stuck upon the Prince Philip Steps in the midst of the Cormorants. His ear was at my shoulder level, so I bent over and said, "What is it, exactly, that you wished my father to do?"

He said nothing. I realized, with some delight, that I was scaring him.

"He stood up to allow you to pass. He and I feel that was enough. We would like to understand, what—exactly—did you wish for him to do?"

The fellow looked around suddenly, with as much industry as that activity allows. He was trying to illustrate the fact that he was a poor innocent tourist, and therefore sightseeing, and if there was a menacing person behind him, he wasn't paying any attention.

"*You*," I said lowly, "are very rude."

The pangas arrived, the Cormorants filed in, the German tourists had their swim in the shadows of the Prince Philip Steps, and that was the end of the fifth day.

Later that evening, we sat upon the topmost deck, my father and I, and drank cervezas. I was feeling pretty good—not about my frightening of the German tourist, although I shouldn't deny a certain residual satisfaction—but about another deal I'd hammered out with my daughter.

We were working out our own Scale of Being. We'd learnt a bit about evolution and were trying to apply it, practically speaking, to our own lives.

After Carson had asked the question, "Can I have a dog?" I said, "No," with finality. She scampered up the ladder to her berth, seeking sanctuary, for she found something alarming in my tone. True, I had said *no* many times before, I'm guessing on maybe ten thousand occasions. But there are many, many ways of saying the word "no," and only one that silences seven-year-old girls.

"Here's what I'm thinking," I said. "A dog is a lot of responsibility. You have to prove you're ready for one."

"How?"

"Let's start small. We'll get a tiny animal. You can care for it, feed it, and see it safely into old age. Then we'll get a slightly bigger animal, you see, and again, you can demonstrate that you can be responsible for the well-being of another living creature. Maybe by that time, you'll be ready for a dog."

"How old will I be?" Carson asked cannily. She was weighing options; she already had the *dog at twelve* offer that had been tabled by her mother.

"That's up to you, isn't it?"

"Yeah but, if I have to wait for these animals to die ..."

"All right, that won't be necessary. You have to demonstrate that they are not likely to die prematurely."

"Suppose they just die?"

"We'll have to judge if there was anything you could have done to prevent it." I had a vision of a little coroner's inquest, robed and wigged judges clustered in Carson's bright pink bedroom, gathered around a cage, solemnly inspecting a tiny corpse.

"Okay," said Carson.

"Hmm?" It was a startling vision; it required some blinking to let go.

"I say *okay*," my daughter told me. "How do we start?"

Those negotiations were still ongoing as she fell asleep. I mounted the staircase to the third deck and found my father. We popped Clubs and sipped long. The *Corinthian* was on the move, from Tower to Bartolomé.

"By the way," said my father, "thanks for taking my side against that silly Bosch."

"Oh," I said, "that's all right."

You know what I was wondering, though? I was wondering if there wasn't a gene for short-temperedness. It wasn't the first time my father's temper had flared. At the Quito airport, for example, when we landed in Ecuador, someone stumbled in front of him, causing my father to double-step and falter. "Watch it," he snarled, raising up his forearm as though he were intent on doing some cuffing. The offender, a young man with a distinctly villainous air, shrank back. I was impressed. Mind you, one can't help but stumble in front of other people at the Quito airport. And back at the Quito airport, as we sat in the departure lounge and waited for the Galápagos-bound aircraft to be made air-worthy, my father once more displayed short-temperedness. In this case, some of the passengers-to-be had opened a door at the back of the room—although it was really the front of the room; this was the door of final transit and outside lay the steaming tarmac. A SAN airway official, hurrying toward the snack bar, advised them that they couldn't do this. The door-openers, a couple of fairly reasonable men, explained that it was very hot and they were just basking in the puffy breeze. "Okay," the airline official said, "just don't go outside."

A couple sat in the plastic chairs nearby. Indeed, the point of this anecdote is only partially to illustrate something about my father, who, as you'll see in the telling, doesn't really do much more than foam and lather; I also wanted to describe this couple. One could tell, at a glance, that they were an insular couple, by which I mean, each had the other for companionship and was satisfied with this. Which is just as well, because the thing about insular couples is, no one much cares for either of the individual components. The woman occupied herself with knitting, her fingers working with mindless mechanicalism. Every so often she would whisper something to the man, and he would launch himself up and go complain to someone. The man was foppish, sporting long hair and a beard. He wore spectacles, but such was his foppishness that in my memory he was wearing two monocles. Both people were dressed strangely, the strangest aspect to their dress the sheer quantity of clothing each was wearing. The woman seemed to admire the fashion savvy of the Amish; she wore a knitted shawl and something I've decided to describe as a dirndl. I know nothing about women's clothing, so I don't know if this really was a dirndl, but it looked as though it should have been. The man dressed like an undertaker: pin-striped pants, a black shirt, a too-tight vest that he kept fully buttoned. The front pulled and yawed over his belly. Beside the man stood a stack of hatboxes lashed together with bungy cords.

Anyway, this fellow would routinely go and complain to people, rarely to anyone who had any affiliation with SAN airlines. And then afterwards, he would wander blithely outside onto the tarmac. The man would suck in some cooler air and fan his armpits. The reasonable men would beckon to him, saying that they could only have the door open because of an agreement not to stand out there. The fellow was unmoved by these arguments.

My father was incensed watching this. He started snapping, and not at any sort of lowered level, hurling invective in this fellow's direction. Carson was deeply embarrassed to have a grandfather who was spouting vileness, even though some of the words were quite novel and would raise her status in the playground. "He's ruining it for everyone," my father explained. Loudly. "The stupid ponce."

My father was right on two counts, because they came and shut the door and the fellow was a ponce. But that doesn't lessen his outburst's severity as a display of ill temper.

I will give one example from my own life. I don't want anyone to think that this book has abruptly taken a nose dive, that
it is in fact one of those accusatory tracts that reveal parental
abuse. But it is gonna be that for the next paragraph. I was
perhaps fourteen, which means that I was a fat little kid who
believed in God because of Dr. Moody's watch argument. I was
also an aspiring musician, and could misplay many musical
instruments. Like many fourteen-year-olds in 1967, I was a
Beatles fan. In our basement was a hulking old piano, and upon
its yellowed keyboard I painstakingly worked out the chords to
"A Day in the Life." "I read the news today, oh boy," I'd sing.
One day I was demonstrating this to my friend Kim, who sat
down beside me on the piano bench in order to watch and listen. When I got to the bridge—"Woke up, got out of bed,
dragged a comb across my head"—Kim, himself a dreadful amateur musician, reached out and started picking away at the upper
keyboard, and he continued doing that as I sang, "I'd love to
turururururururn youoohouooh on ..." Recall for a moment how
that classic recording proceeds. The accompanying orchestra,
under the anomalously laissez-faire direction of George Martin,
executes a slow crescendo that culminates in a fury of cacoph-
ony. Kim and I began to do this, because it was how the record
went, and before long we were pounding at the piano with abandon. The second before I was going to stop all this by playing
that big juicy chord, the second before order was to have been
restored, my head collided with Kim's. It collided with such
force that I still have a flat bit on the right side of my skull,
and I'm sure Kotzma does on his left, and after all these years
I bet they still fit together perfectly. Because my father, you see,
had gathered up our heads, one in each of his huge hands, and
thrown our heads together. "Don't ever do that again," he said,
disappearing back up the stairs. And, I must say, I never have.

What I'm wondering is, do you think there might be some genetic basis to the trait of short-temperedness? DNA can carry lots of information; it really is an extraordinarily efficient system of creature construction, and we know it isn't limited to the physical realm. (Think about instincts that are carried genetically—the salmon's drive upriver, for example, or the cat's reluctance to be dropped into a bathtub of cold water.[1]) Next we could ponder this question: would short-temperedness be naturally selected for? Does it bequeath an advantage vis-à-vis survival and propagation? Well, of course, if you viciously attacked anyone or -thing that approached you, your chances of survival would be enhanced, even if it meant that occasionally you hurt the innocent (people asking directions) as well as the evil (Mormons and purveyors of long-distance savings plans). So maybe, is what I was thinking, my spiritual malaise was really nothing of the sort. True, I had become an irritable fellow, particularly when behind the wheel. I blasted across town with the heel of one hand pressed upon the horn, the other resting on the knob of the window cranker, ever ready to roll down and scream at offenders. After even a short drive, say to the local convenience store, my voice was hoarse and my little eyes were red and inflamed like haemorrhoids. Here I thought there was something wrong with me, profoundly wrong, when really it was just the manifestation of a survival technique that had been passed down intergenerationally, the result of an intricate square dance between adenine, guanine, thymine and cytosine. I didn't need God at all; God couldn't help. Besides, why would He? The biblical God is quite an irritable fellow

---

1 This example is based on experiments performed by my brother Joel and me on our cat Huey. Even when dropped from a considerable distance, five feet, say, Huey would virtually pounce off the meniscus in a flurry of screeching and hissing reluctance.

Himself. How's this for petulance: "I will rid the earth's face of man, my own creation," Yahweh said, "and of animals also, reptiles too, and the birds of heaven; for I regret having made them."

There are implications that I should mention here. For one thing, the story of the Flood helped create the school of thought known as "catastrophism" back in the nineteenth century. Basically, it held that the history of the world was marked by a series of upheavals, after each of which God created life anew. It was, to quote Loren Eiseley, "essentially a device to preserve the leading tenets of Christian theology and at the same time to give these doctrines a scientific cast."

It is interesting to note that God (at least, the God portrayed in the book of Genesis) has not a very clear notion of the science involved. We contain, you and I, all the genetic information about human beings that's available. The same is true of even the creeping thing, that it contains the information for making creeping things. So the God of Genesis, if indeed He was displeased with His handiwork, wasn't going to accomplish much by simply erasing *almost* the whole board. He should have gone right back to square one.

I suppose this would be the time to confess to short-temperedness with Carson, but I have managed to contain myself pretty well in this regard. Perhaps the reason I'm so gnashingly fierce with my fellow motorists is to deflect a lot of simmering and ever-present seething. One time Carson angered me sufficiently, and I turned purple and sputtered with apoplectic rage. She watched me momentarily and then burst out laughing. Now, I should mention that the fact I have only rarely been fiercely annoyed with Carson is more to her credit than mine. She is a very good-natured person, sweet and considerate. Her worst flaw is a fundamental belief that television was invented for her exclusive use and benefit. She will not allow me to click through the frequencies; she will wrest the remote out of my hands whenever the screen fills with fuzzy puppets or those awful children that are bred to appear on American situation comedies.

There is very little that is annoying about Carson. *Except ...* Throughout the voyage of the *Corinthian*, Carson developed a habit of attracting my attention by patting me rapidly on the arm. It felt like the wingbeat of some huge insect. The reason for it was so that Carson would not draw undue attention to herself. If we were sitting in the dining room, for example, she would often want to tell me that she didn't like the food. I would be in conversation with my father, or glancing around the room, and suddenly I would feel this fleshy paradiddle on my upper arm. "Don't do that," I'd say. "I respond to aural stimuli. You could say *Dad*. You could even say *Excuse me, Father*, although I'm not holding out for that." After a day or two I ceased admonishing, merely turned toward her and bugged my eyes open so that the red-cracked whites glistened with threat and malice.

So, while it's true that I've only rarely lost my temper with Carson, I should confess that I often walk around with my eyes bugged thus. It's like I'm topped up with some seething ill humour, and the eyes are little meters that read "FULL." Moral affliction or genetic inheritance, who can say? Like any nature/nurture argument, the answer probably lies in some combination of the two. I will say that environment undoubtedly played a large part, in my case; I drove around Toronto-town screaming "Asshole!" because sometimes I was sharing the slushy streets with nothing *but*, assholes of every stripe careening and caroming down the avenues. In the Encantadas, the world was simplified. A clutch of islands dropped into the endless sea, animals assigned to each. And although each species is well represented, there are only a handful of species. If you believe in the concept of Special Creation, then God was acting with especial finicalness. Perhaps He was nearing the end of His supply, and had to spread them around as best He could. "Okay, um, red-footed boobies over *here*, blue-footed boobies over *here* ..." There was very little in the way of imposed structure in the Encantadas—remember the Prince Philip Steps, which, as I've said, didn't exist in any real or true way. It was easy to see what was *really* there, a series of uneven rock risers that had been fashioned by the ages.

It was easy to see what existed in the Galápagos; it was easy to see what did not.

So, even though God had yet to show His face, the anger level was ever on the decrease; the dipstick of derangement showed less and less black goop residing at the pit of my belly.

There is one trait clearly inherited from my father that I am taking much pride in lately, albeit of a slightly perverse nature.

There were, as I've mentioned, many arguments mounted against Darwin's Theory. Many had validity—the incompleteness of the fossil record, for example, is still debated hotly. The factions line up on either side of the ball, either trusting the existing evidence or taking a leap of faith onto the treacherous grounds of belief. Another argument, kind of a corollary to this one, has to do with intermediary life-forms. If birds evolved from reptiles, why is there no evidence of a creature that is halfway 'twixt the two? This question vexed our friend Charles Darwin. It was put uneasily to rest with the discovery of the fossilized remains of the Archeopteryx, which, it could be argued, is indeed halfway between the two orders. But that didn't really quell any squabbling because, I maintain, it wasn't really what was bothering people. What was bothering people was the step between monkey and man. Many wanted it not to exist at all. Many wondered why it was nowhere to be seen. In short, the search was on for the Missing Link.

Myself, I have no problem accepting that there is none. Don't quote me on this, and demand no support drawn from the scientific literature, but the truth of the matter is, I see no wide gulf between chimpanzees (our closest "cousins" genetically speaking) and humankind. There are wider gulfs that bother exactly nobody; there are variations within varieties that seem far more drastic. All you have to do is spend some time at Doggy Park and you'll see what I mean. Doggy Park is where I take Zoë so that she can play with her mates. It is, technically speaking, the leash-free zone of Withrow Park. But dogs rule the roost there, romping o'er the hills in packs both great and little as their owners stand in the middle, shivering, smoking and making small talk. And there you will find both Winston, a small stuffed snorting sausage skin (a bulldog), and Spencer (likewise one of Churchill's namesakes, the appellation stemming from the flapping jowls), a Great Dane who moves like a marionette controlled by a drunken puppet master.

So where is the great chasm between monkey and man? There is the matter of our hairlessness, a topic I addressed in Chapter Eight. (I addressed it then because I didn't think it would come up again. Guess I was wrong.) Surely it could be argued we are just chimpanzees who have developed a set of specific skills. We are impressed with them, sure, and we prize the artifacts they leave behind (even if much of it is litter), but are we really the best judges? I have a rather glib answer to anyone who, thinking to address the unlikelihood of complexity arising out of chance, asks how long it would take a monkey to produce the works of William Shakespeare. I reply that it would take from the beginning of time until 1616, at which time a monkey with that name lay down his quill and passed away.

Knowing that I am not the best spokesperson for the opposing view, I have secured a copy of a book with the rather catchy title *God—or Gorilla*, written by Alfred Watterson McCann and published in 1922. McCann was obviously a man of great scientific knowledge, because in the tradition of learned men he gave his book a long and cumbersome subtitle: *How the Monkey Theory of Evolution Exposes Its Own Methods, Refutes Its Own Principles, Denies Its Own Inferences, Disproves Its Own Case.* McCann's books, prior to *God—or Gorilla*, dealt with the subject of ingestion: titles include *The Famishing World, The Failure of the Calory in Medicine* and *The Science of Eating.* I suspect he was a chubby little oinker, and likely an annoying one. *God—or Gorilla* has a distinctly irking tone, mostly because THERE ARE SO MANY WORDS WRITTEN IN CAPITAL LETTERS.

Mr. McCann addresses, at some length, the issue of SUPRA-ORBITAL RIDGES. The words written in annoying capital letters refer to a lumpy, sloping protuberance of the brow, distinct in the primates, missing in humankind, or so says McCann. "It was an unfortunate day for the ape-man evolutionist when he began to stress those supra-orbital ridges as proof of relationship to a simian ancestor."

Well, *I got one.* And so does my daddy.[2] Just so you won't think I'm lying or exaggerating, take a look at the author's photo on the back cover. I'm doing something in that picture that I rarely, if ever, do; I'm addressing my left profile to the lens, so that the lumpy ridge—exacerbated by a tumble down a staircase when I was three years old—is evident. My father's supra-orbital ridge is even more pronounced. I once believed that he acquired this skull through a surfeit of grey matter. It was my father himself who disabused me of this notion. He had once

----

2   So did the "beetle-browed" Charles Darwin.

had his own profile X-rayed. Evidently, while at the hospital attending to some other ailment, my father asked that his lumpy brow be examined. This would be typical of him, this curiosity; also typical is the way I'm presuming his own curiosity affected his brothers and sisters in Science. I'm confident that before long my father had the entire medical staff mobilized on his behalf, that a crack team stood around the lighted wall and lifted the black and white transparency to eye level.

"Hmmm," they intoned like priests, full of dark grace. "Hollow."

Fourteen

We panga'd from the *Corinthian* to Bartolomé Island, which lies a-starboard of James. It is a very tiny island, barely visible on some maps, surrounded by a sea littered with a number of austere, blunted pyramids. It is also very Galápagon, and you sense that it was Bartolomé Herman Melville was thinking of when, disgruntled and about to throw in his quill for the exciting new challenges of customs regulation, he scribbled down his bitter and weary, "Take five-and-twenty heaps of cinders ..." Here's the extent to which Bartolomé is a heap of cinders: my young daughter Carson, who tends toward the asthmatic, leapt from the Zodiac onto the rocks, took three steps toward the inland (every footfall raising a little cloud of red dust) and began to cough, wheeze and sneeze. Carson buckled and sat down on a rock, her eyes aflame and her nose leaking. She was allergic to the whole damn island, that much was plain. Now, I knew that we were in for some strenuous trekking. "Wear good walking shoes," advised our guidebooks, highly suspect words indeed. Our guidebooks employed that phrase only twice, once here, once in the section dealing with Hood

Island, with Punta Suarez, with, that's right, the Death March. "Maybe," I said to my daughter, "you might not want to come with us."

Some feet away stood a woman named DeeDee. She was a robust and ruddy woman, with violently red hair and oversized spectacles. She was not a Cormorant. (I believe she was an Albatross, but I could be mistaken there.) "She can stay with me," said DeeDee.

"You're not coming?"

DeeDee was high-coloured and, if anything, breathing with more laboured wheezing than my daughter. "No," she said. "I'm going to stay down here."

"I want to stay here," said Carson. Like a marine iguana, Carson had found a little shadowed nook in the rocks near the sea, and if she sat there, very still, she did not cough and she could breathe.

"She'll be fine with me," said DeeDee.

"Well, if you're sure . . ." I appeared to have lucked into some baby-sitting. My initial impulse was to rush off and try to find a nightclub, maybe take in a show or something, but such opportunities were exceeding rare on Bartolomé. There was, indeed, only the one diversion, climbing the three hundred and twenty steps to the top of the volcano. I made sure Carson had her water bottle and sunblock, because the sky was cloudless and the sun was punishing.

The rest of us—an admixture of Cormorants, Albatrosses and Boobies—began to march. I suppose the guides allowed the groups to mingle because there was no real opportunity to lose people. Some years back the National Park had constructed a wooden staircase on the face of the mount. There were four huge flights imposed upon the rock, angled to each other so that one's assault upon the summit was frustratingly oblique.[1] Connecting these huge flights were resting places, oversized landings equipped with crude benches. I will take us now to the first such way station. Everyone seemed to be in reasonable shape, indeed, only two or three people threw their butts upon the benches. Most took the opportunity to raise up their cameras, to photograph the barren hillside. We had already passed the tree line (or, more precisely, the *Brachycereus* cactus line) and, aside from the occasional lava lizard, the world was now lifeless.

I could see the shoreline, the landing place; the panga was hurrying back to the *Corinthian*. On the rocks by the water sat my daughter and DeeDee. Carson was talking, her hands moving rapidly in front of her face. It looked as though her hands were the conveyance of emotion and meaning; they curled and blossomed and then froze, held a foot or so apart, the fingers aimed inward and trembling with excitement. I recognized the international sign for "Ideal Dog Size." DeeDee then brought up her hands and repeated the sign; indeed, she abbreviated it, pushing her hands closer together. Carson's face lit up with delight and enthusiasm. Apparently DeeDee owned a dog that you could not only pick up, you could stuff it in a backpack along with sunscreen and water.

"All right, Mr. Quarrington, let's go," said Carlos, and I turned away from my daughter and began up the second flight.

I started thinking about middle age. It is not unusual that I thought about middle age; after all, as I neared the summit, three hundred and twenty steps later, I would be thinking about

---

1 The reason being, the stairs were not put there to help Corinthians, or anybody else, up the side of the volcano. They were put there to prevent Corinthians from dislodging tufa and otherwise encouraging erosion.

death. So along about the second huge riser, I reflected on middle age.

I didn't feel middle-aged. (I'm going to tread very carefully here; I'm going to peck at the keyboard with precision, perhaps because it's—that's right—too late at night and I'm sitting in the kitchen, housecoated and sipping at a single malt.) I still felt young, the core of my being was still teen-aged. However, I'm not using this as an excuse for unseemly behaviour; it actually *prevented* me from behaving in an unseemly way. All right, an example. (I'm picking at the keyboard with ever greater care here.) There were, aboard the mighty *Corinthian*, two women from Chile. They were both very attractive women who came to dinner in crisp, wholesome dresses and lounged amongst the sea lions in tiny bathing suits, which, in accordance with the South American style, didn't exist in any appreciable way when viewed from the back. Now, as leering as that sentence may have sounded, I came nowhere near exhibiting the goatish appreciation that these women deserved. One was even given to smiling at me, and although I may have smiled back, it was only briefly, and it was without enthusiasm. What I'm getting at is that a middle-aged guy, feeling his blanched oats, should have gotten all steamy and at least engaged the woman in conversation, or, more likely, babble. I did not; I was preoccupied. The Squabble was ongoing in my heart; not the Great Squabble, but a smaller, more egocentric version. The Lesser Squabble, if you will. I could not pursue any even innocent lechery until it was sorted out. So what I'm getting at is, the Lesser Squabble was preventing me from achieving the next stage in my life. I wasn't fleeing middle age; I was seeking it.

At this point, I would like to introduce my nominee for the Patron Saint of Middle-Aged Guys, William Beebe.

The seminal moment of Beebe's life came on August 11, 1934, when he and Otis Barton descended three thousand and twenty-eight feet beneath the surface of the ocean in their bathysphere. This was, in case you're unclear on the point, much, much deeper than any human being had ever managed to go. At least, living, breathing ones. As they passed six hundred feet, William Beebe uttered, in a somewhat sardonic manner, "Only dead men have sunken so deep." Beebe made this comment over a telephone connected to the world up above, the deck of a ship; his companion and amanuensis, Gloria Hollister, stood up there, recording his words stenographically. For much of the descent, William Beebe was his usual, talkative self. When at nineteen hundred feet a strange fish appeared at the porthole of the bathysphere, Beebe enthused about its beauty, describing the bands of light that were described upon the creature. "I shall call it the Five-lined Constellation Fish," he announced, inventing the Linnaen Latinate right away, *Bathysidus pentagrammus*. My point in mentioning this is not that this fish has never been seen by any other human eyes—it is not, indeed, recognized by science—it is to demonstrate a gabby side to Beebe's nature, because when the bathysphere reached the nadir of its descent, all but twenty feet of the thick iron cabling unwinched on the deck of the mother ship, he suddenly fell silent. Ms. Hollister became quite concerned, but her anxious questions received the same chilled silence. Finally, though, Beebe spoke, and the reason for the long silence became known; he had simply been staring out the little porthole, rendered mute by wonder.

At the time of this historic dive, William Beebe was fifty-seven years old, and already a very famous man. Born in Brooklyn, Beebe began his career as an ornithologist, and immediately after leaving Columbia University became the curator of ornithology for the New York Zoological Society. He was responsible for the famous "flying cage" at the Zoological Park, a huge (fifty-five feet high, one hundred and fifty-two feet long) construction that housed many species of the great water birds. Beebe was also, under the aegis of the Zoological Society, the director of scientific research, and as such led expeditions to South America, the Himalayas, Borneo and Nova Scotia. Many of these journeys were in aid of gathering research for his huge treatise on the pheasant, a bird about which Beebe was the undisputed expert. But many of the things he saw, the adventures he had, could not be contained within the covers of *Pheasants: Their Lives and Homes*, so William Beebe began to compose other books. Titles include *Zaca Venture, Two Bird-lovers in Mexico, Jungle Peace, Jungle Days* and, one of his most popular compositions, *Galápagos: World's End*.

Beebe journeyed to the Encantadas aboard the steam yacht *Noma*, his stated plan being to retrace the steps of Charles Darwin. This he did, in rather telling detail; Beebe not only retraced Darwin's steps, he re-performed many of Darwin's little experiments, for instance, the iguana-toss. Charles learnt much about the marine iguana by throwing specimens repeatedly into the sea, watching with wonder as they lumbered back for more of the same ill treatment. Beebe did that, too, and I would have done it as well, except that Carlos kept stopping me. On Hood Island (Española), Beebe witnessed the elaborate courtship dance of the waved albatross, wherein bills are crossed and clacked like swords and countless gracious bows executed. Spotting an unattached bird squatting nearby, William Beebe approached and gallantly stooped low. The bird immediately returned the bow, and eagerly went at Beebe for a little round of beak-crossing. On the shores of Santiago, William Beebe crawled around on his belly so that he could mix with the sea lions. Although, as we've seen, sociable sea lions don't really require that such pains be taken, and I imagine they followed Beebe about anxiously, their setae quivering with concern.

Like the sea lions, William Beebe exhibited throughout his life a glorious lack of trepidation. This is what I admire most about him, and the quality that I think would serve me best if I ever acquire a middle age. Beebe is a singularly unheedful adventurer, always describing occurrences such as: "Reaching out to help myself by swinging on a branch, I was startled to have part of the dry foliage tear out of my grasp and turn into a large lizard." Or (in an example that, while taken from *Galápagos: World's End*, does not concern his adventures in the Encantadas), "Early in the night I stepped out of the shallows on to a short, half-submerged log, when the log turned into a steel spring, which flicked me backward into a seven-foot pothole." Beebe had stepped onto a crocodile, you see. Which I myself am not likely to do, as skittish as a deer, testing every footfall gingerly. (I am, however, open to attack from the rear— which is how the crocs will get me.)

Whilst poking about the waters that embrace the Encantadas, William Beebe discovered a new fish, a "red-backed azure fishlet," and promptly named it *Eupomacentrus beebei*. Throughout his career, Beebe discovered and named about eight hundred species of fish, and one bird. This imbalance is not really all that unusual, not when you consider that half of all vertebrate species are fish. (I just threw that fact in, not as evidence of any great erudition on my part, more in the spirit of *good news for anglers*.)

William Beebe was, among other things, Teddy Roosevelt's best friend. (Roosevelt also lived a good middle age, didn't he? In the popular imagination he seems forever fiftyish, moustached and portly; the fact that he was the United States' youngest president is all but forgotten these days.) It was Teddy, for instance, who apparently had the insight that a sphere would work better than a cylinder for a watery descent below where only dead men go. (Otis Barton, mentioned above and crouched beside Beebe during the record-breaker, actually designed the thing.) Roosevelt and Beebe journeyed about the world together, in search of the wonders that the earth will yield. At night Roosevelt would drag Beebe out to a clearing, and the two would crane their necks backwards and stare up at the empyrean. After a while, Teddy would say, "All right, Beebe, I think we're small enough now. We can go to bed."

We continued up the side of the volcano, our ranks now spread and thinned, because some people, like Mr. B., took the risers slowly, huffing and puffing and emitting meek groans. Others, like a Cormorant named Alan, raced ahead, oblivious to everything in the world except the attainment of the summit. Indeed, Alan was in the lead, a good fifteen feet ahead of me. This irked me slightly, because, well, I exercise a lot, I belong to the YMCA here in Toronto and have put in many hours there, including many hours on the StairMaster, and here, in the one practical application I was ever likely to encounter, I was being bested by a scrawny little fellow from New York City who smoked too much and ate bad food. Alan had been devastated by the Death March, I recalled; he had returned to the *Corinthian* trembling and ashen, and it had taken many hours for the colour to return. But he went up the stairs sprightly, staring down and concentrating, as if fearful that at any time one of the wooden risers might turn out to be a crocodile. "I have to keep going," he called out to me. "If I stop, I'll never make it."

He made it, of course, and I came second, and one by one Corinthians dragged themselves up the last flight and sought a resting place at the summit, which looked, fittingly, like a druidical burial site. There was a large stone obelisk in the centre of an earthen circle that was only slightly imperfect. A metal plaque was affixed to the monument, and I suppose I should tell you what it said, but I'll have to refer to my notes (I'll have to locate my notes somewhere in the house, and then refer to them) because my attention, like everyone else's, was focussed on the view of the world.

I could take pains now to describe the view, but I don't suppose it will signify all that much, not if I simply tell you that below us lay a huge crater, easily visible through the few feet of water that covered it, the rim just feet away from where my daughter sat talking to DeeDee. Spinning around I could see enchanted islets in all directions, sprung whole out of the ocean, and although the nature and character of each changed (some were naked, others possessed small shrubberies that covered the surface like a spiky buzzcut), I don't think the details are going to help describe what I was looking at. Because what I was looking at—what all of us were looking at, spinning around the barren druidical burial site, struck mute as William Beebe in his bathysphere—was the creation of Earth.

And it seemed freshly minted. The violence of the world-birth was evident. The islets that pierced the ocean glistened, as though they had arrived just yesterday and hadn't quite dried. The lava seemed newly solidified; the craters were finely etched and perfectly round, as though time hadn't had a chance to smooth and obscure them. I could imagine a world filled with smoke and fire, the briny a-boil and bubbling, all of this orchestrated, all of this conducted by the Lord Almighty. This was the closest I came to spotting God. I wanted to yell down to my daughter, away down there below me—"Hey, Carson, come on up here, I think I see Him!"—but I knew she wouldn't hear, and besides, she and her new friend DeeDee were discussing dogs.

I'm going to speak, for a bit, about the age of the world.

I'm going to invent a place. I'm going to call it Our Valley of Stones. It is not my intention to enter the realm of fantasy here; I intend this to represent a place that could exist on the planet, at least as an exaggeration of many places that do. Our Valley of Stones is well named, for it is just that, a deep, deep gorge half-filled with huge boulders. And rising on either side of the gorge, huge mountain faces, surmounted by more huge boulders. Now, a handful of folk live there, doing what I don't know, and they are all greatly alarmed one day when one of these huge boulders away up on top of the mountains suddenly falls over and joins the other boulders in the gorge below. The young priest checks the local records to find out if such an awesome thing has ever happened before; he finds he has to go back many years, hundreds and hundreds of years, but there in some forgotten prelate's immaculate hand is the record. Then a realization sets in, an Insight. The valley was once empty, and it has been filled, over time, by rocks falling from the mountains. And the huge gorge is half full, so there are thousands and thousands of rocks, falling every thousand years. The young priest doesn't have to consult his mathematical tools to realize that the world is much older than anyone suspected.

Certainly much older than six thousand years, which is a figure bruited about with considerable assurance in the nineteenth century.[2] It was arrived at by working backwards through the

---

2 John Ray, who some consider the first great naturalist, gave "the novity of the world" at "not yet 5600 years." Archbishop Ussher was more precise still, naming the date of Creation as the twenty-sixth of October, 4,004 BC. At nine o'clock in the morning.

Bible, through the generations and litanies of "begats," gathering up the Tribes of Israel, checking off forefathers, pushing aside Cain, Abel and Seth to get at Adam, and then subtracting six days for the actual work of Creation. And that seemed to be about six thousand, give or take a month. So many people challenged the Theory of Evolution on the grounds of unassailable logic: there simply wasn't *time* enough for it to have done all that Darwin alleged it did.

Charles got fortuitous support, however, because geologists were investigating places like Our Valley of Stones, and they were pretty much agreed that this six-thousand figure was way out of line. Jean Fourier (1768–1830) was one of the first to essay calculations based on observable physical phenomena extended to the world by analogy; in this case, cooling. It had not escaped people's attention that as you, say, descended a mine shaft, the temperature rose. From this they conjectured that the earth was, in the beginning, a huge ball of red-hot molten stuff, spit out into the icebox of space. Isaac Newton, in his *Principia*, judged that it would take an Earth-sized glob of molten iron fifty thousand years to cool down. Fourier was more exacting in his work, first of all studying the way heat flows through solid objects and then developing equations based upon the processes. He assembled all his data, invented formulae, did all the necessary calculation, but as far as anyone can tell, he never wrote down the answer, which would have been a hundred million years.

Aging the world became quite a popular pursuit, and Darwin benefited from it. People made calculations based on the cumulative thickness of strata, estimating the age of the earth's crust. People made calculations based on glacial accumulations, which are influenced by orbital eccentricity, which I take it means that at either end of the world you can take off a slice and

count rings, much as you would age a tree. People made calculations based on the erosion of geological formations (a
process which has the pleasing name of "denudation"). People
counted the number of huge boulders that had tumbled into
Our Valley of Stones. Underlying all of these methods is the
notion of "uniformitarianism," proposed by Charles Darwin's
great hero and mentor Lyell, which had it that these processes
were steady. Each estimate would send the time reeling backwards, two hundred million years, a thousand million years, a
billion. Darwin, growing old, let these men do their arithmetic,
now rarely leaving Down House. Occasionally he would go to
Malvern for the Water Cure, because his illness did not abate;
otherwise he would stay at home and putter in the garden.
Charles had a new consuming interest, orchids.[3] What little
strength he had was devoted to these flowers, and to work upon
a new manuscript, every bit as weighty as *The Origin: On the
Various Contrivances by Which British and Foreign Orchids Are
Fertilised by Insects.*

Then came William Thomson, Lord Kelvin (1824–1907),
considered by many to be the greatest physicist of the nineteenth century. His name sounds familiar, not because he
invented electronic appliances, but because he is honoured by
the eponymous scientific temperature scale measuring from
absolute zero. Lord Kelvin was one of the formulators of the
basic principles of thermodynamics, particularly the second law.
(You know the second law of thermodynamics, don't you? It's
the one dealing with entropy, the Big Freeze, the slowing down
and the coming to silent rest.)

---

3   My father's consuming passion is the primula. He once travelled to Seattle to attend
    a primula convention. Charles Darwin published a paper in the *Journal of the Linnean Society* entitled "On the Two Forms, or Dimorphic Condition of Primula."

Lord Kelvin stands out in this story for a significant reason: he appears to be the one individual who really got Darwin's goat. Charles had a legion of denouncers and detractors, as we know, but he shrugged off their criticisms with a remarkable show of equanimity, even with what we might call Christian good will.[4]

Not so Lord Kelvin, whom Darwin referred to as an "odious spectre." Lord Kelvin based his estimate concerning the world's age on three factors: the cooling of the earth, tidal retardation, and the age of the sun. The third is based upon the notion that the sun is dissipating its energy at a rapid and steady pace. "Unless new sources, now unknown to us, are prepared in the great storehouse of Creation," Kelvin wrote in an article entitled "On the Age of the Sun's Heat," "it seems ... most probable that the sun has not illuminated the earth for 100,000,000 years." Kelvin was willing to grant the earth an age of about twenty-four million years, not enough time, in evolutionary terms, to do much of anything.

Charles Darwin lamented, poetically, "I take the sun much to heart." He wrote, "I am greatly troubled at the short duration of the world according to Sir W. Thomson, for I require for my theoretical views a very long period before the Cambrian formation."

This is mostly of historical interest, because Kelvin was wrong; he himself fingered the problem in the statement cited above, for there is a new source prepared in the great storehouse of Creation, atomic energy. But there is an aspect to the story which has, at least for me, a more immediate and heart-felt meaning.

---

4 Darwin was under constant attack by one of the most famous and influential scientists of his day, Richard Owen, and all he could say was, "What a strange man to be envious of a naturalist like myself, immeasurably his inferior."

Charles Darwin and his wife Emma had quite a few children, ten in all. The births were clustered rather tightly together; nine took place within twelve years of the Darwins' marriage. The last child, Charles, born in 1856, was retarded and sickly, and died at the age of eighteen months. Some scholars nowadays think he had Down's syndrome, but Darwin saw the death of his namesake as further evidence that whatever strange malady possessed and cursed him was somehow being inherited by his offspring. The very mystery that haunted him professionally—the mechanics of heredity—seemed to mock him in his private life. Still, given the infant survival rate of the times, the Darwins were fortunate. Another daughter, Mary, had been taken when she was wee, just three weeks old, but the other children survived, although not all to adulthood.

So this is an aspect to Darwin that we shouldn't lose sight of, that his house was filled with children who, no doubt, interfered with his study, demanding that some situation be given due attention and diplomatic resolution. His daughter Annie was Charles's clear favourite; although Annie, unfortunately, seemed most afflicted by the malady. She was often forced to keep to her bed. Darwin's daughter Etty was a sensible and well-spoken young lady. She seemed to share with her father the knack for uncluttered, communicative prose; indeed, she helped Charles with the composition of *Descent of Man*. The last daughter, Bessy, was a quiet and sullen sort. She never married and remained at Down House, attending to small chores in the house and garden, never saying much of anything to anybody.

Of the Darwins' five sons, three followed their father into the sciences. (Leonard entered the Royal Military Academy, eventually achieving the rank of major, and the eldest, William, became a banker.) The three who went to Cambridge had varied careers. Horace, the youngest of the children, set up a scientific instruments company. Francis became a botanist, although he is better known, at least more appreciated, for other things. He was a fine writer, Francis was, composing in a slightly whimsical style books that dealt not only with his vocation but with his avocation—for he was an accomplished amateur musician—and his family. It is through Francis's *Reminiscences* that we have the clearest picture of Charles in his dotage.

But I really meant to tell you about George. His career was the most brilliant. He attended Trinity College and graduated second wrangler and Smith's prizeman in 1868. (I lifted that delightful phrase from the *Dictionary of Scientific Biography*. Of course, I have no idea what graduating "second wrangler" means, but please join me in accepting that it's a good thing.) In 1883 George was elected Plumian professor of astronomy and experimental philosophy at Cambridge, a position he held for the rest of his life.

George was rather a man of leisure, producing abstracts infrequently, although the collective weight of his life's work was enough to earn him a knighthood. (Francis was knighted too, I hasten to add, exhibiting my reflex for parental fairness.) But one of the things George applied himself to was, you may have guessed, the aging of the earth. He chose to approach the problem from the point of view of tides. Let me see if I can't confuse you concerning the science here. Basically the thought is that the moon, pulling upon the water that covers the globe, exerts a certain amount of what I'm choosing to call "braking" action. None of the scientific tomes I currently have gathered about me use this expression, so it may be that I've misunderstood, but they all seem to agree that at one time the earth was rotating much more quickly than it is today, and that one of the things that has slowed it down has been the action of the tides. Allow me to quote something for you:

The whole of this argument reposes on the imperfect rigidity of solids and on the internal friction of semi-solids and fluids; these are *verae causae*. Thus changes of the kind here discussed must be going on, and must have gone on in the past. And for this history of the earth and moon to be true throughout, it is only necessary to postulate a sufficient lapse of time.

I got this from the eleventh edition of the *Encyclopaedia Britannica*, where the long article under the word TIDE is signed G.H.D. These words, then, are George's, and reflect his thinking that previous calculations based on tidal braking (it was one of the thrusts of Lord Kelvin's attack) failed to take properly into account the fact that the globe is not *covered* with water, but only mostly so. The effect of friction at the seams of the land masses had to be factored in, and that was what George was intent on doing.

When I read of this, I nodded and sighed as I had sighed when movies ended happily ever after at the Don Mills Odeon. Yes, I thought, this would have been a wonderful gift for his father, to grant the Theory of Evolution by Means of Natural Selection enough time to do its work simply, to do its stuff obviously and for all the world to see. I wish I could give my father such a gift. I wish I could live in Our Valley of Stones, and watch a huge boulder teetering in the sky.

But listen. Again I lift from the *Dictionary of Scientific Biography*:

> This [George Darwin's] work was directly inspired by Lord Kelvin, whose great interest in the young Darwin may be said to have been the chief influence in his decision to make science his career.

Whoa. There are some interesting dynamics going on when one's father is Charles Darwin, but one decides upon a life in the sciences because of the odious spectre himself, Lord Kelvin. I imagine a scene enacted upon the immaculate lawns of Cambridge, not a scene of gay donnish wrangling, rather one of a dark figure emerging from behind the statuary: "Psst. Hey, kid. You know your old man's wrong, right?"

I have found no evidence of a great rift between father and son; indeed, the opposite is true. Charles was ever and remained a proud and affectionate father to all of his children. Whatever conflict existed within George seems not to have had permanent effect—although we read of him in middle age, concerned with his health and afflicted by strange maladies, walking about "with a shawl over his shoulders; this was a regular sign of feeling 'seedy.'"

And I am somewhat gratified to note that when, in 1886, George Darwin was asked to make the Presidential Address before the British Association, he meekly called for open-mindedness concerning the earth's age until more precise knowledge was available.

CHAPTER

Fifteen

Late Saturday afternoon, I finally stepped upon the same shores as had Charles Darwin, the sea-sprayed lava fields of Santiago, or James, Island. Sullivan Bay was a bleak but busy place, the tidal pools spitting weed and surf, the wind full of birds, the land claimed by the Galápagos' full assortment. The marine iguanas swam from rock to rock, crawling out of the sea in laboriously slow motion, each one reenacting that Great Moment, the Commencement of Life Ashore, for the tourists and their cameras. Sally Lightfoots scuttled across the eerie terrain, which looked like nothing so much as black plastic melted on a stove top.

We had already been upon the same islands as had Charles. He set foot on four—San Christóbal, Floreana, Santiago and Isabela—and it is only the last that the *Corinthian* steered away from. Longer cruises circle Isabela (Albemarle), the largest of the Encantadas, sneaking around its westward side, riding through the channel lying between it and Fernandina (Narborough), in order to spot the famous flightless cormorant. I'm sorry to have missed seeing those birds, for they exist in that one place and there alone, and who knows when or if I will ever get back?

Santiago is the place where the young Darwin (and Bill Beebe after him) came to toss marine iguanas into the surf. Carlos wouldn't let me repeat the experiment. He suggested that such an activity would land me in jail, and I understand that conditions are very rough in Ecuadorian prisons, especially for people convicted of iguana-tossing. So I demurred, although the experiment has significance and merit. You see, Darwin was attempting to show that the sea was not the natural or preferred element for the poor, cursèd creature; because as many times as the lizard would be tossed into the briny, it would struggle back to the rocks and crawl unerringly toward the huge, mysterious entity who (it should soon have become apparent) was only going to toss it back again. Clearly there were things in the water that the iguana didn't like.

So I obediently followed along behind Carlos, stepping gingerly upon the lava, which had been spit-polished by the surf until it was slick and treacherous. In places the lava was lapped up so that it formed ropey, sharp ridges; this sort of lava is called (take special note, all Scrabble enthusiasts) "aa."

Carson and I were busy with our avian checklist, checking off those species that we hadn't seen before. We checked off the lava heron, the yellow-crowned night heron (what a delightful name that one is) and the American oystercatcher. The latter is rather a plain-looking bird, although I have abundant affection for it. I think, after all my feeble rumination, that I like animals called by what they *do* and not by what they are calculated to be. If you see what I mean. The oystercatchers jumped about, usually in couples, checking in the tidal pools for something to eat. ("How about oysters?" "Sure, yeah, oysters sounds good.")

Carlos gestured toward the oystercatchers and told us, "They are not good parents. A month ago, right over there, there were two birds and two eggs. A week later, one bird, two eggs. Then one bird, one egg. Then one egg. Then nothing." Carlos shrugged his shoulders and marched away. The Cormorants followed.

The lava fields were spotted by grottos, the sheet of shiny obsidian rock undercut by catacombs where the sea could spill in and fill the pools.

We came upon a hole in the earth, a circle having a diameter of perhaps four feet. Every few moments water would rise and gurgle up the tube; with a huge sucking noise it would disappear. I watched this process for several minutes, transfixed by the regularity. "Ah yes," said Carlos, noting my interest. "Darwin's Toilet."

Not only was Charles allowed to hurl marine iguanas into the surf, apparently he was allowed to ... *well, never mind,* I told myself. I did suddenly get a very clear picture of the young man, all of twenty-six years of age when he walked upon these shores. Having conducted his experiments for the day— in addition to hurling iguanas, Darwin also submerged tortoises, jumping upon the carapaces and riding the beasts underwater, anxious to find out how long they could survive without air— young Charles unbuttoned and hunkered over this convenient opening in the rock. More than convenient: there, if anywhere, was proof of an intelligent and benevolent God. Not that Darwin needed any proof back then, back when he was young and mettlesome and full of an energy that burned brightly and seemed like love.

As it neared late afternoon, so the sun became both lower and stronger. It heated up the black rock and spread over it a coating of light, oblique and glistening. All about the isle, sea lions alternately lounged and cavorted; the place was therefore as wet, splashy and crowded as a public pool in the dog days. Offshore, the young sea lions blasted out of the water and disappeared again, leaving behind ribbons of mist. They then threaded through the narrow cuts in the lava and materialized inland, leaping out of pools for a quick and renewing languish on the hot rock. But the call of the Great Cavort was strong, and no sea lion lounged for long; bellowing with excitement, the creature would roll and push up onto its flippers. The beast would find the quickest route back to the sea—either down through the holes in the world or directly across the black belly—and begin again its frenzied gymnastics.

There's one thing you should know about sea lions, one evolutionary adaptation that became very evident that day. Because —and you'll remember this from a chapter near the beginning of this little book—life for a sea lion is both carefree and treacherous, there exists within a sea lion colony a certain number of orphans. And these critters are doomed. That's the way it goes. Sea lions don't adopt. It's policy; it may be hardhearted, but it's the way the whole thing works best. We Cormorants had already witnessed, a couple of times, little strays trying to get in on some nursing action, nuzzling between two playmates to get at a teat which, after all, wasn't being used by anyone. The lounging mother's head would cock up abruptly, setae all aquiver. (It's the smell, the odour of otherness, that gives the interloper away.) The mother would drive the orflink off, shoving at it with her snout, brutally ignoring its pleaful bleats.

We'd seen that. Today we saw the logical conclusion. We had, unaccountably, been spared up until that moment. But now we stumbled upon a stretch of black lava, barren except for a few pools of brackish water and a dead pup. The pup lay half in, half out of one of these pools, as though sensing, in its desperation, that water and life are bound inextricably, that they curl around each other like the beautiful helix of DNA. It was plain enough that the pup had starved to death. Its head seemed enormous compared to the windsock that was the body, a matting of dull fur covered emptiness, and was rippled with the outline of brittle bones.

I put my hands on Carson's small shoulders and led her away.

Annie Darwin had suffered throughout the winter of 1850-51, her small body wracked with spasms and seizures. Annie's head swelled with pain and her stomach could hold no food. Her skin had been spoiled and her eyes had gone dull. Charles had no idea what was wrong with his daughter—except, really, he *knew* what it was. It was the same tormentor that he held inside and it had made the generational leap, somehow. Darwin didn't know how, he didn't know the mechanics of inheritance, but here it was shown plain enough, and if, should he ever decide to publish his secret notebooks, miscreants challenged him on this basic point, that characteristics were passed on from parent to child, he need only point to poor little Annie.

Charles likewise didn't know how, or why, Dr. Gully's Water Cure worked. He had heard explanations, but he mistrusted them. The explanations evidenced no strict thinking; they glossed over informational gaps with speculation and fancy. But the Water Cure had worked for him, improved his health to the point where he could work for more than an hour or two a day. So he took Annie to Malvern. He stayed with her a few days, walking with her to the natorium, his hands on her little shoulders. He gasped and grimaced when she was thrown into the icy water, her naked body blue and rattling with shivers. Still, after three or four days she seemed stronger. She was able to sit up in bed and take a few spoonfuls of broth. Confident that this was the right course, Charles left her in the care of Dr. Gully and journeyed back to Down House. He needed to get back to his barnacles.

Several days later, Charles received an urgent message from Dr. Gully. When he arrived at Malvern he found, not Annie, but a pale husk that contained his daughter's trembling bones. Annie looked at her father but her eyes registered nothing. Her lips moved but only silence issued forth, silence and, sometimes, words that made no sense. Or, more precisely, words that may have made sense, but not there, only in a place very far away. A place where the sun shone and flowers bloomed and bird flitted from blossom to blossom. For example, it seemed to Charles that every now and again his daughter would ask for a pet dog.

Charles did not leave Annie's side for a week. At the end Annie asked for a drink of water. When Charles gave it, she whispered, "I quite thank you," and passed away.

He did what he could for sweet Emma, and she for him. They would spend long days at Down House, days that seemed almost endless, their hands wrapped together, each trying to draw strength from the other. Eventually, exhaustion would drive Emma to bed. And then Charles could go to work. He'd open up the secret notebooks and write, now with an industry that bordered on fury. Charles had established his course, and he would sail it with the single-mindedness of his somewhat batty old friend Captain FitzRoy.

Charles Darwin knew exactly what he was doing.

He was killing God.

I look at it this way. (I am pretending to be Dr. Moody now; indeed, I believe that I now bear that man some slight resemblance. I am dressed in a sober-sided suit, the tie knotted so tightly that I am starved for air and my face is alarmingly cheery. I hitch a ham over the side of my desk and lean even closer toward you.) Suppose I were to come across an old house, the door opened invitingly. Suppose I were to walk inside and find evidence of strange happenings. There might be papers dense with writing spread across the floor. They are dirtied by ashes from a fireplace many feet distant. Candlesticks lie flat on tabletops. Paintings—of people we don't recognize, of places we've never been—are crooked upon the wall.

Now (I, like Dr. Moody, fold my hands even more tightly), my first assumption is that the house has an owner, and I next assume that the owner is responsible for whatever goings on went. I therefore try to imagine motive and reasoning. He left the door open so that I might come in. These papers on the ground, I might hypothesize, he put there because he wanted me to read them. Why then did he soot them with ashes? Perhaps to make my reading them slightly more difficult, so that understanding, when it did come, might be even more complete. Why did he lay the candlesticks down? Obviously it is a sign that he doesn't want me to use them. And why did he make crooked the paintings? Maybe to indicate that these pictorial representations are false, not to be trusted.

Yeah. Yeah, that's it.

If it were then suggested to me that the wind blew open the front door and was responsible for everything that I saw, suddenly all these signs would be without significance and meaning. I like meaning and significance as well as the next fellow (and he loves it), but I could live without it. Particularly if, suddenly, the mysteries appeared to vanish.

Of all the mysteries in the abandoned house, I think the greatest is indifference.

I am not confusing indifference with cruelty. I did not, for example, stifle sobs upon the sight of the dead sea lion pup, I did not wipe tears away hurriedly so that Carson wouldn't see. Indifference is neither cruelty nor kindness; that's the whole point, isn't it? But it is, when contemplating God, a deep and chilling mystery.

Indifference is manifest everywhere. We, those of us who abide 'neath glass towers, see relatively little of it. We may see the homeless lying upon and clutching the grate above the subway, or accident victims bloodied and twisted on the side of the road. We see little enough of it that it is almost dismissable, God's clerical oversights. Other people see vastly more. They see disease culling the population with the cheerful assiduity of an amateur botanist pruning bushes.

Why would a God cause that to happen; why would a God tolerate it? Here is the impasse. A believer would inform me that this is all beyond my comprehension. To which I can only respond, well, um, get lost. Why should I believe something that I am not capable of even contemplating? Why shouldn't I embrace the notion that disease is, after all, just another form of DNA replication and propagation? It's a crowded world and competition is fierce; sometimes, very often, the disease wins.

Moreover, let's get over this species-ism. Let's consider the other creatures that dwell upon the little blue stone. It is a world of predation and death. The odds in what we graciously call the "animal kingdom" are something along the order of four to one in favour of the prey, which might seem, at first blush, evidence of a kind of benevolence or mercy. But it means that at any time roughly a quarter of the creatures on the planet are being consumed. I'm sure that as you near Earth from outer space the collective howling becomes louder and louder—actually, I don't suppose you can hear it until you enter the atmosphere, but at that point it becomes almost deafening.

Some might say, *Yes, it was the wind that blew through the house, but someone opened the door to let the wind in.* In other words, God began the process of evolution. His reasons for doing so, if they are even *reasons* in any of the senses in which we use the word, are so far beyond our intellectual grasp that the extent to which we cannot fathom them is absolutely unfathomable.

Well, fair enough; what can I say? Maybe, four and a half billion years ago, God created this planet. He waited a billion years before creating some really rudimentary bacteria. Three and a half billion years later we arrived, which is just what he intended.

Okay, what's time to God? Granted. And if you accept the existence of a God, I guess you also buy into the assumption that, having started the process, He was prescient enough to foresee *our* arrival, even though we only exist somewhere in the middle of one of a billion pathways. But where does any of this get you?

When I was a boy, I owned a series of painted turtles. This was before the universe had soured, before you could contract the disease of salmonella from little pet reptiles. This is why creatures of this ilk were never negotiated by my daughter and myself, because I have forbidden them in my role as Parental Unit. But back then they were okay; indeed, they were readily available to any little porker with half a buck and the where-withal to get himself to the pet store beside the bowling lanes. (In the parking lot immediately outside these conjoined establishments I once found a dead squid. Oh, those were the days.) These little turtles I would keep in a glass terrarium, and I would lord over them, in a very literal sense, for a couple of hours every day. At least for the first day or so, and then my boyish ways would send me outside and the notion of turtleness would drift further and further from me. The turtle would die, which happened in silent, dignified agony. (The little corpses were never far from where I'd last seen them; no panicked raking of the glass walls had taken place.) Eventually I would stumble upon the little turtle corpse, and my finer feelings would come to the fore. I would feel great sadness and bury the creature in the back yard. Remorse would send me back to the pet store beside the bowling lanes, where I would solemnly lay two quarters on the countertop.

You got here long before me, I'm sure; you saw this point coming from a distance. But as a boy, as a boy given to overly ambitious lofty thinking, it occurred to me that I was the Turtle God, at least to the specimen in the glass box. An indifferent and inept Turtle God, to be sure, but undeniably the Turtle God. It amused me to think that, by analogy, a huge God could exist outside the glass box that is the world.

But now I emulate the tiny painted turtle itself, who never squandered a single thought on the possibility of the existence of a Turtle God outside the glass walls. It concerned itself with the realities of its life, with the stale water, rocks and handful of grass that comprised its tiny world. If the painted turtle had ever stopped to ponder the grass itself—you have to play along here; besides, who can say for certain that humankind are the only animals to philosophize?[1]—then simple science and logic

---

1   As Charles Darwin writes in *Descent of Man*, "The difference in mind between man and the higher animals, great as it is, certainly is one of degree and not of kind.... If it could be proved that certain high mental powers, such as the formation of general concepts, self-consciousness, et cetera, were absolutely peculiar to man, which seems extremely doubtful, it is not improbable that these qualities are merely the incidental results of other highly advanced intellectual faculties."

would indicate that Someone had ripped it out of some distant ground and transported it to the glass box. Perhaps (and only perhaps) you or I could apply science and logic to some aspect of our glass box and surmise the existence of a Great Turtle God. But today I prefer not to, because He has wandered off, probably gone to find something to eat.

It is not lost upon me that many people would decry the low flying level of my thoughts. People have wrestled with His existence for thousands of years; I have made up my mind during a week-long cruise. People have written huge tomes, each page stained by the salt of labour and tears. I have read a few books (and there's no concrete evidence that I finished any). I seem to have spent no more than a few hours, total, in contemplation.

And yet I claim to be done with the central conundrum.

I won't champion the quality of my spiritual journey, because in an ideal world I would read some of those thick tomes. I'd live in a cloister with book-lined walls, and every day I'd drag leather-bound parchment over to a huge ink-stained table. That, I agree, would be the way to do things. But there isn't time. You and I simply don't have enough time. As superficial as my search may seem, it was as much work as I could manage. I bring up this point, not to dodge accusations of shoddy thinking, rather to encourage you to decide. Too many people wave their hands vaguely and pronounce the question imponderable, which is true. But I suppose my feeling is—now—that one should decide, finally, what is out there, so that we may then concern ourselves with what's inside the glass walls.

When I saw the dead sea lion pup, I thought, simply, *no*. I'd come to the Galápagos Islands, the Encantadas, to find God;

instead I'd discovered that He wasn't there. And I felt, suddenly, like the boy on the back of the turtle, watching the ship fade away, clutching onto the rim of the rippled carapace and wondering where I might go next.

I looked up from the sea lion carcass and saw the rest of the Cormorants standing a few yards away, arrayed in a small semicircle, their heads bent. Some, like Mr. B.'s, were bent under the weight of photographic equipment, but most were bent out of reverence. The sun, resting now just above the horizon—moving across the face of the waters—back-lit my fellow Cormorants. Their white clothes sopped up the silver light; their dark human shapes were outlined with radiance.

Sixteen

The *Corinthian* plowed through the swells, sailing from Santiago to Santa Fé, that being a small island just to the east of Santa Cruz.

My father sat in one of the plastic chairs on the Jacuzzi deck, staring up at the night sky. He had his hands folded across his chest and every so often would heave contented sighs. An empty cerveza can sat on the plastic table in front of him, but such was his mood, and his peacefulness, that he made no move to replace it. Sad-eyed Hugo, reading a newspaper, would glance up occasionally and cock an interrogative eyebrow, but my father never responded. He was too busy staring up at the sky.

I gave Hugo my custom, of course; I grabbed a can of Club and joined my dad.

He lifted a finger and stabbed it at the stars. "The Southern Cross."

"Oh yeah, that's right, we went back over the equator again." Indeed, and, unlike our crossing on the way north, *this* time the sailors did something about it. After dinner, under the pretence that they were getting up to the shenanigans customary on a cruise ship as it neared the end of the voyage, they enacted a bizarre ritual. First of all one of the sailors appeared dressed as Neptune, his arms crossed over his chest. One of the women from Chile stood beside him, wearing a beaded bra, her lower parts sheathed in some metallic fabric. The rest of the crew and guides appeared in various garb. It looked as though some cut-rate costume store had had a going-out-of-business sale, to which the *Corinthian* crew had arrived late. There were sailors in stagy pirate's garb, true, but there were also sailors dressed up like Spiderman. Carlos—whom we recognized because of his broad-shouldered lope—was wearing a white robe with gorilla mask, and brandished a hangman's noose that he would toss playfully around the passengers' necks. Judy the Purser stood at the back of the room and hollered into the wall mike, explaining exactly what was going on. Only no one knew what was going on, certainly not Judy. It was simply too weird a scene, as if Cowley and Dampier and the rest of the Jolly Bachelors had overrun the Love Boat. And that was before Orlando came in dressed like the Pope, a mitre balanced on his head, a monstrance at the ready. Man, we were tapping some heavy motherlodes in the Ecuadorian psyche. My father fled. My daughter sat there, aghast. I stared at the woman from Chile. Then the sailors came and grabbed a passenger, selecting the other woman from Chile, which was a good choice, and hauled her up to the front and forced her to kneel before the Pope. She was given communion, a biscuit laid upon the tin-foiled paddle. And then horns sprouted out of everyone's forehead and we all peeled off our clothes and rutted like billy goats. Mr. B., as things turned out, was really *Beelzebub*, and . . .

"It's good for a man to see the Southern Cross in his lifetime," noted my father.

I nodded with agreement and appreciation, because I could

see and discern the Southern Cross. Other constellations require too much imagination. Orion the Hunter, for example. What strange distillate gave birth to that notion, what hemlock-addled Greek glanced up at the sky and said, "Look! A big guy with a bow!"

I sort of know the answer to that, humankind being what we are. They *all* said it, all at the same time, because we all seek a Heavenly Father, even if he seems a little dangerous.

Which reminded me. Although I certainly had my hunches, and knew exactly where I'd place any big money, I didn't know for certain where my father stood on the issue.

I led my father down a twisted pathway that I hoped might end in the Garden of Revelation. I began by asking if his parents—Joe, the castor bean plant grower, and his wife Vera, a beautiful and regal woman—were religious.

"They went to church," my father remembered. "They went to Hope United at Danforth and Main." My father grew up in Toronto's East End, where I live now. I often count this as coincidence; as a twenty-odd-year-old I moved to the Annex, which is westward, and spent years there, and was only drawn across town when I met my wife-to-be. But sometimes I'm struck, and made glad, by the cyclical aspect to my life. The streets I inhabit now are the same streets I was perambulated about during the first year of my life, before the move three miles north to Don Mills. At any rate, I knew the church at Danforth and Main. "But I think my parents were more interested in the social aspects. My father enjoyed being with the other men. My mother was part of some women's group. They would perform every year at Christmas, banging away on pots and pans.

"There was a time my father got into trouble with the church elders."

"Oh? Why's that?"

"Oh, he came under criticism, because he became a follower of Denton Massey. Massey was a very popular fellow at that time. He preached a sort of softened-down Christianity which emphasized fellowship and concern for other human beings. I imagine God was in there somewhere."

My father, sitting there beneath the Southern Cross, told me that he had gone to Sunday school, although he was drawn mostly by the teacher, a fellow who had achieved legendary status with my dad's friends. He seemed to be, from the way my father was talking, one of those strapping young men who liked to take boys to the gym and have them box. We don't much care for those guys these days. But my father remembers him fondly, and the friends he made at Sunday school stayed with him late in life.

"But at some point—and I can't put an exact age to this, fifteen perhaps—it occurred to me that all of this religious stuff was nonsensical. And back then, I thought that Science was the bee's knees."

"What do you think now?"

"Oh, well, I suppose I still think it's the bee's knees. But one would be a fool if one didn't wonder what all this was about." My father rose to his feet and moved along the gangway; I followed behind. We went down the steel staircase and up to the bow of the boat. The anchor winch occupied most of the deck there, a huge horizontal drum wrapped in the thickest chain. My father moved into the curved V of the prow, and stared into the night.

When you stare into the sky at night, you are looking at the edge of time. If the universe were infinite, if there were no end to either space or time, then the sky would never darken. The light from billions and billions of stars would culminate in a heavenly vault of perpetual radiance. The reason the sky is dark at night is that there hasn't been enough *time* for light to arrive from the more distant suns. So time had a *beginning*, and that fact is plainly evident. Science will tell you that time was born, along with everything else, with the Big Bang, some fifteen billion years ago. The other side holds that God made it, I suppose, although He himself holds no truck with time. God abides eternity and invites us all to live with Him. Religion is, finally, not so interested in the beginning of time as it is in the *end* of it.

My father had made his decision, long ago. Still, he turned away from the heavens and fixed me with a steady stare. "I wouldn't mind being surprised," he said quietly.

On the last full day of the voyage of the *Corinthian* we made two stops: in the morning on the shores of Santa Fé, in the afternoon back at Indefatigable.

Santa Fé (the English name is Barrington) is one of the smaller islands, and is noteworthy because of the land iguana that is endemic there, the cleverly named Sante Fé land iguana. It lives in the midst of a forest of giant opuntia cactus. The landing beach[1] is festooned with sea lions and, by the way, we saw something on Santa Fé which, for some odd reason, we hadn't really seen up till then in our explorations: sea lion shit.

---

1 Because one spends, on all of these day trips, a lot of time standing on the landing beach, I witnessed the following sight: a panga appeared, ferrying only two passengers. These two people were dumped unceremoniously upon the shore, along with a number of hatboxes. I recognized the couple: it was the dour woman and the poncey man who had so annoyed my father at the Quito airport. The poncey man said something to the panga jockey, who nodded curtly and roared away. A few minutes later the marinero returned with two water bottles, which he more or less tossed at the poncey man and his wife. Then the panga disappeared. I guess there is some explanation for this, but it looked for all the world as though they were being abandoned there, perhaps to start a race of dour, poncey people.

I don't know if this was just happenstance, or if there is some fundamental difference between these sea lions and their brethren from other islands, but the Barrington sea lions just let fly wherever they were, and the beach was spotty with dung.

It occurred to me with some force, upon the isle of Santa Fé, that the Galápagos archipelago is really quite a strange place to have become a tourist attraction. "Take five-and-twenty heaps of cinders," began Herman Melville all those many years ago; to said recipe we can now add, "Sprinkle liberally with sea lion shit." Despite which, something on the order of sixty thousand people make the voyage every year. Sixty thousand people cower in the airports in Quito and Guayaquil whilst all about them is naught but confusion. Sixty thousand people are herded upon aircraft; they are discharged upon the ground and made to march past little wooden huts. Men in uniforms assess assizes and levy taxes. Finally, sixty thousand people take to the seas, in ships of all sizes.

I don't know how many people come because it is the last place on earth. Certainly a number of people have put off the Encantadas, journeying first to other lands and islands, with the result that they arrive in the Galápagos of a certain age, and, although I don't mean to be cruel, decrepitude. Like Mrs. B., who has gotten short shrift in these pages. Just as she received at the wrinkled hands of her husband, who routinely shoved her aside to take advantage of the photo ops. I cannot recall Mr. B. ever turning the Supercam upon Mrs. B. and intoning, "And here she is in all her glory." Mind you, there's no telling what they got up to at night. The point is, Mrs. B. was a valiant and stalwart soul. She made every expedition with enthusiasm, even though this took its toll health-wise, demanding every trace of her energy. She also dropped once or twice, felled by slippery black lava.

If this book has any practical advice to offer, it is this: go to the Encantadas when you are young, like Charles. Or if you are in robust middle age, like William Beebe. Don't put it off for the Golden Years, because you will be sent upon the Death March, you will be made to climb a cliffside where there is only the fanciful suggestion of "steps," you will be trooped up a volcano. These are health and safety issues, and they are to be taken into advisement. There is also a spiritual price to be paid if, like me, you had gone expecting to find Our Father, white-bearded and beaming, the man who holds the keys to the Great Hereafter.

Mind you, many people come to the Encantadas because they are, already, Disciples of Science. There weren't many on the *Corinthian*. There was Mr. Perdomini, I think. He evidenced faith in Science by fighting seasickness with the little flesh-coloured patch on his jugular vein. And he was always reading books that seemed very scientific, although the titles were in Italian so I couldn't be entirely sure.

Speaking of this, there is quite a market in trade in books about Science these days. And do you know what you find if you open those pages? *Squabbling.* It's true. This is not the Great Squabble, because what they're squabbling over is the precise way in which evolution works. There are people who endorse theories of saltation, which has it that evolution takes place in sudden spurts. This is opposed by a school known as gradual-ism. There is a compromise on the table, termed punctuated equilibrium ("eek-peek," in evolutionary shoptalk), put forward by Eldredge and Gould. The latter is Stephen Jay G., author of all those wonderful books, who, because of eek-peek, finds himself squabbling with people like Richard Dawkins, author of other wonderful books.

There is a theory that calls for a new perspective on the whole thing; don't think about complex organisms adapting, think in terms of the smallest units of life, the mitochondria and bacteria, building more complex and specialized vessels in which to live and get around. And then some apply that kind of thinking to the whole Big Blue Ball, which is called the Gaia hypothesis, which suggests that the earth itself is a living thing.

These writers squabble over how life actually got started. (And in doing so help the cause of the Deists, who of course have their pat answer at the ready.) You can read in these books various suggestions. One that, ironically, has a kind of biblical resonance is that life literally came from clay, that the earliest prototypes of DNA in a sense "learnt" the replicating procedure from clay crystals that spontaneously form copies of themselves. Another theory—advanced by no less a personage than Crick, of Watson and Crick, co-discoverers of the double helix—is that life came from elsewhere in the universe. Panspermia, this theory is called, so the theory gets big points on the basis of name alone. There are two ways panspermia could work. One is fairly reasonable, and has it that life might exist inside interstellar clouds, where conditions could be right for its creation. The other way panspermia could work is that some agency, somewhere, "fired" life at us, "seeded" the planet, if you will.

I will tell you one more thing about these books. I tend to collect them from libraries, secondhand shops and garage sales. The copies I buy are uniformly filled with marginalia. Here, for example, in a copy of *Microcosmos*[2] (which was taken from the

2   By Lynn Margulis and Dorion Sagan, 1986. This book puts forward what is perhaps the only radically different evolutionary thought since Darwin and Wallace. Basically, the authors argue that life on our planet has everything to do with microbes. We, humankind, are essentially vehicles for microbes to get around in.

library, tsk, tsk), I find in the right-hand margin of page 205 a very neatly lettered "slightly inaccurate."

You find such annotations in books about religion, don't you? I purchased my copy of the New Jerusalem Bible at a garage sale, and while the previous owner didn't actually scribble in it, he did laden it with several bits of paper, covered in neat, orderly typewriting. One that tumbled out was entitled "A Thought for the Day" and was set down in poetic verse.

> Whenever I see lilacs blow
> My heart rejoices, and I know
> That in the world far off, somewhere,
> There is a God who answers prayer.

So the battle wages on. Admittedly, rarely on so simple a level as I tend to pitch it, Darwinists versus Creationists, although that does still occur. But both teams have drafted new players, hired whole new coaching staffs. There are the Neo-Darwinists, the term simply indicating a synthesis of related sciences. The most important of these is genetics, because Darwin knew nothing of the mechanics of heredity. On the other side we have a kind of intelligent Christian faith that *of course* doesn't take Genesis literally and is chiefly concerned with matters of the spirit. These people are even willing to accept evolution as a reasonable hypothesis, if that makes you feel any better, if that helps you "understand" the workings of the Lord, Our God. This intellectual generosity is somewhat disingenuous, of course. They leave the Neo-Darwinists to squabble and bicker publicly, and disagreements over tiny specifics of the operation tend to colour and obscure the whole theory.

Let's pitch the battle at its most fundamental: Science versus Religion. I suppose I was situated rather uncomfortably in the *Religion* camp. I suspected I didn't really belong, because the other people there had scholarly airs and dusty tomes. They had tools of self-flagellation and the appurtenances of ritual and sacrifice. I had a scrap of paper with the words of Dr. Moody scribbled upon it. "Where things are most wondrous and astounding," it read, "it is there you shall seek God." So I stood near the fringes of the camp, and I craned my neck and peered across the field into Science, trying to see what they had. They had scholarly airs and dusty tomes. They had the tools of experimentation, the appurtenances of research and development. From a distance, it looked pretty much the same as the Religion side. There was one huge difference, at least to me—my father was settled comfortably over there, lounging on a deck chair with a frosty can of cerveza in his hand.

In the field between the two sides, Charles Darwin and God had grappled, long ago. Now the field was empty, naught but mud and black rock. The ground was turned up, roiled and gouged; people from both camps used the map of disturbance to bolster their own arguments, pointing toward a rut and claiming it as proof that God had fallen, pointing to a huge hole and stating that Charles Darwin had stumbled therein, and that's the last anybody ever saw of him.

The field was empty, although occasionally people would bolt from one camp and run screaming toward the other. Sometimes they never made it; sometimes the muck sucked them up and they disappeared. It was better to stay in one camp, most people decided.

Still, when I saw a little girl wandering through the mire, lost and confused, I decided to bolt.

I didn't make it.

For one thing, I don't, like my father, think that Science is the bee's knees. If you want a concrete and tangible reason, how about this? In 1905 the *Academy* arrived in the Encantadas, a huge ship full of scientists from the California Academy of Sciences. These learned people descended upon the isle of Santa Cruz, doing what scientists do, perhaps even grabbing marine iguanas by the tail and flinging them into the weedy surf. They collected specimens—8,691 birds, 166 tortoises—and then departed for the United States.

On that same island were eight suffering sailors, shipwrecked off the Norwegian bark *Alexandra*.[3]

In the midst of the wandering Cormorants, three unlikely people found themselves walking together for practically the first time on the trip: my father, my daughter and myself. Carlos was leading us through the forest of opuntia cactus to find the land iguanas. For some reason, this journey struck the three of us, all at once, as somewhat whimsical. We didn't put all that much effort into it. Carson was still concentrated on birds, my father far more interested in the cactus itself, and I was ever vigilant for finches. Time was running out and I'd yet to have an Insight. Losing my God was not an Insight; at least, not one I could easily sneak past the perpetually cheerful Publisher. So I looked for finches, the little birds that had blessed Charles Darwin with vision, and often I'd call out, "Hey, Carlos! Is that a finch?"

"No, Mr. Quarrington. It is a Galápagos dove."

"Oh, yeah."

The little Quarrington subgroup allowed the Cormorants to move past. Carlos was lecturing on something, but I can't report what, because I wasn't paying attention. My father, of course, never paid attention. My dutiful daughter always paid attention, but this was a chore and a burden, as she understood little and

3   A survivor tells the ghastly tale to Bill Beebe in *Galápagos: World's End*.

cared for none of it. On this last day of the trip, she allowed the Cormorants to march away from her, and didn't nod or comment to those who had become her special adult friends. Peter even made some comment—"Come on, Carson, you have to help us find land iguanas"—but Carson shrugged cryptically and did not fall in beside Peter and Carmen. Carson did, by way of politeness, casually indicate a lizard lying just to the side of the pathway.

Soon the three of us were pretty much abandoned, and found ourselves within a forest—not of cactus, but of actual trees. What sort, I couldn't say. They were strangely North American-looking, if you want my opinion, but my opinions on matters arboreal are less than worthless. Anyway, there was a rock underneath one of these trees, near the trunk; sitting on the rock, enjoying the shade of the thick branches, was a Sante Fé iguana. My daughter spotted it, jerking her thumb and inform-ing us of its presence very offhandedly, remaining much more focussed on birds. I peered through the branches. The iguana nodded civilly. My father appraised the tree, long and hard. I assumed he found something of botanical note, because he often stared at trees long and hard and then went "Hmm!" Some-times, much to Carlos's distress, my father marched up to the tree in question and tore something from it. He would turn a leaf or piece of bark over in his hands, squinting at it as though there were printing he couldn't quite make out. "Hmm!" So he stared at this strange tree, and he glanced several times at the lizard, and after a time he said to his granddaughter, "Shake that branch over there."

Carson obediently walked over to the branch in question, one of the lower- and outermost, and gave it a quick wiggle. Then there was wiggling within the tree itself, a motion car-ried through with the whimsical logic of a Rube Goldberg machine, at the end of which the thick branch directly above the iguana descended and gave him a smack on top of the head. The creature looked up, wondering what bastard done that.

We laughed heartily, the three of us.

Now let me take you with us for the afternoon trip, to the Charles Darwin Research Station. Don't worry, this won't be boring, because the Charles Darwin Research Station was closed, as it was Sunday. But Carlos, being trained by these people—as are all the guides in the Galápagos; at least, they're all supposed to be—took us in there and led us around.

The facility is trying to undo the damage that humankind has done to the islands. They devise strategies to combat the castor bean plants and elephant grass. They work out ways of dealing with the feral goats and cats. Now, as I say, the place was closed, so I can't tell you exactly how they're doing these things. But I know they're trying, and trying hard. I *can* lead you with us to the pens that surround the scientific compound, so that we can visit a more visible aspect of their work.

It is in these pens that I finally saw the symbol of the Encantadas—in both a poetical and a literal sense, because "Galápagos" means "tortoise" (although, remember, it actually means "saddle," which means "tortoise" by figurative extension.)

In one pen there were three adults, two males and a female. There were slabs of cracked pavement. The perimeter was marked with meagre shrubberies and trees. There was a pool of stagnant water, algae-green and stale. Tortoises, as a rule, don't move when they don't have to, but we were fortunate enough to witness what amounted to a flurry of activity. One of the males was poking around the greenery and came as close as a tortoise can to breaking a sweat. He decided to have a swim in the fetid pond. The other male, who had been in the pond, decided to have a look around the shrubbery, which he did with impressive torpor, as though he were bathrobed and hungover and wished the boy could fire the paper closer to the front door. Anyway, these two fellows met on a yard-wide pathway. They butted up nose to nose, and then, hearing the ancient voice within scream, "War!" they did battle. They both opened their mouths and began to hiss. Despite Herman Melville's assertion that this is "the chief sound of life," these were the first real hisses I'd heard on the Encantadas. They were pretty impressive, too, loud and grainy and thick as radio static. The tortoises kept their eyes locked and then slowly began elongating their necks. As one would gain height, the other would summon forth a few more inches from the carapace, and this game of one-upmanship continued until both creatures had nearly three feet pulled out. Then one, his hiss turning into something that was more properly *howl*, came up with an extra quarter-inch or two. The hisses ended, very abruptly; the necks shrank back into the shells, and the loser politely moved out of the way.

In a large pen lived one of the most famous residents of the Galápagos Islands, Lonesome George.

The most visible work the Charles Darwin Research Station does has to do with the restoration of the populations of tortoises that once inhabited the Encantadas. These huge, ancient creatures—for they can weigh up to six hundred pounds and live for a century and a half—once lumbered about the place in great numbers. But over history they have been subjected to a series of calamities. First came the pirates and sailors, who rendered the beasts into "sea pie." They would toss the tortoises into their ship's dank holds, and, even a year later, the animals would be alive, fresh and and ready for the cauldrons. A total of over 15,000 tortoises is recorded in the logs of 105 whaling ships that sailed between 1811 and 1844. Tortoises were also taken back to the old country and displayed in local zoos. Lord Rothschild's private zoo, in Hertfordshire, boasted several prize specimens. Then came the settlers, with their exotic animals, pigs and goats, and the tortoise populations were decimated further. Pigs would root out the eggs, smash them and lap up the insides. Goats would attack the baby tortoises that managed to hatch. In the thirties came oil hunters. They killed thousands of creatures, rendering them into exotic grease. And some years back, fishermen, reacting to restrictions on their catch in the local Galápagon waters, slaughtered hundreds as a protest.

Scientists think there were, at one time, as many as fourteen different varieties of tortoise, each endemic to a different isle in the Encantadas. Each was driven to the brink of extinction. They managed to reestablish eleven of the populations, which is extraordinary, although one variety still teeters, quite observably, on the brink of extinction. Because Lonesome George is the *only* survivor of the tortoises that hail from the island called Pinta.

We saw him; at least, we saw his huge butt end sticking out of a little hut where he'd gone to seek shelter from the sun. At least, I suppose it was the sun Lonesome George was avoiding, although he may be heartily sick and tired, after twenty-some years, of being gawked at by tourists. Lonesome George probably wears his fame uncomfortably, seeing as it is based upon the fact that he simply cannot get laid.

These populations of tortoises do not interbreed, so George cannot mate with a female from, oh, Santa Cruz. Now, those of you who have been paying attention to the science may be thinking, *Hmm, if they can't breed with each other, wouldn't that mean each variety is a species unto itself?* Good point. But apparently, the problem here is the carapace, moulded and formed in particular ways on particular islands. Two creatures from different places often simply do not fit together, so although Lonesome George has met girls, has even laboriously climbed aboard with his eyes crossed and his tongue sticking out of his mouth, no mating has taken place. The search is on for a female from Pinta, or a female from anywhere with a shell that is Pintese. Until she is found, Lonesome George will remain lonesome.

We left the Charles Darwin Research Station and wandered into the town of Puerto Ayora. This is perhaps the strangest town in the world, and I would gladly live there, except that (a) it is, undeniably, a little out of the way and (b) I can't say the name. I don't know why this is; it may not have *just* to do with my loose, flabby mouth, it may be universally a very hard thing to say. Try it: *Puerto Ayora*. How did you do? Just as I suspected. The name becomes a sort of incantation or spell; speak it aloud and *poof*, you are transported to this tiny, ensorcelled city. The main street is adorned with statues of iguanas. There are many shops (the oddest is a small concrete hut that lacks right angles; it belongs to a jeweller who, the sign outside announces, also has a shop on New York City's Fifth Avenue) and a handful of tavernas. The clientele inside these places is mixed. The tourists cluster in small groups, eagerly downing cervezas, pleased to be free of their guides. The larger tables, the rims and corners of the stand-up bar, are occupied by buccaneers, or their descendants, grizzled men who devour shot glasses and laugh for little or no reason.

There was even ... well, let me back up a little bit here; let me return to the march into Puerto Ayora. The research station is a quarter mile or so away from the town, so Carlos dismissed us, directing us toward the settlement and ordering us to gather at the town docks in two hours. So the Cormorants set off down the dirt road. My father lumbered along in his safari garb, sweating profusely. Though white-haired now, as I've said, in his boyhood he was red-, he was one of those florid, freckled kids who cannot naturally tolerate the sun. So he suffered, but was not alone, because that day Sol was raging and there was not a cloud in the vault.

(The day before, as I strapped my goggles over my eyes and cinched my bathing trunks, I said to Carson, "I'm going swimming."

("Why?" she demanded.

("I like to look for fish."

("I like to look for birds," Carson said, clutching her yellow list, a pencil poised nearby, even though we were aboard the *Corinthian* and inside the pitching closet.

("Yes, that's right," I said. "I like to look for fish, and you like to look for birds and Grandfather likes to look for—"

("Shade," completed my daughter.)

On the outskirts of town is a cemetery, contained within a low wall. The people in that part of the world don't bury their dead so much as crate them, and stack the boxes in blindingly white necropolises. The dirt road suddenly became crudely cobbled; we turned a bend and were immediately walking down the main street. Off to one side sat the wooden skeleton of a ship, the kind of vessel upon which Herman Melville took to the seas.

The shops offered keepsakes and mementos, and in one my father bought a small canvas tote bag that displayed the logo of the Charles Darwin Research Station. "Here," he said, presenting this to Carson.

"Thank you," she said, genuinely touched. I gave Carson her own water bottle, which she placed in the bag. I handed her the yellow sheet of paper and a pencil. She opened and refolded the bird list, making sure none of the checkmarks had disappeared, and placed that inside her new bag. She gingerly set the pencil therein. We continued on our way.

A few minutes later, Carson and I were in another shop looking at seashells, judging their merit as potential gifts. My father came up behind us and thrust something toward Carson. "I'll only do this *once*," he said, somewhat chilling words that took me back to my childhood. In his hand, of course, he held the bag with the Charles Darwin Research Station logo.

"Thank you," said Carson, hooking the bag over her shoulder and racing off to find Carmen and Peter.

"Sheesh," said my father.

My father and I walked in silence for a few yards until I spotted something that made me genuinely excited. "Look," I pointed, "Beck's."

Like the farmer who won't complain about the weather, grateful for the wheel of seasons, I don't like to say anything bad about a brand of beer, but, well, Club couldn't be faulted for tasting too good. That's why I was excited by the sign that proclaimed Beck's. This was not a manufactured sign, by the way, this was a piece of Bristol board with that word lettered upon it in black marker. It was mounted on the façade of a small shop, a single block with double doors thrown open. On the patio out front there were two or three little tables. "Care for a beer?" I asked my father.

"I'm buying," he answered.

Before sitting down I investigated the interior of the shop and found that it sold used books and beer. My kind of place, indeed. And the proprietor was appealing, too, a dark-haired woman who wore a loose blouse that fell from her shoulders. It didn't really look as if it could be shaken off by a hearty laugh, like the blouses of the buccaneers' consorts back at the Don Mills Odeon, but I was determined to be as witty as possible, just in case. We ordered two bottles of Beck's beer. She went to a small freezer to fetch them and then charged us some reasonable amount.

My father was smitten, although not by the woman. A small tree struggled upward beside our patio, thin and generally naked. It did hold, in the bony hands of its upper branches, a blossom, variously hued.

"What is that?" my father asked.

"A lantana," answered the woman, in a husky voice only slightly coloured by accent. I was expecting a shrug, maybe even half-hoping for it; still, I was pleased, for my father's sake, that she had a ready answer. The woman pointed across the cobbled street. "There's more over there," she said, touching the air in several locations. Lantana bushes seemed to appear magically.

My father gazed at the flowers. "We have them where I come from," he said, "but not as big as that."

"Where do you come from?" she asked.

"Canada."

"What do you do there?"

"Oh," my father responded, after a long pull at his cerveza, "I'm a gardener."

"You know what?" I demanded suddenly. I felt a strange sensation in my skull, a throbbing near the back of the brain. It was a kind of labour pain, and indicated the advent of Insight, but I didn't realize that at the time; I only realized that I wanted very badly to tell something to my father. "I guess over the week I've strolled along an impressive amount of beachfront property."

"Oh, yes."

Dr. Moody's loud and polished voice rang in my ears. "Suppose you were walking along a deserted beach," he'd had me suppose when I was just a lad of thirteen. *Well, okay, Dr. Moody,* I was thinking, *now I've done it.* "You know what?" I continued. "I never found a pocket watch."

"No," commiserated my father, almost as if he knew what I was talking about. And maybe he did.

I was about to tell my father about the dead sea lion pup when my daughter Carson reappeared with her hands buckled on her hips. "It's time to go to the docks!" she informed us, her voice laden with censure.

I did not move, because I was delivered of my Insight. Bear in mind that sometimes Insights can be speculative and wonky and maybe way wide of the mark.

I rose from the table and took my daughter's hand.

It was late in the afternoon, so the sun (up at six, down at six, there on the equatorial line) was sinking toward the sea. "Come on, Father," I said. "Let's go back to the ship."

Seventeen

All right, then. Let me roll up my sleeves and do some heavy-duty ruminating. Let me darwinize, at long last, but remember that in doing so I salute not Charles but the fuzzy-eared Erasmus. Allow me my scientific conjecture, because this is what occurred to me as I sat on that patio in Puerto Ayora, this is my Insight. It was inspired by the memory not of the dead sea lion pup but of the image that followed, the sight of the people standing upon the black rocks of the Encantadas, the sun illuminating their sunsuits and making them seem incandescent. Because in that moment, even though I had lost God, I saw that there was *holiness*.

And I conceived a theory. Like Darwin, I repaired to my home—I live still in Toronto, Ontario, not three miles from the Don Mills Odeon, which is now a fitness club, crammed full of sweaty people who have taken that "survival of the fittest" thing far too literally—and I worked out my theory slowly, over time, questioning and challenging it. This, I've concluded, is why my father always held up Charles Darwin as an exemplar, this is the lesson my father meant to teach me: that one must question every idea and notion that one has. Ideas are beautiful but fragile things; you don't want them smashed by big bullying arguments you hadn't seen coming. So it's up to you, the creator, to find their weaknesses, then to make them stronger, to prepare them for the fray. This process didn't take as long for me as it did for Charles, because my theory is much simpler.

Here goes.

Let us accept the possibility that there is, at death, not an abrupt cessation of energy, rather a dispersal. This seems more than reasonable to me. Mind you, I've owned a series of old cars, and I'm used to turning off the motor only to experience a series of rumblings and explosions that would shame many a volcano. This is the sort of thing I'm conceptualizing, a kind of clunky running-on. And just as some cars are more susceptible to this behaviour, so people vary in the length of time, and the force with which, their energy sputters and gasps.[1]

Okay. Now, let us go back in time, back to a simpler era before calories and co-dependency, where we see humankind living a tribal existence. I am imagining a scene wherein a woman bears a child. This would be biological success enough for some creatures, but not us, because our offspring cannot immediately fend for themselves. This has to do with the fact that our ancestors, who were hairier than even your Uncle Mel, made a decision to stand up. This in turn altered our body shapes; it affected the female in that it rendered the pelvis too small to allow the birthing of a larger, more viable child. (This is not my theory, in case you're wondering why, all of a sudden,

---

1 By the way, I've just thought of another model for this phenomenon, not exactly a pleasant one: body odour. Does body odour simply stop at the moment of death? I think not; I think it clicks over to the big gears, becomes reinforced and augmented.

things have the ring of authenticity.) What I'm looking for is a reasonable explanation as to why the tendency toward post-mortem energetic run-on might be important in an evolutionary sense, and I think this is it: because our newborn offspring are utterly helpless. All right. The mother that I imagined, she has the genetic coding for long and emphatic noncorporeal rumblings. Now I am imagining that something goes wrong in the delivery process. The baby is born and is fine, but the mother is losing far too much blood, she is headed for the Big Blackness. She clutches her child to her breast and frantically scans the area for another human being. But everyone else is hundreds of yards away; it will be a while before anyone thinks to see how she is doing, by which time she will be dead. As will her child, carried off by predators. Unless, you see, the dispersing energy, the insubstantial pops and rumblings, can scare the marauders away for those precious few minutes.

My example is overly dramatic, but it is not wholly unreasonable, and it serves to make this genetic mutation a player at the evolutionary table. You see what I'm getting at: a biologically and evolutionarily sound model for the *soul*. (I didn't say I'd achieved it.) Let's conceive of the soul as an aura that human beings wear on their backs, as cumbersome as a tortoise's carapace. Some are larger than others. It seems reasonable that, in general, ours are larger than our distant forefathers', just as we are, in general, a little bit taller. And there is certainly nothing in my idea that is undone by theories of Sexual Selection. If anything, it explains why the unlikeliest of candidates are chosen. "He's bald, he's pudgy, he's myopic and little-dicked," says a hypothetical female, "but he's got a soul the size of fucking Brooklyn."

A soul need not necessarily be benevolent, but we can conjecture that it serves the propagation of the race, because mostly everything does so, perhaps in ways like scaring off intruders (which our society interprets as the work of "ghosts") or providing protective envelopes for offspring and progeny (we call them "guardian angels").

Let me tell you this story. There's no hope of stopping me at this point, anyway.

Here in Toronto, and in Canadian cities across the land, we hold, in late September, an event called Word on the Street, a huge fair dedicated to things bookish and literary. We close off a portion of Queen Street, and let me just explain for those of you unfamiliar with the city that we do indeed also have a King Street, which lies to the south of Queen. Those two avenues are separated by Adelaide and Richmond, which run one-way east and west respectively. Got it? In 1995, I was scheduled to read from a book that was newly published, *Fishing with My Old Guy*. It was so newly published that I had never actually seen a copy. I rushed over to the booth operated by the Publisher— at least, his ambassadors and minions—and there I was presented with a lovely little volume. The cover featured a pair of muck-flecked chest waders, my name was spelt correctly. It was all in all a delightful thing, so I grabbed it and started searching through for an appropriate passage to read aloud. I decided to walk south, toward King Street, where I might find a coffee shop with available seating. I flipped through the pages as I strolled. And what happened was, I somehow lost track of the streets, and by the time I reached King—my nose still stuck inside the little volume—I thought I had only achieved Richmond. Anticipating traffic from my left, I checked and then strolled, still engrossed in my small book (which you'd think I'd already have read, wouldn't you?). Anyway, halfway across the street, I tripped. I fell flat on my face, and as I got up I saw, to my right, a car stopped but still shaking, the driver smiling at me with the compassion reserved for helpless but harmless idiots. Because, apparently, I had almost strolled nonchalantly into her path; King is a two-way street. Now, the thing is, there was no good reason for my tripping, which is to say, there were no banana peels or piano wires. I am among the clumsiest of men, but it is still extremely rare for me to actually tumble. Think about it: when was the last time that you, without ben-efit of strong drink, actually hit the asphalt?

Why then had I gone down?

One reason might be that if I hadn't tripped, I'd have been hamburger.

When this sort of thing occurs, people often say that there was some power greater than themselves at work. This sounds reasonable. I am just suggesting that it is not necessary to equate "greater than ourselves" with "stretched across the heavenly vault." It could mean "just slightly greater." A cocoon of energy that we carry with us, that is capable, under some conditions, of affecting physicality. (Maybe the soul can "jam" the system, so to speak; maybe it overloaded my brain with conflicting impulses and directions, causing the legs to quaver and blam, down I went. Maybe.)

Furthermore, I conjecture that the totality of all these souls is what constitutes the Godhead. I mean this in the same sense as the "Leviathan" of Thomas Hobbes, whereby man, that is, everyone together, creates "that great Leviathan called a Com-monwealth or State, which is but an artificial man, though of greater stature and strength than the natural, for whose pro-tection and defense it was created."[2]

---

2   In rereading my Hobbes I stumbled upon this most excellent quote, which I'm bung-ing down in the name of bolstering my theory: "Seeing there are no signs nor fruit of religion but in man only, there is no cause to doubt that the seed of religion is also only in man."

And that leads me to my Insight: God was not there at the beginning of evolution; God is what lies at the end of it.

"Ever since I had read the *Vestiges of Creation*," wrote Alfred Russel Wallace, "I continued to ponder on the great secret of the actual steps by which each new species had been produced."

This is a strange place to arrive, but my journey to the Galápagos (which, as we know, entailed a journey through my somewhat patchy spiritual past) has led me finally to the mysterious fellow who shares credit with Charles Darwin for the Theory of Evolution by Means of Natural Selection. He has been called "Darwin's Moon"—as in, "He was the moon to Darwin's sun"—but the sobriquet is misleading, with its implication of algidity and silence. This is a man who was propelled upon his adventures—and he had adventures, by gum—by Robert Chambers's tome *Vestiges*, mentioned in Chapter 3. For those of you reluctant to flip backwards (and I can understand such a reluctance, the end of the book draws tantalizingly near), let me remind you that *Vestiges* was full of bold ideas and scientific twaddle. Darwin could see nothing in it, but it lit a fire under Alfred Wallace.

When he was a young man, barely into his twenties, Wallace assessed his own character, crediting himself for an appreciation of beauty and a passion for justice, and listing, on the debit side, sundry faults: no ear for music, no sense of humour, no assertiveness and no physical courage. As a teen-ager he had collected flowers and beetles, writing down thoughts for lectures which he delivered to an imaginary audience. In the photographs that survive of Wallace as a young man he appears both pudgy and poncey, soft pale flesh crammed into severe clothing. (Wallace looks almost exactly like the pudgy, poncey man who annoyed my father in the Quito airport.) It was this somewhat strange young man who, with Henry Walter Bates, set off for equatorial South America in 1847.

I mean to fast-forward through the exploits and trials that make up the centre of Wallace's life. (I can recommend David Quammen's book *The Song of the Dodo*, in which there is a long section entitled "The Man Who Knew Islands.") Although he set off for equatorial South America (where the Galápagos lay waiting to enchant), his peregrinations ultimately led him to the other side of the world, to the Malay archipelago. And there Wallace got sick, and suffered from a fever. "Every day during the cold and succeeding hot fits," Wallace recorded, "[I] had to lie down for several hours, during which time I had nothing to do but to think over any subjects then particularly interesting me. One day something brought to my recollection Malthus's *Principles of Population* [*sic*]." This book, remember, was the key to Darwin's Insight. It speaks about the tendency of a human population to outgrow its means of support; it discusses "checks to increase" that occur: disease, famine, accidents, war.

> It suddenly flashed upon me that this ... process would necessarily *improve the race*, because in every generation the inferior would inevitably be killed off and the superior would remain—that is, *the fittest would survive* ... The more I thought about it the more I became convinced that I had at length found the long-sought-for law of nature that solved the problem of the origin of species. I waited anxiously for the termination of my fit so that I might at once make notes for a paper on the subject. The same evening I did this pretty fully, and on the two succeeding evenings wrote it out carefully in order to send it to Darwin by the next post, which would leave in a day or two.

Why did he send it to Darwin? He'd long admired him, for one thing. Wallace had read the *Voyage of the Beagle* as a young man and was immediately taken with the author.[3] That book, perhaps as much as *Vestiges*, had propelled Wallace on his adventures.

There has been much scholarly debate over Darwin's subsequent conduct, but the clearest-eyed view, I believe, has Charles behaving as we might expect him to, with honour and honesty. The two men shared credit on the paper delivered before the Linnean Society. And Wallace's letter finally convinced Darwin to publish the contents of the secret notebooks. Charles saw that he had to hurry lest he be obscured in history, so instead of the long book he had been planning, *The Origin of Species* is (in his own terms) a "brief." Given that the version I've been reading is four hundred and seventy pages long, scholars must also give thanks here to Alfred Russel Wallace.

Darwin wasn't obscured, and Wallace was. He died penniless and was buried in a pauper's grave. There is no Alfred Russel Wallace Research Station in the Malay archipelago, and sixty thousand people a year don't sail there on ships. Although it sounds like a fascinating place, and I'm thinking about making the journey. Perhaps one day I'll take my other daughter, Flannery, and we will pay homage to the forgotten man. I am more drawn to Wallace than to Darwin because Alfred Russel Wallace's thinking, like my own, bumped up against a wall in his heart: "It will probably excite some surprise among my readers to find that I do not consider that all nature can be explained on the principles of which I am so ardent an advocate." The wall in Wallace's heart had to do with human beings,

---

3 "His style of writing I very much admire," wrote Wallace, "so free from all labor, affectation, or egotism, and yet so full of interest and original thought."

Homo sapiens; Wallace liked them, indeed, had an almost over-vaulting opinion of their nature and capabilities. Wallace argued that if Natural Selection were the only process ongoing, then the brain of a "savage" would only be adapted a "few degrees superior to that of an ape." Instead, writes Wallace, the brain of a savage is little inferior to that of a philosopher: "They possess a mental organ beyond their needs." Darwin and Wallace bick-ered over other matters as well; our hairlessness, for one, and that is now the third time the subject has come up here in my book. Darwin agreed that that "nakedness of the skin" proferred no direct advantage to human beings, and suggested that we had lost our fur "for ornamental purposes." (This of course brings up the subject of Sexual Selection, which Wallace seemed to view with a certain amount of Victorian squeamishness.) Hairlessness, he claimed, was a physical exemplar of those things about human beings which could not be explained by Darwin's science, things that included "the constancy of the martyr, the unselfishness of the philanthropist, the devotion of the patriot."

Some would have it that Darwin power-grabbed the glory and left Wallace to languish in obscurity,[4] but Wallace was very well known in Victorian England, for a time, until his penchant for matters spiritual made men of Science hurry away or cross the road at his approach. Interpreting this as a lack of under-standing, Wallace wrote a book entitled *Miracles and Modern Spiritualism*. His confreres were less than enthusiastic, all except for Robert Chambers, author of *Vestiges*, who exclaimed, "I have for many years *known* that these phenomena are real."

---

4 In fact, the truly obscured man here appears to be Patrick Matthew, who published, in 1831, a theory which, according even to Darwin, "completely anticipates the theory of Natural Selection." Matthew's mistake was to have published this in a work entitled *Naval Timber and Arboriculture* and, even then, in the appendix.

Spiritualism was then much in vogue, and Wallace became convinced that seances were genuine, that bridges were being found into the Great Beyond. When "Doctor" Henry Slade was hauled into a London court, Wallace testified on his behalf. Slade was a man who claimed to be in contact with the dead, who would communicate to the living through writing on small chalkboards, slates held, rather conveniently, by Dr. Slade. The great magician John Nevil Maskelyne appeared for the prosecution, and apparently ticked the judge off by making writing appear on a number of slates, so much so that the judge eventually forbade their introduction in the courtroom. The high point of the trial came when Alfred Russel Wallace appeared for the defence, testifying that Slade was an honest man, "as incapable of an imposture as any earnest inquirer after truth in the department of Natural Science."

It was this sort of behaviour, and not Darwin's treatment of him, that caused Wallace to find disfavour in the scientific community. Indeed, when before long he was reduced to grading examination papers for a living, it was Darwin who petitioned the government and his fellows to provide Wallace with a small pension. Charles was eventually successful at this, although he encountered a great deal of resistance. Joseph Hooker told him, "Wallace has lost caste terribly."

Still, though some of his notions were barmy (don't forget, many people thought the Theory of Evolution by Means of Natural Selection pretty barmy, and many still do), I prefer Wallace's writings to those of any of his contemporaries, including Charles Darwin, because Wallace was capable of joyous and ecstatic rhapsodizing:

Man is the one being who can appreciate the infinite variety and beauty of the life world, the one being who can utilize in any adequate manner the myriad products of its mechanics and chemistry. Man is the only being capable, in some degree, of comprehending and appreciating the fore-ordained method of a supreme mind. That is surely the glory and distinction of man—that he is continually and steadily advancing in the knowledge of the vastness and mystery of the universe in which he lives.[5]

It is Alfred Russel Wallace who leads me to suspect that God versus godlessness is not the real issue here, not the main fall-out from the Theory of Evolution by Means of Natural Selection. After all, one of the co-discoverers of the Theory felt no need to abandon his Father. And even Charles himself ended his life simply not knowing. In his youth he had been a believer (perhaps more out of convenience than anything else). Then came the Galápagos, where he saw the finches, tortoises and accursed iguanas. Darwin repaired to Down House and worked on the Theory, and there he lost his God. (Perhaps, grieving the loss of Annie, Charles may have even had a hand in His disappearance.)

But at the end of his life, he simply didn't know.

> I may state that my judgement often fluctuates ... In my most extreme fluctuations I have never been an Atheist in the sense of denying the existence of a God. I think that generally (and

---

5   One finds no such beauty in the books written by Charles Darwin, only clear and workmanlike prose. My favourite passage was written in a letter to his wife Emma (from Malvern, where he was taking the cure) and reveals a kind of whimsical weariness: "At last I fell asleep on the grass, and awoke with a chorus of birds singing around me and squirrels running up the trees, and some woodpeckers, laughing, and it was as pleasant and rural a scene as ever I saw—and I did not care one penny how any of the beasts or birds had been formed."

more and more as I grow older), but not always, an Agnostic would be the more correct description of my state of mind.

So maybe it is not the God/No God question that is the sticky point. Perhaps the ugglesome bit is this: if you accept Darwinism, you accept that at the most profound and fundamental level *things change.*

Charles Darwin and Alfred Russel Wallace, men who loved islands, helped us discover rivers. This is the analogy that I find most satisfying, because rivers go somewhere, don't they, and they go with what looks like wilful determination, but they don't *progress* (although there is a *progression* that makes much sense in terms of rivers). Myself—the man who loves rivers— I don't consider the headwaters to be in any way inferior to the mouth, although I acknowledge the differences in character. I think Wallace and Darwin made clear to us that life is a river. I don't mean my own individual life (and I certainly don't mean *yours,* you self-involved so-and-so), I mean the whole gamut of things that live on the little blue stone. Humankind is but a little patch of foam bobbing along near one of the banks. (I put "near one of the banks," but my first temptation was to write "down the middle." Humankind is vain.) It amuses me to imagine this little bit of flotsam with thought bubbles popping overhead: "This river was made for us! This river was made to take us where we were always meant to be, glug." And I can make a slightly unsavory analogy to theology, because I can imagine a debate over the origin of the tiny hurtling patch of foam: was it created by natural forces, the river pounded over rubble and roots, or did someone gob into the water?

Life is one of the rivers that Wallace and Darwin helped us find, as is Time. Time is the mightiest of them all, powerful and huge beyond our imagining. If we are a tiny bit of spit in the

River of Life, what must we be in the River of Time? One of a billion bubbles that pop upon the surface. I suppose, however, that while a bubble may burst and disappear, it was created by the river and goes back to the river, nothing is lost and nothing gained, so we are in the River and will complete the journey with the River. Time began—my father and I watched it from the *Corinthian*, bobbing in black waters amongst the cownosed rays and dolphins—and time will end.

Speaking of endings, I have two for this little book.
One big, one little.

THE BIG ENDING

This may be hard to swallow, but I actually researched this book quite diligently. As I wrote it, I read books about Science. Indeed, these volumes are beguiling, as seductive as any golden-tongued preacher. I began reading about the particulars of Evolution, because I wanted to make no, or very few, factual errors. I was led down some very interesting side roads, too. Particularly intriguing is the fledgling science of memetics, which was created by Richard Dawkins. Let me briefly mangle that one for you. Basically, a meme is an idea, a concept, a notion. It is analogous (although mostly as an intellectual exercise) to a gene. Just as genes "find" suitable mediums for self-replication, so do memes. According to the science of memetics (at least, my shaky understanding of it), my book here contains a number of memes: the notion of God versus godlessness, for example. That is a meme that finds expression many places, to be sure. It was particularly healthy in the nineteenth century, when people found themselves called upon to come down on one side of the fence or the other. (Nowadays, we are not required to make a decision; we are allowed to both know a little of the science and mumble about a *force*. In a sense, most of us have been avoiding the question.)

As I say, I was merrily reading these books about Science, which led me in two directions, inward and out-. For instance, some of my reading became more and more particular and minute in focus: the mechanics of genetics, the structure of DNA, the interaction of atomic particles. The other road rippled outwards, from the finches on Albemarle to the troposphere and beyond. Finally, I was reading about the universe.

I read about the Goldilocks Phenomenon, a phrase coined by the scientific community to reflect the apparency that the universe seems to be *just right* for us. (Just right for the creation of life, although, like most of my ilk, I conflate *life* with *being human*.) Perhaps the most arresting example of the Goldilocks Phenomenon is that the universe could very easily not exist at all. As John Gribbin writes, "One of the most surprising things about our universe is that it is just about as big as it could be without being infinite." Expanding out from the "singularity" that was the Big Bang, gravity is exactly enough to cancel out the expansion. The universe is held in a delicate balance. Gribbin offers the analogy of someone throwing a ball skyward from the surface of the earth. If you or I threw it, it would simply fall back to the ground. If a greater being threw it, someone to whom we ascribe superhuman strength, the ball would simply rip free of the atmosphere and be gone forever. It would require a being possessing extraordinary strength *and* skill to throw the ball at *precisely* the right speed so that gravity would almost stop it but not quite, so that the ball would almost rip free but not quite.

That gave me pause. Gives me pause as I write it now, on a wintry night in Toronto. I glance up from my little computer, have a small sip of whiskey, and stare through the frosted window at the heavenly vault.

Perhaps, I reflect, Dr. Moody's mistake was in thinking too small. It shouldn't be *Suppose you found a watch on the beach*; it should rather be *Suppose you found the universe, as big as it could be without being infinite*. There indeed is evidence of design.

But, if there ever was a God (I reflect and refill my whiskey glass), then, like Tangaroa, he has gone away. Or cosmic winds have blown and separated the Captain on the ship from the boy on the back of the turtle. Although I'd like to think, as long as I'm thinking along these lines, that this was no accident. My sister Christine, the youngest of the children, sent me a letter written by my father in response to her concern about the proper role of the parent. My sister felt this was sage counsel for all parental units, and I agree. "With regard to optimum parenting," my father wrote, "it is a snare and a delusion. All the evidence to date indicates that parenting which is 'good enough' is all that can be done to enhance the development of a child. This will take some explaining which I won't attempt here, but will tell you about sometime soon. The point is, no one can identify the best way to raise a child—as long as basic needs for growth, social attachment, and cognitive development are met, nothing more done will have any further enhancement on development and can (depending on the nature of the excess) have negative effects. So take heart, you are managing very well, indeed."

Perhaps this is God's point of view, as well.

THE LITTLE ENDING

Some weeks after our visit to the Galápagos, a big fat crow, exhausted from its struggle against the late winter winds, landed on our front lawn. He started picking through the snow and evidently found something he liked, garbage, I'm guessing, garbage leaked through a squirrel-hole in a green plastic garbage bag long since carted away by the refuse collector. The crow pecked and began a euphoric bouncing, alternately hump-shouldered and exultant.

Carson happened to turn herself around on the sofa at this moment, away from the television set. She peered, through the slats, out the window, and saw the fat crow doing its stuff.

"Dad!" she hollered. "Dad! Come quick!"

I was in the kitchen with the newspaper, trying to keep track of various woes and wars; I threw it down and bolted into the living room, alarmed by the urgency in my daughter's voice. "Look," she said, quiet now. "Look outside."

I looked at the crow bouncing on my lawn, as joyous as a prize-fighter who's just knocked down the leading contender.

"Huh. You know what that is?" I asked my daughter. "That's wondrous and astounding."

Allen, Thomas B. "William Beebe." In *Into the Unknown: The Story of Exploration*. Washington: National Geographic Society, 1987.

Anderson, D. T. *Barnacles: Structure, Function, Development and Evolution*. London/New York: Chapman & Hall, 1994.

Asimov, Isaac. *Asimov's Biographical Encyclopedia of Science and Technology*. Garden City, N.Y.: Doubleday, 1982 [1964].

Barber, Lynn. *The Heyday of Natural History (1820-1870)*. London: Jonathan Cape, 1980.

Beebe, [Charles] William. *Adventuring with Beebe: Selections from the Writings of William Beebe*. New York: Viking Press, 1960.

———. *Galápagos: World's End*. New York: Dover Publications, 1988 [1924].

Blunt, Wilfrid. *The Compleat Naturalist: A Life of Linnaeus*. New York: Viking Press, 1971.

Boyce, Barry. *A Traveller's Guide to the Galápagos Islands*. San Jose: Galápagos Travel, 1990.

Brackman, Arnold C. *A Delicate Arrangement: The Strange Case of Charles Darwin and Alfred Russel Wallace*. New York: Times Books, 1980.

Brower, Kenneth (ed). *Galápagos: The Flow of Wilderness.*(2 vols.) San Francisco: Sierra Club, 1970.

Burchfield, Joe D. *Lord Kelvin and the Age of Earth*. New York: Science History Publications, 1975.

Burney, James [Lord Monboddo]. *On the Origin and Progress of Language*. (6 vols.) Marston, England: Scholar Press Facsimiles, 1967 [1773].

[Chambers, Robert and Chambers, William]. *Vestiges of the Natural History of Creation*. Leicester: Leicester University Press, 1969 [1844].

Cronin, Helena. *The Ant and the Peacock: Altruism and Sexual Selection from Darwin to Today*. Cambridge: Cambridge University Press, 1991.

Dampier, (Captain) Wm. *A New Voyage Round the World: Describing Particularly the Isthmus of America, Several Coasts and Islands in the West Indies, the Isles of Cape Verd, the Passage by Tierra Del Fuego, &c*. London: Adam & Charles Black, 1937 [1697].

Darwin, Charles R. *[The] Descent of Man, and Selection in Relation to Sex*. Princeton: Princeton University Press, 1981 [1871].

———. *Journal of Researches into the Geology and Natural History of Various Countries Visited by H.M.S. Beagle in a Voyage Round the World, Under the Command of Captain FitzRoy, from 1832 to 1836*. New York: Hafner, 1956 [1839].

———. *[A] Monograph on the Subclass Cirripedia, with Figures of All the Species*. London: Ray Society, 1854.

————. *(On) The Origin of Species By Means of Natural Selection, or, The Preservation of Favoured Races in the Struggle for Life.* London: John Murray, 1859.

————. *[The] Voyage of the Beagle.* New York: Signet/Mentor, 1988 [1845].

Darwin, C. and Wallace, A.R. (deBeer, Sir Gavin, ed.) *Evolution by Natural Selection.* Cambridge: Cambridge University Press, 1958 [1858].

————. "On the Tendency of Species to Form Varieties: and on the Perpetuation of Varieties and Species by Natural Means of Selection." *Journal of the Proceedings of the Linnean Society (Zoology)* 3: 45–52, 1858. [reproduction, de Beer, Sir Gavin, ed.] Cambridge: Cambridge University Press, 1958.

Darwin, Erasmus. *The Botanic Garden: A Poem in Two Parts.* London: J. Johnson, St. Paul's Churchyard, 1791.

————. *Zoonomia, or, The Laws of Organic Life.* (2 vols.) London: J. Johnson, St. Paul's Churchyard, 1974–6.

Darwin, (Sir) Francis. *Rustic Sounds and Other Studies in Literature and Natural History.* London: John Murray, 1917.

Darwin, (Sir) George. "Radioactivity and the Age of the Sun." *Nature.* London: September, 1903.

————. *Scientific Papers.* (5 vols.) Cambridge: Cambridge University Press.

———— [signed "G.H.D.] "Tides." *Encyclopedia Britannica* (11th ed., Vol. 26). 1910.

Dawkins, Richard. *The Blind Watchmaker.* London: Penguin, 1988.

————. *The Selfish Gene.* Oxford: Oxford University Press, 1976.

Dennett, Daniel C. *Darwin's Dangerous Idea: Evolution and the Meaning of Life.* New York: Simon & Schuster, 1995.

Desmond, A. J. *Archetypes and Ancestors: Palaentology in Victorian London, 1850–75.* London: Blond and Briggs, 1982.

Desmond, A. J. and Moore, J. *Darwin.* New York: Norton, 1991.

Dobshansky, T. G. *Genetics of the Evolutionary Process.* New York: Columbia University Press, 1970.

Eiseley, Loren. *Darwin's Century: Evolution and the Men Who Discovered It.* Garden City, N.Y.: Doubleday, 1958.

FitzRoy, (Captain) Robert. *Narrative of the Surveying Voyages of His Majesty's Ships "Adventure" and "Beagle" Between the Years 1826 and 1836 Describing Their Examination of the Southern Shores of South America and the Beagle's Circumnavigation of the Globe.* London: Henry Colbourn, 1839.

Ford, Edmund Briscoe. *Mendelism and Evolution.* London: Methuen, 1960.

Gaines, Richard. *The Explorers of the Undersea World.* New York: Chelsea House Publications, (c.) 1994.

Geikle, (Sir) Archibald. "Geology." *Encyclopedia Britannica* (11th ed., Vol. 11). 1910.

Goethe, J. W. von. *Theory of Colours [Zur Farbenlehre].* Cambridge, Mass.: MIT Press, 1970.

Gosse, Edmund. *Father and Son: A Study of Two Temperaments.* New York: Norton, 1963 [1907].

————. *The Life of Philip Henry Gosse, F.R.S.* London: Kagan, Paul, Trench, Trubner & Co., 1890.

Gosse, Philip Henry. *Actinologia Britannica: A History of the British Sea Anemones and Corals*. London: John van Voorst, 1858.

———. *Omphalos: An Attempt To Untie the Geological Knot*. London: John van Voorst, 1857.

Gould, Stephen Jay. *Bully for Brontosaurus: Reflections in Natural History*. New York: Norton, 1991.

Gribbin, John R. *In the Beginning: After CODE and Before the Big Bang*. Boston/Toronto: Little Brown, 1993.

Gulick, (Reverend) John Thomas. *Evolution, Racial and Habitudinal*. Washington, D.C.: Carnegie Institute of Washington, 1905.

Haber, Francis. *The Age of the World: Moses to Darwin*. Baltimore: Johns Hopkins Press, 1959.

Haeckel, Ernst. *The Evolution of Man: A Popular Exposition of the Principal Points of Human Ontology and Phylogeny*. (2 vols.) New York: Appleton, 1897 [1879].

Hallam, Anthony. *Great Geological Controversies*. Oxford: Oxford University Press, 1989.

Harris, Michael. *A Field Guide to the Birds of Galápagos*. London/New York: Collins, 1974.

Heyerdahl, Thor [Arne Skjślsvold]. *Archaeological Evidence of Pre-Spanish Visits to the Galápagos*. Millwood, N.Y.: Kraus Reprint Co., 1974.

Hickman, John. *The Enchanted Islands: The Galápagos Discovered*. Dover, N.H.: Tanager Books, 1985.

Hitching, Francis. *The Neck of the Giraffe: Darwin, Evolution, and the New Biology*. New York: Signet/Mentor, 1983.

Hobbes, Thomas. *Leviathan, or, The Matter, Form and Power of a Commonwealth Ecclesiastical and Civil*. London: Collins/Fontana, 1962 [1651].

Huxley, T. H. *Darwiniana: Essays*. New York: Appleton, 1896.

Idyll, Clarence P. *Abyss: The Deep Sea and the Creatures That Live in It*. New York: Cromwell, 1971.

Irvine, William. *Apes, Angels and Victorians: Darwin, Huxley and Evolution*. New York: McGraw-Hill, 1955.

Jackson, Michael Hume. *Galápagos: A Natural History Guide*. Calgary: University of Calgary Press, 1985.

Jones, Thomas Rymer. *General Outline of the Organization of the Animal Kingdom and of Comparative Anatomy*. London: John van Voorst, 1871.

Kammerer, Paul. *The Inheritance of Acquired Characteristics*. New York: Boni and Liveright, 1924.

Koestler, Arthur. *The Case of the Midwife Toad*. New York: Random House, 1971.

Kohn, David (ed.) *The Darwinian Heritage*. Princeton: Princeton University Press, 1985.

Lamarck, Jean, etc. *Zoological Philosophy*. London: Macmillan, 1914 [1809].

Leeming, David A. and Leeming, Margaret A. *A Dictionary of Creation Myths*. New York/Toronto: Oxford University Press, 1995.

Linné, Carl von [Linnaeus]. *Systema Naturae*. Delft: Coronet Books, 1964 [1735].

Lovejoy, Arthur O. *The Great Chain of Being*. Cambridge, Mass.: Harvard University Press, 1936.

Lyell, (Sir) Charles. *The Principles of Geology: Being an Attempt to Explain the Former*

Changes of the Earth's Surface, by Reference to Causes Now in Operation. (2 vols.) London: John Murray, 1830–3.

McCann, Alfred W. *God—or Gorilla: How the Monkey Theory of Evolution Exposes Its Own Methods, Refutes Its Own Principles, Denies Its Own Inferences, Disproves Its Own Case.* New York: Devon-Adair Co., 1922.

McDanell, Colleen and Lang, Bernhard. *Heaven: A History.* New Haven: Yale University Press, 1988.

MacDonald, David W. *The Encyclopedia of Mammals.* New York: Facts on File, 1984.

McKinney, H.C. *Wallace and Natural Selection.* New Haven: Yale University Press, 1972.

Malthus, Thomas Robert. *An Essay on the Principle of Population, As It Affects the Future Improvement of Society.* London: J. Johnson, 1798.

Margulis, Lynn and Sagan, Dorion. *Microcosmos: Four Billion Years of Evolution from Our Microbial Ancestors.* New York: Summit Books, 1986.

Mattison, Chris. *Frogs and Toads of the World.* New York: Facts on File, 1987.

Melville, Herman. "The Encantadas, or Enchanted Isles." In *The Shorter Novels of Herman Melville.* New York: Liveright, 1956.

————. *Pierre, or, The Ambiguities.* New York: Hendricks House, 1962.

Mendel, Gregor. "Experiment in Plant Hybridization." In *Classic Papers in Genetics.* [Peters, J., ed.] Englewood Cliffs, N.J.: Prentice-Hall, 1959.

Milner, Richard. "Charles Darwin and Associates, Ghostbusters." *Scientific American,* Oct. 1996.

Moore, Ruth. *Charles Darwin.* London: Hutchison, 1957.

Moorehead, Alan. *Darwin and the Beagle.* New York: Harper & Row, 1969.

Nelson, Bryan. *Galápagos: Islands of Birds.* New York: Morrow, 1968.

Ortel, Abraham [Ortelius]. *Theatrum Orbis Terrarum [Atlas of the Whole World].* Antwerp: at Christopher Plantin's Press, 1570.

Paley, William. *Natural Theology, or, Evidences of the Existence and Attributes of the Deity, Collected from the Appearances of Nature* [2nd ed.] Oxford: J. Vincent, 1828 [1802].

Parsons, Geoffrey. *The Stream of History.* New York: Scribner's, 1928.

Quammen, David. *The Song of the Dodo: Island Biogeography in an Age of Extinctions.* New York: Scribner, 1996.

Quarrington, Paul. *Fishing with My Old Guy.* Vancouver: Greystone Press, 1995.

Raverat, Gwen. *Period Piece: A Cambridge Childhood.* London: Faber & Faber, 1952.

Robinson, William A. *Voyage to Galápagos.* New York: Harcourt, Brace, 1936.

Rogers, Stanley R.H. *Freebooters of the Pacific.* London: Blackie, 1941.

Rogers, Woodes. *A Cruising Voyage Round the World.* London: Cassell, 1928 [1730].

Sagan, Carl. *The Dragons of Eden: Speculations on the Evidence of Human Intelligence.* New York: Random House, 1977.

Salaman, Redcliffe. *The History and Social Influence of the Potato: With a Chapter on Industrial Uses.* Cambridge: Cambridge University Press, 1949.

Semon, Richard Wol. *The Mneme.* London: Allen Unwin, 1921.

Soule, Gardner. *The Ocean Adventure: Science Explores the Depths of the Sea.* New York: Appleton-Century, 1966.

Steadman, David W. *Galápagos: Discovery on Darwin's Islands*. Washington, D.C.: Smithsonian Institution Press, 1988.

Strauch, Dore. *Satan Came to Eden*. New York/London: Harper & Bros., 1936.

Sutton-Vane, Sybil. *The Story of Eyes*. New York: Viking Press, 1958.

Swedenborg, Emmanuel. *Small Theological Works and Letters of Emmanuel Swedenborg*. London: Swedenborg Society, 1975.

Taylor, Ian T. *In the Minds of Men: Darwin and the New World Order*. Toronto: TFE Publishing, 1984.

Thomson, Wm. [Baron Kelvin]. *Popular Lectures and Addresses*. London: Macmillan, 1891–4.

Thornton, Ian. *Darwin's Islands: A Natural History of the Galápagos*. Garden City, N.Y.: published for the American Museum of Natural History Press, 1971.

Toulmin, Stephen and Woodfield, June. *The Discovery of Time*. London: Hutchison, 1982 [1965].

Treherne, J. E. *The Galápagos Affair*. New York: Random House, 1983.

Wallace, Alfred Russel. *Darwinism: An Exposition of the Theory of Natural Selection, with Some of Its Applications*. London: Macmillan, 1889.

———. "On the Tendency of Varieties to Depart Infinitely from the Original Type." *Journal of the Proceedings of the Linnean Society* (200) 3: 53-62, 1858.

———. *[The] Malay Archipelago: The Land of the Orang-utan and the Bird of Paradise, a Narrative of Travel with Studies of Man and Nature*. London: Macmillan, 1869.

———. *Miracles and Modern Spiritualism*. London: G. Redway, 1896.

———. *My Life: A Record of Events and Opinions*. New York: Dodd, Mead, 1905.

Weeks, David Joseph and James, Jamie. *Eccentrics: A Study of Sanity and Strangeness*. New York: Kodansha America, 1995.

Weiner, Jonathan. *The Beak of the Finch: A Story of Evolution in Our Time*. New York: Knopf, 1994.

Welker, Robert Henry. *Natural Man: The Life of William Beebe*. Bloomington: Indiana University Press, 1974.

White, Alan. *Galápagos Guide*. Quito: Imprenta Europa, 1972.

White, Michael and Gribbin, John. *Darwin: A Life in Science*. New York: Dutton/Penguin, 1996.

Wilkinson, Clennell. *Dampier, Explorer and Buccaneer*. New York: Harper, 1929.

Wittmer, Margret. *Floreana*. London: Anthony Nelson, 1989.

WEBSITES

Darwin & Darwinism: www.stedwards.edu/cfpages/stoll/iv/darwin.htm

Evolution Entrance: www.ucmp.berkeley.edu/history/evolution.html

SAGE *[The Society for the Advancement of Genetics Education]*: www.genetics-ed.org

Evolution Echo Jargon File: Compiled by W.R. Elsberry: www.rtis.com/nat/user/elsberry/projs/jargon.html#SciCre

Goethean Science: gate.cruzio.com/~eOyes/eOyes.main/goetheanscience.html.

The Church of Virus [memetics]: www.lucifer.com/virus

A C K N O W L E D G E M E N T S

The author wishes to thank, with much sincerity, the following people: Rob Sanders (for he is the Publisher); Dean Cooke, David Johnston and Sue Gillespie (for they are the Agents); Barbara Pulling (a wonderful editor, even if she failed to catch that in an early draft I gave my grandmother the wrong name); Tony Quarrington (who helped immeasurably with the research); Keith Wade (who kept me honest); Joel Quarrington (for, among other things, receiving a rock to the head); Christine Quarrington (because she is scientific); Bruce and Carson Quarrington (for coming with me); and Stuart McLean, who said to me, "Write about that. It's what you're talking about, isn't it?"